Locally Delicious

Recipes and Resources for Eating on the North Coast

Ann Anderson
Martha Haynes, Ann King, Carol Moné,
Lauren Cohn-Sarabia and Suzanne Simpson

Published by:
North Coast Co-operative
811 I Street
Arcata CA 95521
707-826-8670
David Lippman, General Manager
davidlippman@northcoastco-op.com
www.northcoastco-op.com

Contact Editorial Team at: info@locally-delicious.com
Visit: www.locally-delicious.com

Supporting Organizations:

Humboldt Bay Center for Sustainable Living
P.O. Box 238
Eureka CA 95502
707-822-5583
info@eco-hostel.org
www.eco-hostel.org

Humboldt Community Alliance with Family Farmers
922 E Street, Suite 202
Eureka CA 95501
707-444-3255
humboldt@caff.org
www.caff.org/regions/humboldt.html

Editor-in-Chief: Ann Anderson
Associate Editors: Martha Haynes, Carol Moné, Lauren Cohn-Sarabia
                and Suzanne Simpson
Consulting Editor: Dr. Corey Lee. Lewis, Ph.D.
Copy Editor/Proofreader: Ann King
Proofreader: Amanda Carter
Photographers: Chris Wisner, with additional photographs by Ann Anderson,
  Sharon Letts, Harvey Raider, Lauren Cohn-Sarabia and Karen Wehrstein
Farm Directory Fact-Checker: Joyce McGibbon
Restaurant Directory Fact-Checker: Janet Vail
Graphic Consultants: Allison Hooper and Janet Vail

ISBN 978-0-615-31507-2

Contents

Acknowledgments

Locally Delicious is the work of the Humboldt Community. We especially thank the North Coast Co-op, the Humboldt Community Alliance with Family Farmers (Humboldt-CAFF) and farmers, ranchers, store and restaurant owners, food producers, faculty from Humboldt State University, North Coast Growers Association, Southern Humboldt Farmers' Markets, Humboldt County's Department of Agriculture, and interested citizens for their contributions of insights, information, references and recipes.

Shail Pec-Crouse and Sean Armstrong, Tule Fog Farm
Kevin Cunningham and Melanie Oldstead, Shakefork Community Farm
Janet Czarnecki, Redwood Roots Farm
Jeff M. Dolf, Bruce Bryan and Lynda Powell, County of Humboldt,
    Department of Agriculture
Karina Green, Jacob's Greens
Dr. Steven Hackett, Ph.D., Humboldt State University
Josephine Johnson, Food for People
Everett King, Southern Humboldt Farmers' Markets
Dr. Corey Lee Lewis, Ph.D., Humboldt State University
Lewis Litzky, Humboldt Bay Center for Sustainable Living
David Lippman, Jacque Torre, Matt Reed, Bob Stockwell
        and Melanie Bettenhausen, North Coast Co-op
Ed Mata and T Griffin, United Indian Health Services, Inc.
Carol McFarland, Freelance journalist
Susan Ornelas, Arcata City Council
Melanie Patrick and Michelle Wyler, Humboldt-CAFF
Mark Randall, Trident Lightning Farm and Orchard
Cheryl Siedner, Wiyot Tribe
Eddie Tanner, Deep Seeded Community Farm
Karen Wehrstein, Nutritionist and Photographer
Chris Wisner, Photographer
Zierer Family, Flora Organica

Special thanks and appreciation for financial contributions from Topeka Community Foundation and Lon and Nancy Lewis, and Ann Anderson.

As Editor-in-Chief, I wish to thank the core team for their insights, creativity, and hard work in bringing this project together. They have contributed ideas, found resources, solicited and received help and information from the community, showed up for meetings rain or shine, made pickles, took photographs, written recipes, tested recipes, helped keep the book on course and generally put up with my many requests. They encouraged me, fed me, and put up with me when I went a little nuts.

Forward

We, on the North Coast, are blessed with a temperate climate and a varied set of environments from oceans and rivers to coastal plains, valleys and forests. Each environment provides us with wonderful foods. We are also blessed with people who care about our food. Our farmers, ranchers, fishers and dairymen/women work hard to make healthy food available. Local grocers and restaurants support the farm community and we have organizations supporting our food system. We have the potential to sustain ourselves with local food.

The first goal of *Locally Delicious* is to encourage you to obtain a larger percentage of your food from our region. Your personal choices in eating can make a difference in your own health, the health of our community, our nation and the world at large. Eating within our region gives you better-tasting food, improves your nutrition and our local economy, and enriches our community. It reduces our carbon footprint and reduces the pollution and disease generated by industrial agriculture. Some of your choices can also contribute to solving issues of hunger on a global basis.

The second goal of the book is to contribute to the further development of the regional food economy and any profits will be spent on projects to further this goal.

Locally Delicious is a community project. Perspectives in the first chapter are from local professors, farmers, cooks, nutritionists, community advocates and some who are just passionate about local food as a means for a better life here and globally. The chapter on history and our future comes from many resources including the Humboldt County Agriculture Commissioner, and the Humboldt Chapter of Community Alliance with Family Farmers (Humboldt-CAFF). Recipes are from many community members. Our reference section had much help from Humboldt-CAFF, North Coast Growers Association, Southern Humboldt Farmers' Markets and the North Coast Co-op.

We hope this book inspires you to include more local foods in your diet and makes it easier for you to eat locally by showing you where to find the food and how to prepare it. We hope the book helps to create a better life for our farmers, local food producers and every resident and visitor to our region.

Each of our contributors wishes you *bon appétit!*

Ann Anderson
Editor-in-Chief

Digging In

By Dr. Corey Lee Lewis, Ph.D.

The damp, rich aroma of the earth rises from our fingers as we knead the soil with our hands, piling it up into soft, rounded mounds. My two sons, who are eight and five years old, wrestle and play as they dig, getting almost as much dirt onto each other as they have in their own garden plots. This year my wife and I have given each boy his own 5- by 5-foot garden plot to plant whatever he wants.

"We can plant Jack-O-Lantern pumpkins, and corn on the cob!" Hunter exclaims. One of his favorite autumn activities is getting lost in the corn maze and picking out giant, too-big-to-carry pumpkins from our local farms along the Mad River and out at Blue Lake.

"Yeah, punkins!" Bodie shouts with similar excitement, "and sumflowers, and watermemons, too!"

So, on this cloudy spring day we are mounding up soil with our hands, pushing small seeds into the earth and looking with hope to the future. Although our family is by no means self-sufficient, we have been growing more of our own food each year, our garden growing in size, our harvests growing in number, and our meals growing in taste and nutrition.

We are beginning the important process of digging in, of putting roots down in a place, and learning how to belong here. Northern California poet and environmental philosopher Gary Snyder, who makes his home not far from here on the San Juan Ridge, calls this process "re-inhabitation," and believes it is our most urgent purpose for the 21st century. In essence, re-inhabitation is a reversal of much that industrialization and globalization have wrought in the last century, a return to more regionally based economies, more locally controlled politics, and less energy and resource-intensive ways of living. In one sense, "digging in" means re-weaving the threads of our environmental and social communities that have become so frighteningly unraveled, especially those making up the food-web that supports and sustains us.

I grew up on a small family farm in the Midwest and witnessed much of this unraveling firsthand. During the farm crisis of the 1980s especially, we watched as family after family left their farms, businesses closed, and what used to be thriving rural communities became ghost towns full of vacant store fronts and broken windows. At the start of the 20th century, more than 30 percent of Americans were farmers and most of our food was grown within a few hundred miles of our own homes. Now, 100 years later, less than 1.8 percent of our population farms, and the average piece of food travels 1,500 miles from farm to fork. This was the American heartland I grew up in, where wheat for the entire world was grown, and where you couldn't even find local lettuce or a tomato grown within the state. In fact, Wavoka, the great spiritual leader of many Native American Nations, started the Ghost Dance, and spoke his haunting prophecy in the Midwest, the heart of our agricultural land, saying: "I have seen their future brothers. They shall sit beside their square houses and starve." Now, a century later, agricultural experts and historians are beginning to see this same specter of food insecurity and starvation looming on the horizon.

Industrial agriculture, as we are finally beginning to admit, is amazingly fragile and not sustainable over the long term, especially because it is dependant on cheap and abundant supplies of fossil fuels that are rapidly running out. Because industrial agriculture relies on massive amounts of fossil fuel at every stage of the process—from planting and spraying crops, to harvesting, processing, transporting, and storing them—it makes up almost 20 percent of our total fossil fuel use as a nation. Shifting to local and organic agriculture is one of the most effective means we have not only for creating a sustainable food system capable of feeding us in the future, but also for reducing our dependence on foreign oil and combating climate change.

With wide-brimmed hats for protection against the sun, my wife and I are planting potatoes and peas, garlic and onions, lettuce and tomatoes and many other things the boys won't put in their garden plots, but may still eat off their plates. Like many others here, we also attend the farmers' market religiously, where the boys play with friends on their favorite climbing tree, and we hula-hoop, talk with our own friends, or dance to local music. And, as a part of our process of "digging in," we recently joined a local Community Supported Agriculture Farm (the Arcata Educational Farm), where student farmers provide free gardening and cooking advice along with the weekly baskets of food. These are special events for us, enjoyable weekend routines that pull us through the hectic work week; attending them doesn't feel like my other "activist work" or "community service." Eating locally is not a sacrifice.

Eating locally is not just about supporting local farmers and food producers to ensure that we, and our children, can avoid starvation, but that kind of food security is important. Eating locally is also about eating better, tastier and healthier food, protecting both our biospheres and our bodies. We lost my bother, Bart, to cancer last year; his was caused in part by living in the Midwest and being exposed to several of the 66 known carcinogens routinely used as pesticides and herbicides. Toxicologists now estimate that over 90 percent of the 1,570,000 new cases of cancer each year are caused by the chemicals we are putting into our environment, and recognize farming as one of the nation's top 25 "cancer industries." Since the average middle-aged American has over 177 different organochlorides in his or her body, it is no stretch to say that industrial agriculture is currently poisoning those it professes to feed.

"You can either pay now, or pay later," my wife is fond of saying, and we have decided to pay now. Instead of paying with costly medical care, prolonged chemo treatments, futile surgeries, and untimely funerals, we are paying with dirty fingers, hours of planting and pulling, and time spent in the kitchen cooking together. These are costs we can accept; in fact, they are their own reward. And, yes, sometimes we do pay a little more at the store for organic and local varieties of meat, milk, cheese, bread and produce, but that little extra goes to people we know, stays here in our community, and comes back to us in many ways. For most food purchased in the U.S. (that is non-local food), 80 percent of the purchase price goes to advertising, packaging and shipping, while only 20 percent goes to the farmer. Locally produced food, however, significantly changes these figures. Each farmer gets more of our food dollar when we buy locally, not only making local farmers able to compete in the marketplace and stay in business, but also able to further support our local communities through local taxes and spending. Without committed local support, rural counties like Humboldt soon become colonies, places from which natural and human resources are continually extracted and funneled off.

For those of us who live here, and especially for those of us with children who we hope will be able to make a living here, we must also eat here. Right now, American agriculture is undergoing a renaissance of re-localization and de-industrialization, as more and more Americans realize the benefits of moving away from corporate agri-business and global markets toward supporting local, organic farmers and farmers' markets. While it is common wisdom to recognize that "You are what you eat," we are also beginning to realize that "You are where you eat."

Corey Lewis and Family
Photograph Supplied by Corey Lewis

The boys are harvesting strawberries at an approximate rate of "one for the bucket, and one for the mouth," while I braid some more garlic for drying. We will add these strawberries to some early-season blackberries and a little wood sorrel, or "sour flowers" as the boys like to call it, for dessert. The dried garlic will be used along with stored potatoes from last year, and new carrots and onions from this year, and finished off with local whole milk and Humboldt cheese, for my favorite Potatoes au Gratin. Others are bringing the Humboldt grass-fed beef, the locally caught and smoked salmon, the tossed salads, locally made wines and homemade beers.

This local potluck, shared with close friends and neighbors, won't pay profits into any corporate stocks, nor will it add massive amounts of carbon and toxins into the environment. It is a true "added value investment," in both the present and the future, one that will continue to pay back in dividends of well-formed friendships and cohesive communities.

The kids are coming in, running around and circling tables like moths, looking for parents and friends to sit with. We circle up in one large group, young and old, and stand together hand in hand: some hands are slender and soft, others weathered, cracked and calloused; some belong to farmers and cooks, others to teachers, bank tellers, and mechanics, to husbands, wives, and children. We take a moment to look around the circle, our eyes moving from one beaming smile to another, as we learn the faces of our place in the world, and get to know the people with whom we live.

I whisper a quick prayer for us,

> "Together let us eat, and our children grow.
>
> Together let us reap, just what we sow."

And, then, we all begin "digging in" . . .

Chapter 1: What Is Local Food And Why Is Eating Locally Important?

What is Local Food?

There is no standard definition, either in government or industry, for "local food." To some, it means food grown within an arbitrary distance in miles. To a large U.S. corporation, it may mean food grown within the United States. But we do know that "local food" is a hot topic and that even the largest grocery chains are incorporating it into their marketing messages.

For this book, "local" means a natural biological region (bio-region) or foodshed that has the necessary active or potential food resources to sustain its population. Our natural bio-region is the area drained by our six rivers, called the Six Rivers Region. This roughly corresponds to Del Norte, Humboldt and Trinity Counties (Tri-County), or our core region. Our extended region pushes the boundaries to about 250 miles and includes the northern part of the Central Valley of California to the east, Sonoma County to the south, and Southern Oregon to the north. By including this extended region, we gain such foods as rice, olive oil and a few more great cheeses.

We currently supply only 8 to 15 percent of our food needs from our core region. As a comparison, in the first half of the 20th century we supplied 80 percent of our own food. The Tri-County area can supply each of our residents with more food than we need at about 3,000 calories per day. Clearly, we have the potential to feed ourselves.

Looking at food miles alone addresses the pollution and climate-changing effects of transporting food over great distances—industrial food travels an average of 1,500 miles from farm to fork—but it does not address the other negative impacts of industrial agriculture. To account for these impacts, our local food also needs to be grown in a sustainable way, free from the negative effects of excessive use of fertilizers, and the use of herbicides, pesticides, antibiotics and hormones.

The resources listed in the appendices cover the core region only—Del Norte, Humboldt and Trinity Counties—with a few exceptions that are noted. Recipes include foods from the core and extended regions, plus spices. We included spices because they are a long-standing part of culture and have been traded sustainably for centuries. They are not used in great volume, don't weigh much, and thus can be produced non-locally.

As you read and consider the issues presented in this book, we hope you will start adding more local foods to your shopping baskets and diet. The important thing is that you become aware of the source of your food and of the effect growing it has had on Planet Earth. As your awareness of your eating practices increases, you may find that you naturally start looking for more locally sourced items. You may even decide to start growing some of your own food.

Two of our editors, Carol Moné and Suzanne Simpson, have been on this journey a long time. They share their views with you here.

Constraints to Becoming a Locavore
By Carol Moné

Eating Local? What does it mean? How extreme can one get with the idea of being a locavore? These questions are addressed in other sections. For now, let's look at some factors which prevent us from being true locavores.

Amazingly, people have a hard time eating locally. One difficulty is addiction. The big imports—coffee, tea, chocolate and sugar—are not foods so much as drugs. Regular consumption of these items was, until very recently, only for the wealthy. Some say addictions can be broken, but I will remain happily addicted to caffeine so long as my morning coffee is fair trade and organically grown.

A second hurdle is desire. Spices are nice to have, but our overall nutrition doesn't depend upon them, and obviously one would never consider sourcing cinnamon locally. Spices are "extras." Native plants exist with the medicinal properties inherent in many imported herbs and spices, making this a good topic for further exploration. But in spite of recent research illustrating medicinal properties for cinnamon and cardamom, exotic spices are, nonetheless, true taste luxuries. Look for organic non-irradiated spices. Certain spices may be "fair trade" products.

A third problem is expectation. An imported orange in December was a big treat a mere generation ago; now it is the norm. Grocery stores have trained us to expect and want everything year round, which has bred confusion about both seasons and food origins and ultimately has led us to simply not care: it's there, I buy it. Eating becomes an exercise in unawareness. A plethora of cookbooks requiring exotic and manufactured ingredients does not lessen this expectation. As one moves toward local eating, one's awareness of seasonal eating effortlessly increases, and expectations magically change.

Economics is a fourth enormous obstacle. The hidden costs of eating subsidized commercial foods and food products—both an expectation and a habit now—are only recently being explored and addressed. But because of these subsidies and hidden costs, healthful food is often more expensive at the checkout counter. Avoid the checkout counter in favor of the farmers' market. There is no such thing as expensive zucchini in August. Eating seasonally and canning or drying the excess will ameliorate this problem. Knowing your producers—farmers, cattlewomen, goatherds, shepherds, gatherers and fishers—is far more powerful than knowing from which country your food originated. China is quite large. Look more toward knowing the reputation of your food producers and suppliers than relying upon federal organic certification in local products. Often farmers go far beyond federal requirements for organic. Observe their practices firsthand. Organic is good, "more-ganic" is even better.

Confessions of a Reformed Big-Box Shopper
By Suzanne Simpson

Those of us who grew up in the last half of the 20th Century have known more abundance than at any other time in history. From a cornucopia of plenty, we consumed without a thought to where the food came from, the living conditions of the people who grew it, the treatment of the animals we ate, or the costs of our excesses to our planet.

For me the process started when I was a very young schoolteacher. My best friend called to tell me about the opening of a new, fabulously large discount store, the Price Club. It was unbelievable, the excess of cheap things that were available. Although I had little money, I came out of the store carrying large packages of things I could never use up, like ten dozen cookies and a giant ham. Like most Americans, I was mesmerized by the aisles of plenty in these big-box stores, and tantalized by their cheap conveniences. I was hooked.

As big box stores and shopping malls sprung up in our towns like mushrooms, and massive agri-businesses took over family farms, we succumbed to the siren call of plenty, like children in a candy store. "By God, we are Americans and this is our due. If I can have one, why not two? If my best friend has it, I want it also."

In the late 1980s, my husband and I bought and cleared five acres of blackberries just east of Willow Creek on the Trinity River, and I planted my first garden.

In those early days of gardening, I think Mother Earth must have sprinkled some fairy dust on me. Like a butterfly emerging from a cocoon, I awakened to a new and wondrous world. Enthralled, I loved the texture, feel and aroma of the rich, loamy earth. I held a tomato seed the size of a pinhead in my hand and felt such awe, knowing that it could grow and produce 40 pounds of fruit. I gave up manicures and panty hose and roamed the garden barefoot, drunk on nature. *Mother Earth News* and *Organic Gardening* magazines became my bibles. I was insatiable. There was no end to what could be learned about seeds, soil, bugs, weather and harvesting.

My first garden, which was over 3,000 square feet in size, was a disaster. It had been an exceptionally wet year with the rains continuing into May. Excited and impatient, I planted rows of corn, eggplant, tomatoes, squash and basil into soggy soil, leaving my neighbors snickering and shaking their heads over the dumb city slicker. A week later when I returned, the plants were limp, yellow and more or less drowned.

The next year, determined, I planted more corn with a better knowledge of Mother Nature's timetable. With a humbled sense of accomplishment, I watched the green shoots spring up and develop into full, ripe tasseled ears of corn.

Alas, my hubris suffered another blow one evening while sitting with my husband in the garden, watching the full moon rise over nearby Ironside Mountain. As we watched incredulously, in marched a marauding horde of raccoons, rattling the corn stalks as they took advantage of my garden's largess. Armed with an arsenal of green tomatoes, we furiously lobbed missiles at the nasty beasts, only to be met with hisses and snarls as they stripped the corn off the cobs.

Our neighbor, a retired professor, patted me on the back the next day, told me not to despair, and said with wisdom, "The only life worth living is the experimental life. Life is a grand experiment." A good lesson to take to heart.

After that first year, my mission was to restore our five-acre patch of blackberries into a place where Mother Earth could sing and dance. I studied the plants that grew best in the Trinity River area, talked with locals and exchanged seeds. I learned patience. Drawn to that tiny piece of earth, I became rooted and found a profound sense of belonging to the land.

Over the past 20 years of growing food, I have learned the importance of sustainable living in all aspects of our lives. It was an incremental process of patience and learning. As my gardening experience grew, I began to question and change my lifestyle and habits of consumption. It has been a challenge, as well as an exhilarating process.

We now eat less meat, and only that which is local and organic. I read the labels on packaged goods to check for nutritional value, and I won't buy canned goods since many cans are lined with bisphenol A, with its several negative health effects.[1] We support local farmers, and eat fruit and vegetables in season when the taste is much better.

We now produce well over 75 percent of the fruit and vegetables that we consume. In our temperate climate we are able to grow healthy vegetables all year long. By canning, dehydrating and freezing our harvest, almost all of our food is home grown. It feels good to give something back to our Mother Earth and to participate in a community that is on its way to becoming sustainable.

From my own experience as a woman working 40-plus hour weeks for many years while maintaining a large garden, it took serious budgeting of my time. For families who are crunched for time and want to plant a garden, I suggest that you sit down as a family and talk about the importance of growing a garden. Come to an agreement as to how much time each family member can contribute. For young kids and even for teenagers, it can be rewarding to take a small amount of time each day, to give up their computer games for a little while and go outside, dig in the dirt and discover the joys of gardening. There is something magical about planting beans or squash at any age, watching them grow, and harvesting the fruits (literally) of their labors.

The only big boxes I use now are for carrying the vegetables and fruits that we grow, and those are recycled from the North Coast Co-op.

For me, all of these wonderful changes started with the planting of one tomato seed in a little pot. This simple act became a defining moment in my life.

Why is Eating Locally Important?

But first, a note from the Editor-in-Chief. Much of what changed my eating behavior was the hard facts about industrial agriculture. The following section provides an overview of the positive reasons for eating locally-produced organic food and describes the problems created by industrial agriculture. The main text will provide you with the core information but if you would like to digress into the Sidebars you will find details, some of them technical and some a bit scary. These are the details that changed me.

The list of reasons for eating locally is long and sometimes complex and the story of how we came to rely on non-local agri-business is complicated. This book can tell only a part of that story. If you want to dig deeper we suggest reading all or some of the following books and/or watching some of the movies listed.

The Omnivore's Dilemma, by Michael Pollan, is an insightful description of the current state of our food system. *The End of Food*, by Paul Roberts, is a thorough and fact-filled discussion of the origins of our current agri-business based food system. It covers issues at the local and international levels and discusses some possible scenarios for starting to solve the problems. For a delightful description of one family's adventure in local eating, read *Animal, Vegetable, Miracle* by Barbara Kingsolver. Among the informative movies are *Food, Inc., King Corn* and *Super Size Me*.

The Pleasures of Eating Locally

Local food tastes better, supports the local economy, helps to build "community," and protects agricultural land and open space.

Locally grown food tastes better.
Fresh food, picked when ripe, just tastes better! Peaches are juicy, fragrant and delicious, carrots are crisp and sweet, and to-matoes are flavorful. Food from the garden or purchased from the farmer has probably been picked within 24 hours of your eating it. Local food from locally-owned grocery stores is likely on the shelves sooner than food shipped from a great distance.

Food also tastes better if it's ripened *before* being picked. Industrial produce is often picked unripe and engineered to appear ripe days or even weeks after being harvested.

Having a wide variety of food also adds to our eating pleasure. Local farmers grow many varieties of our favorite veg-etables and fruits—many varieties that we may not have seen before. They often bring heirloom fruits and vegetables back into production. Contrast this with some facts about industrial agriculture:

> - Industrial agriculture has reduced the varieties of fruits and vegetables available by 75 percent since the beginning of the 20th century.
> - Today, 75 percent of the world's food is generated from just 12 varieties of plants and five animal species. For example, iceberg lettuce, frozen and fried potatoes, potato chips and canned tomatoes make up almost half of U.S. vegetable consumption.[2]

Local fresh food is healthier for you.

Local organically-grown food that is eaten soon after being harvested is higher in nutrients and does not contain pesticides and added hormones found in industrially-produced food.

> A recent study showed that fresh produce loses nutrients quickly. In the week or longer delay between harvest and the dinner table, sugars turn to starches, plant cells shrink, and produce loses its vitality.[3]
>
> Most local farmers use organic farming methods. These methods build soil and soil fertility. Paul Roberts states, "Soils rich in organic matter have a greater capacity for additional nutrients—that is, they can absorb more fertilizers, whether natural or synthetic, and convey those nutrients more readily to plants."[4]
>
> Pasture-raised chicken and grass-fed beef are free from the antibiotics used to stimulate growth and to control the spread of pathogens within Concentrated Animal Feed Operations (CAFOs). Organic, grass-fed beef and dairy products are free of growth-stimulating hormones.

Buying local food helps build our economy and our community.

When money is spent locally, more of it stays within the community. Several studies have shown that every dollar spent in a locally-owned store has three times the effect of a dollar spent at a store owned by a distant corporation.[5] Economics Professor Dr. Steven C. Hackett, Ph.D., Humboldt State University, explains:

> . . . appropriate substitutions of local food for imported food create benefits for the local economy. One can think of the income circulating in a local economy as being analogous to the level of water in a bathtub. Like the spigot that adds water to a bath, new income is injected into the local economy when people outside of the area purchase locally-produced goods and services. Some of that income is spent locally, and thereby becomes income for others as the pattern repeats itself in a process referred to as the multiplier effect. Like the drain at the bottom of a bathtub, however, when we buy goods and services from outside the area, income leaks out of the local economy. The more imports we buy, the more income leaks out of the local economy, and the smaller is the multiplier effect. Gold Rush mining camps, for example, needed to import most all goods and services, and oftentimes became ghost towns when the ore played out.

When we make the conscious decision to buy locally-produced food instead of food produced outside the area, we are reducing the leakage of income out of the local economy. By doing so, we increase the multiplier effect, meaning that a given dollar injected into the local economy generates a larger quantity of new income for local residents. Conscious consumers also know that we shape our local economy and our local community by the way we spend our money. Our spending can be thought of as votes cast for the types of farms, businesses, and products that we want in our community. By buying locally-produced food, we are casting our dollar votes for local farmers, as well as the businesses and organizations that process and market these goods to the public. We come to recognize that supporting our local farmers helps preserve the open space and working landscapes that are a keystone of our quality of life. Over time these commercial relationships expand into something more—a complex set of relationships built on trust and reciprocity serving as the "social capital" that give communities the capacity to find common purpose, adapt, and thrive.

In addition to putting more money back into the local economy, buying locally creates a greater level of charitable giving. On average, local businesses contribute four times more money as a percent of revenue than distant corporations.[6]

Eddie Tanner, owner of Deep Seeded Farm and author of *The Humboldt Gardner,* writes his perspective on building community:

Eating locally is more than just a great way to get the freshest foods and to support the local economy. It is a way to connect with our environment and strengthen the ties that make us a community. Eating is our most fundamental link to the natural world, and by looking to local sources we become attuned to the abundance and the limits of the soil under our feet and the climate we dwell in. Never before in history have we had more opportunity to separate ourselves from our environment, and thus it has never been more important to consciously make that connection. In taking this action, we become more in touch with our humanity. By sharing local foods and recipes, and by connecting with local producers, we come to a fuller realization of what it means to be a member of the community.

Deep Seeded Community Farm
Chris Wisner, Photographer

Local food preserves open space and supports a clean environment.
The Humboldt Community Alliance with Family Farmers explains:

> As the value of direct-marketed fruits and vegetables increases, selling farm-land for development becomes less likely. A well-managed family farm is a place where the resources of fertile soil and clean water are valued. Good stewards of the land grow cover crops that prevent erosion and replace nutrients used by their crops. Cover crops also capture emissions and help combat global warming. In addition, the patchwork of fields, hedgerows, ponds and buildings is the perfect environment for many beloved species of wildlife. That landscape will survive only as long as farms are financially viable. When you buy locally-grown food, you are doing something proactive about preserving the agricultural landscape.

Problems Avoided by Eating Locally

Eating locally-produced food avoids many problems caused by the industrial food system. These problems include contributing to climate change through carbon dioxide (CO_2) and nitrous oxide (N_2O) emissions; poisoning of our waterways, our food and our bodies; spreading of pathogens; contributing to poor health through processed foods high in fat, sugar and salt; and practicing farming techniques that strip land of top soil and soil nutrients. Many of these problems contribute to food insecurity and all are damaging our bodies and our planet.

High Energy Cost

One of the first benefits that comes to mind when considering local food is that less energy is used in its transportation.

> Locally-produced food requires 17 times less petroleum than does a diet based on food shipped across the country.[7]

Dr. Steven Hackett, Humboldt State University:

> My friends and I who enjoy long-distance cycling eat particular foods to help our performance. Many cyclists believe that bananas, being rich in potassium, will help prevent muscle cramps during a long ride. I prefer avocados, which contain nearly twice the potassium of a typical banana, as well as B_6 and oleic acid, a great mono-unsaturated fat. While these great foods help me ride many miles on my bicycle, they themselves must travel even longer distances as freight from where they are grown to my grocery store. The banana I eat on a ride may have been hauled by diesel truck from the plantation to the Guatemalan port of Quetzal, transferred onto a freighter (powered by bunker oil) to Port Hueneme, and again loaded onto a series of diesel trucks that brought that banana to a grocery store in Humboldt County, California. The fossil fuel burned in order to transport a banana more than 2,500 miles results in greenhouse gas emissions that contribute to global climate change. If one were to tally up the greenhouse gas emissions each year from the foods we eat, the goods and services we buy, the vehicle miles we travel, the electricity we draw from the grid, and the natural gas we use to heat our homes and businesses, we would arrive at the carbon footprint associated with how we choose to live our life.

It ends up that many locally-grown foods provide good sources of potassium and other nutrients. Examples include the potatoes, blueberries, and strawberries growing in my vegetable garden. In good years, I am able to get a few tomatoes from early-maturing varieties I try to grow in my cold frame, and those tomatoes are also an excellent source of potassium. By appropriate substituting local food for imported food, we can continue to enjoy a rich and varied diet while reducing our carbon footprints.

Water and Air Pollution

Use of excess nitrogen fertilizer, common practice in industrial agriculture, pollutes waterways, killing aquatic animals. Nitrogen in water also causes illness in humans, and removing it from water supplies is a great expense for many cities. Organic farmers do not use artificial fertilizers.

> Dead zones in bodies of water are created when excess nitrogen causes algae blooms. The algae dies and sucks oxygen from the water, killing fish and other oxygen-dependent animals. The number of dead zones in our oceans has risen to more than 150—up by a factor of over two from 1990, as reported by the United Nations Environmental Program.[8] The loss to commercial fishing amounts to billions of dollars a year and means less food for people.
>
> Excess nitrogen is also linked to a number of human health risks, including miscarriages and cancer. Federal and State environmental agencies now regard farming as one of the biggest polluters of the nation's water system.[10] Including pesticides, annual cost of surface-water contamination was calculated to be $16 billion.[11]
>
> Excessive amounts of nitrogen also pollute the air. Nitrogen combines with oxygen to form nitrous oxide (N_2O), a greenhouse gas 300 times more potent than carbon dioxide.[12]

Pollution by Pesticides

Organic farmers do not use pesticides (herbicides, insecticides and fungicides) and thus do not poison and pollute waterways and soil. Most of our local producers use organic methods.

> One of the most widely used herbicides (weed-killers), Atrazine, is linked to heart and lung congestion, muscle spasms, degeneration of the retina, and cancer, as well as the wholesale extinction of some species of amphibians. Atrazine is the second most frequently detected herbicide in water from drinking wells.[13]
>
> Insecticides and fungicides, many based on organophosphates, are heavily relied on by growers of alfalfa, almonds, carrots, grapes, apples, strawberries, peaches, walnuts, corn and cotton, which together account for half of all organophosphate use.[14] These products disrupt a pest's central nervous system. Organophosphates not only affect the pest, they also poison people, helping to make farm work one of the most dangerous occupations in the world.[15]

> Less obvious is the fact that insecticides also kill beneficial insects such as bees, as well as insects that prey on the pests. Finally, the pests can develop resistance, which requires the development of new or stronger chemicals, in a never-ending cycle.[16]

Loss of Topsoil

Organic farmers use cover crops and manure to build and fertilize soil. Industrial agriculture causes loss of topsoil.

> The National Academy of Sciences has determined that cropland in the U.S. is being eroded at least ten times faster than the time it takes for lost soil to be replaced. Many of the industrial agricultural processes leave land bare and subject to topsoil loss from both water runoff and wind. Food production increases with the use of nitrogen fertilizer but the soil needs to be replenished with organic matter as well. The future food supply depends on soil and soil high in nutrients for plants.
>
> One encouraging developement is that a few otherwise industrial farms are starting to use no-till practices that protect the soil as well as sequester carbon.

Why I Changed the Way I Eat
by Ann Anderson

I grew up in a large city and knew very little about agriculture. Of course I knew about organic food, but did not pay much attention. I just thought of it as more expensive. My life changed about ten years ago, when I heard a radio interview with Robert F. Kennedy Jr. The subject was hog CAFOs. I had never heard of a CAFO but learned that it meant a Confined Animal Feeding Operation, where animals are jammed together in buildings or in feedlots. The hogs are so close together that they often bite off the tail of the animal in front of them, so tightly confined that they cannot even turn around. The inhumanity to these other living creatures horrified me. I knew the animals were slaughtered for food but I thought they had a decent life until that dark day.

Added to the treatment of the hogs was the fact that hog CAFO operations seriously poisoned both land and water. I learned that a hog produces about three times the waste of a person and that there could be tens of thousands of hogs in one facility. How shocking to learn that these buildings were classified as agricultural facilities and did not come under the same sanitation rules that would be applied to a city. A CAFO might be creating the same amount of waste as a medium-sized city, but was not required to have a sewage treatment plant. The waste was simply dumped on the soil and collected in "ponds." The waste killed the soil, seeped into aquifers and found its way into rivers, where it polluted drinking water and killed aquatic animals.

I have not eaten pork since that day.

I later learned about poultry CAFOs—even some of the large "organic" poultry producers were not much better. I now only eat chicken that is raised in pastures. It's a bit harder to find but some of our local groceries are researching their suppliers carefully and buying from producers that are truly "organic" and humane in their operations. We may also soon have chicken from small local farmers.

Then I read books by Michael Pollan and Paul Roberts. There goes the beef! CAFO-raised beef creates some of the worst environmental damage. We are lucky in our region to have several ranchers who grow their beef on pasture land, where the animals can eat grass. Grass-fed beef has a much lower impact on the environment, uses less petroleum energy and is better for your heath. I still do not eat a large quantity of beef, but I do enjoy a hamburger once in a while.

As I read more and saw a few of the films about industrially-produced food, I became more aware of its negative effects. I became serious about fruits and vegetables, as well. I want to avoid eating pesticides. I want to reduce my carbon footprint by buying local and organic. I am not yet and may never be a 100 percent locavore, but I have started my journey. I have more to learn, but it is a journey that I am happy to be on.

Living in this small community, I've also learned that I can talk to the owners and managers of the groceries where I shop (at least the local and regional ones), and they listen to me and answer my questions. For convenience, I shop at Murphy's in Trinidad and the Co-op in Arcata. The butchers are knowledgeable and can tell me where their various meat and fish products come from. They can tell me how the animals were raised and processed. They have listened to and accommodated my requests when I tell them about a meat producer that uses a humane and organic method of production. When I asked the Trinidad Murphy's manager to put labels indicating which farm local produce came from, he did it! I now know that if I ask questions and make requests, I can help influence what food will be available. I believe that our other local and regional markets would respond in a similar way to the ones at which I shop.

For those of you who wish to learn more about CAFOs, disease and pollution, read on. Otherwise, skip to page 18 to read about food security or page 19 to read about obesity. (Okay, I know this is not fun stuff but it is the stuff that changed my behavior.) You can skip to page 21 for some suggestions about what we, as individuals, can do to address some of these problems.

The Problems with CAFOs

CAFOs were created in the last half of the 20th century as a way to produce more meat on less land and at lower cost. The idea of lower-cost production of meat was appealing, but many of the costs were not recognized.

One reason the production cost is lower is that subsidized feed (largely corn) is sold to the CAFO operator below its actual cost of production. We are making up the difference in the form of subsidies paid from our taxes. The main beneficiaries of these subsidies are the large agri-businesses that control our food economy. But money is not the only issue. CAFOs, like other industrial food production, externalize many of the costs.

CAFOs are major polluters but the cost of cleaning up fouled water supplies and the cost of lost land is not counted in the price of food.

> On June 21, 1995, an eight-acre hog lagoon in North Carolina gave way, unleashing twenty-five million gallons of excrement in what one account described as a "two-hour, knee-deep stream that destroyed the cotton and tobacco crops of a neighbor's field, crossed the highway, and drained into the New River, where it killed all aquatic life for 17 miles."[17] When animal waste (manure) is used in a small integrated farm, however, it fertilizes the crops or pastures, without destroying the land.

CAFO practices are putting us all at risk because they contribute to reducing the effectiveness of antibiotics needed for treating human illnesses. Animals raised in close quarters require sub-therapeutic doses of antibiotics in order to avoid the sickness induced by confinement in CAFOs. The bottom line for the meat producer is more profit. The cost to our own health is ignored. Bacteria become resistant to antibiotics and these antibiotics may no longer help us if we become ill.

> Decades of heavy sub-therapeutic antibiotic use by livestock producers, which now accounts for nearly half of all antibiotics used worldwide,[18] has produced numerous new strains of bacteria that are immune to entire classes of antibiotics. Mary Gilchrist, University Hygienic Laboratory in Iowa, warns of a "'post antibiotic era' . . . a period where there would be no effective antibiotics available for treating many life-threatening infections in humans."[19] Small farmers do use antibiotics to treat infections in their animals, but the wholesale use of antibiotics to keep animals alive and for growth promotion in feedlots and CAFOs is the critical issue. Unlike local farmers, CAFOs must give daily doses of antibiotics to their animals because so many animals are kept confined in their own excrement. This daily regimen of sub-therapeutic antibiotic use may be quickly pushing us into Gilchrist's "post-antibiotic era."

CAFOs also breed pathogens. Centralized distribution helps spread them. A deadly version of the common *E. coli* bacteria evolved as a result of CAFO practices. *E. coli* has caused illness and death and is the reason for many nationwide food recalls. Again, these costs are not accounted for.

> In 1982, an outbreak of *E. coli* sickened 47 McDonald's customers. Many more incidents of *E. coli* have been reported since then. By 2008, even Whole Foods was forced to recall ground beef because of an outbreak. *E. coli* is not just found in meat anymore. It has been found in fresh spinach from California, peppers from Mexico, and cookie dough in Toll House products from Nestlé, all causing illness and major food recalls.

We have heard much about *E. coli,* but this bacteria was not a problem in our food supply until the late 1970s. Two contributing events occurred late in the twentieth century: *E. coli* merged with the shigella bacteria and acquired shingella's dangerous traits. As cattle were increasingly fed corn, their guts became more acidic, and a new strain—acid resistant—of *E. coli* (O157:H7) emerged. This new bacteria could withstand the acid in human stomachs *and* carried the dangerous traits of the shigella bacteria. This nasty new bacteria shuts down protein synthesis in the victim's intestinal wall, the wall perforates, and the toxins enter the bloodstream. There they begin killing off red blood cells and in about five percent of cases, destroy the kidneys.[20]

Many of the meat recalls due to *E. coli* have been for hamburger. Hamburger and other industrially-produced food is processed in relatively few facilities, and contamination can quickly spread. A single hamburger may contain meat from 1,000 animals. The meat is quickly and widely distributed to groceries and to fast-food and other restaurants in many states over a period of a few days. By the time illness appears, the *E. coli* may already be widely distributed.

Two other bacteria, salmonella and campylobacter, cause illness in millions of Americans each year. Again, these bacteria have become more of a problem since CAFOs came into existence.

Another nasty bacteria is salmonella, which sickens far more than a million Americans, six hundred of them fatally, every year.[21] In 2006, 16.3 percent of whole broilers and 32.4 percent of ground chicken contained salmonella.[22] In 2008, even peanut butter was the subject of a national recall, due to salmonella contamination. So far, lobbyists for the food industry have succeeded in preventing the USDA from classifying salmonella as a "food contaminant," which would bring it under regulation.[23]

In addition, more than half of all raw chicken meat is contaminated with *Campylobacter jujuni*[24], a bacteria that causes two million annual human illnesses and is increasingly resistant to the antibiotic ciprofloxacin.

Viruses have always been a threat to humans but that threat may be greater as a result of the industrial food system.

The Avian influenza virus (H5N1) has jumped from birds to humans in a limited number of cases with frequently fatal results. World health organizations are keeping a close eye on H5N1, hoping it does not develop the ability to jump from human to human with the potential of causing a dangerous global pandemic. Our current swine flu *has* become a global pandemic, but as of this writing, has a low death rate. Swine flu (H1N1) may be a virus that jumped from hogs to humans and may have evolved in a CAFO. We don't know that this is the case, but it is a possible scenario.

Industrial Agriculture adds to food insecurity.

The term "food insecurity" refers both to the actual availability of the food supply and to its safety. It's the central theme in Paul Robert's book, *End of Food*, which provides great detail on this large and complicated issue. One of the points Roberts makes is that regional food systems can add greatly to food security of both types.

Knowing your food producer increases food safety. Consumers can know who is accountable for the safety of the food if it is local. Producers of industrial food are largely anonymous and the source of bacterial outbreaks can be difficult, or sometimes impossible, to trace.

As described in Dr. Hackett's essay, industrially-produced food requires a great deal more petroleum energy than does locally-produced food. Availability of oil and the price of that oil affects food availaility and affordability. When oil reached $4.00 a gallon in the summer of 2008, food appeared to be scarce. We had our own small food panic in Humboldt County. Local TV news showed some of our neighbors buying such large quantities of basic food supplies that the Eureka COSTCO had to restrict the number of bags of rice each customer could buy at one time. As energy becomes scarce and more expensive, local food will become even more important to our food security.

> Industrially-produced and processed food is heavily dependant on petroleum fuel. The U.S. food system uses ten times more energy than it produces in the form of food calories.[25] Used to fuel transportation and farm equipment, petroleum is also used in fertilizer, many pesticides, and in processing and packaging foods. Petroleum fuels have heretofore been cheap and abundant, but that scenario is changing. As many other parts of the world grow and develop higher standards of living, the demand for and the price of oil goes up. As oil becomes more scarce, the price will rise.
>
> Oil prices rose enormously in 2008. The effect on the global food system was rapid and dramatic. Global food prices increased almost 50 percent.[26] Some countries stopped exporting food; there were food riots in others.

Two additional issues threaten food security: scarcity of water and global climate change. Industrial agriculture uses more water than is provided by precipitation in the form of rain or snow. Agricultural water is coming from ancient aquifers and is being used faster than those aquifers can be recharged. Weather patterns are changing. Draught conditions exist in many parts of the world. Farmers in the Central Valley of California dramatically reduced their planting in 2009 because they did not have enough water. Less planting means less food, and food at higher prices. Industrial agriculture is a contributor to these global climate changes.

Three of the major greenhouse gases are carbon dioxide (CO_2), nitrous oxide (N_2O) and methane. Industrial agriculture is major contributor of CO_2 and N_2O. Livestock production alone creates 18 percent of greenhouse gasses globally.[27] We cannot know all of the effects of climate change, but this we do know: where and how the world produces food will change.

Supporting local agriculture now means that we will have the farms and local food system infrastructure needed for our future.

The industrial food system contributes to obesity.

Obesity has reached epidemic proportions in our county. High amounts of fat, sugar and salt in the processed and industrial foods found in our fast-food restaurants, supermarkets, and often schools, contribute significantly. For many reasons, industrially-produced food is often cheaper than fresh, organic, local food, adding to the problem. We cannot fully cover this issue in this book, but Paul Roberts has an extensive discussion in his book, *The End of Food*.

According to the Center for Disease Control and Prevention (CDC)[28],

In the U.S., approximately two-thirds of adults and one-fifth of children are obese or overweight. Being either obese or overweight increases the risk for many chronic diseases (e.g., heart disease, type 2 diabetes, certain cancers, and strokes). Reversing the U.S. obesity epidemic requires a comprehensive and coordinated approach that uses policy and environmental changes to transform communities into places that support and promote healthy lifestyle choices for all U.S. residents.[19]

The report noted above lists 24 recommendations for reducing obesity, acknowledging that being obese is more than a matter of individual choice. For people to make healthy choices, healthy food options must be available and accessible. The report suggests steps that communities can take to create these healthy options. Three of the recommendations that relate to local food are discussed below.

Communities should increase availability of healthier food and beverage choices in public service venues. As a community, we have started on this work. Humboldt-CAFF is working to bring more fresh local food into our schools and restaurants. Mad River Community Hospital has started their own garden to provide fresh food for their patients, and Food for People (the local foodbank) works with farmers and gardeners to provide fresh food to people in need. United Indian Health Services grows fruits and vegetables on its two-acre Arcata farm and provides the food to the local Indian community as one way to help prevent and control diabetes and improve health in general.

Communities should improve availability of mechanisms for purchasing food from farms.

> According to M. Hamm of Michigan State University, in the CDC report:
>> Mechanisms for purchasing food directly from farms include farmers' markets, farm stands, community supported agriculture, "pick your own," and farm-to-school initiatives. Experts suggest that these mechanisms have the potential to increase opportunities to consume healthier foods, such as fresh fruits and vegetables, by possibly reducing cost of fresh foods through direct sales; making fresh foods available in areas without supermarkets and harvesting fruits and vegetable at ripeness rather than at a time conducive to shipping, which might improve their nutritional value and taste.

The Tri-County region of Del Norte, Humboldt and Trinity has moved toward this recommendation. This area has 13 farmers' markets, 13 CSA farms and several grocery stores actively promoting local food.

Communities should provide incentives for the production, distribution, and procurement of foods from local farms.

> According to the CDC report,
>> Incentives to local food production can include forming grower cooperatives, instituting revolving loan funds and building markets for local farm products through economic development and through collaborations with Cooperative Extension Services. Additional incentives include but are not limited to farmland preservation, marketing of local crops, zoning variances, subsidies, streamlined license and permit processes and the provision of technical assistance.

Our local communities have taken a few steps, but there is much more work to be done. Projects exist in Del Norte and Humboldt Counties, funded through grants or economic development groups, for food processing and preservation facilities. None are in operation yet but the projects are moving in the right direction. A commercial or cooperative infrastructure is needed, as are county and city policies that protect agricultural land, making it easier for farmers to produce the food we need.

A Note From the Editors:
We realize that eating regional food is not the single answer to all the issues of the global food system. It is, however, one important answer over which we have control. Every time we spend money for food, we vote for the future that we want. Changing our food system to be more energy efficient and healthier for us as individuals, as a local community, and for the entire world starts with each of us. We may not be able to control our national or state gov-

ernment and effectively blunt the influence of the handful of agri-businesses that now control the national and even global food system, but we, and the tens of millions of other people who are aware of the issues, can change the system from the dirt up.

Please use our resource lists in the appendices and the recipes in the cookbook section of this book to help you get started.

Ed Cohen, Earthly Edibles Farm
Chris Wisner, Photographer

Chapter 2: Where to Find Local Food

Food produced in our core region is abundant. The rivers and sea provide fish and shellfish. Farmers and ranchers produce a wide variety of vegetables, fruit, meat, eggs, dairy products and wine. Extending the local area to about a 250-mile range adds rice, more varieties of cheese, olive oil, vinegars and even more wine.

There are three options for acquiring local food: buy it, grow it or find it through foraging, fishing or hunting. If you're lucky, you have a friend with a farm or garden who likes to share. Many people do like to share, especially their zucchini!

Where to Buy Local Food

Food can be purchased directly from farmers and producers at farmers' markets, farm stands or CSA farms. You can also buy it indirectly through retail groceries and restaurants.

Farmers' Markets

The farmers' markets operate from spring through fall. There are currently 13 markets in Del Norte, Humboldt and Trinity Counties. The Arcata Plaza market, run by the North Coast Growers Association, is the longest-running farmers' market in California and has been in continuous operation since 1979.

> The U.S. Department of Agriculture estimates more than a million people visit a Farmers' Market weekly. More than 20,000 farmers use farmers' markets to sell to consumers.

You can find complete list of farmers' markets in Del Norte, Humboldt and Trinity Counties in Appendix B.

Farm Stands, U-Picks and Buying Directly

Some farmers, ranchers, and producers have farm stands or stores or will allow you to pick your own produce. Others have on-line sales. Appendix C is a list of farms, ranches, dairies and fishers. The list indicates what each producer grows, raises or catches and how their products are sold directly. Appendix C also has a web site link to RedwoodAg, where you can do an interactive search for a particular food. Redwood.Ag is sponsored by the University of California Agricultural Extension Office.

Grocery Stores

Many local and regional grocery stores purchase produce, meat, dairy and packaged products for resale from our local producers. Appendix D has a list of grocery stores that sell locally-produced food. When you shop, let the store owner or manager know that you appreciate their support of the local agricultural community and ask if they can do more. Encourage them to label the source of the fresh products. Look at the labels on packaged products and buy as locally as possible.

Restaurants

Don't want to cook but want good local food? Eat at some of the restaurants that use and feature local food. Humboldt Community Alliance with Family Farmers (Humboldt-CAFF) has started a program to encourage restaurants to create special local meals—look for the "Buy Fresh, Buy Local" sign at the participating restaurants.

If your favorite restaurant does not use local food, encourage them to do so. Use the restaurant list in Appendix E when choosing a restaurant and let them know that you appreciate their use of local food.

Locally-Packaged-Food Producers

Some locally-packaged-food producers sell directly to the public; most sell through retail groceries. Although many of these companies buy few (or no) ingredients from nearby primary producers, they are included in this book because buying locally-processed food in some respects lessens the carbon footprint, while at the same time encouraging and supporting a regional economy. Local producers are also more likely to incorporate local ingredients as they become available. Appendix F lists local packaged-food companies.

Community Supported Agriculture Farms (CSAs)

This region supports 13 Community Supported Agriculture Farms. Humboldt County's Democracy Unlimited provides an excellent definition:

> This method of farming allows the farmer security in knowing that the crops are sold right from the start of the season. Members purchase shares in the output of the farm and receive a box or bag of fresh food each week during the season. Buying a share in a CSA is a way to lower the overall cost of the food for the consumer and get the freshest food available. It also helps to support and extend local food production. You can even go see your food growing - what fun!

The CSAs are listed in Appendix G. Some CSAs have internships available for those who want to learn how to grow their own food.

Grow your own food?

In the Yard

Growing your own food can be economically rewarding as well as provide the absolutely freshest food. The convenience can't be beat—just walk into your garden for today's salad and vegetables. Go to the chicken coop for eggs. Children will find this all fascinating (adults, too).

During World War II, the government encouraged citizens to plant "Victory Gardens." Resources for transportation of all sorts were becoming scarce, so local production became more important. (History may be repeating itself, with the cost of gasoline and diesel fuel rising.) Nearly 20 million people started gardens. Judge Marvin Jones, acting as War Food Administrator, stated that these gardens produced 8 million tons of food supplies, which added up to an astounding 40 percent of all vegetables grown for consumption in the United States in 1942.[1] Eleanor Roosevelt started a Victory Garden on the White House grounds. And today, for the first time since World War II, we have an organic garden on the lawn of the White House, tended by our First Lady, Michelle Obama.

Appendix H provides more information on growing your own food.

Garden-share

You may have a yard or some land that would make a wonderful garden, but can't grow the food yourself. You may be able to find someone who would love to grow food on your land. You provide the land, someone else provides the labor, and you both share in the produce.

> Urban Garden Share is a web-based service located in Seattle, Washington, that matches gardeners to gardens. See their site at www.urbangardenshare.org. They describe themselves: "Urban Garden Share pairs together eager gardeners with eager gardens. When neighbors come together and cooperatively grow food, dirt flies and good things happen." The possibility exists locally for such a service.

Or simply hire someone to put the garden in for you. We have a new category of businesses focused on creating food gardens. We listed them in Appendix H, but you can also ask your local garden store or landscaping service if they can help. Check with a local farmer—some might like the opportunity to "foodscape" your yard.

Community Gardens

Lacking land, you can grow food in a community garden. Working with other people can be fun. Check local zoning laws to see where gardens are permitted. Consult the agricultural extension office to see if there is an existing community garden near your. Appendix H lists all the community farms we could find. We hope more will be created.

Living off the Land: Foraging, Fishing and Hunting

Humboldt County has a wide variety of native foods which can be gathered, caught or hunted. Appendix I provides some initial guidance.

Summer provides a bounty of berries. Go for a hike and your snacks are there for the picking. Bring a pail and fill it with blackberries or huckleberries. Go home and make pies, tarts, jam and other treats. Teas are made from some native plants which may already be growing in your yard. Gather seaweed for sushi, pickles and broth.

Fall and winter are mushroom seasons. Regionally, we have a huge variety of mushrooms, many of them edible. *Be sure you gather in a legal area and that you know for certain which can be eaten and which are toxic.* Guide books and information on the local Mycological Society are in Appendix I.

With many rivers and the ocean nearby, local fish and seafood are available if not always abundant.

Carol Moné
Foraging

And finally, quail, grouse, geese, ducks and deer are among the birds and animals that are hunted in this region.

What about winter and early spring?

One of the challenges of eating locally is to find produce and fruit in the winter and early spring. Here are several solutions.

Keep it Growing
Fresh produce will grow throughout the year in a greenhouse. In our temperate climate, many Asian greens can overwinter outside. Broccoli, carrots, celery, chard, collard greens, fennel and kale also grow as winter crops in much of our region.

Storing and Preserving Food
Preserve foods when they are abundant and use them in winter through early spring. A chapter in the Recipes section of this book is devoted to food storage and preservation.

Cold Storage is an easy option for foods such as winter squash, onions, garlic and root vegetables. Food can be kept for extended periods of time if kept cold either in a cool room such as a root cellar or in a refrigerator.

Broccoli, corn, cauliflower, green beans and peas freeze well. Freeze sliced apples and berries in a bag. Cut up sweet peppers or onions and freeze them—they'll be ready for cooking any time of the year. Roast hot peppers and freeze them for later use. Turn vegetables into stock and freeze the stock to use in a mid-winter soup.

Vegetables that pickle well include cucumbers, beets, string beans, carrots, watermelon rind and cabbage (as sauerkraut or kim chee.) Bull kelp can be successfully pickled as well.

Drying is a good option for fruit and tomatoes. Dried apples, plums, peaches or pears make quick tasty snacks. Sun-dried tomatoes are fabulous in appetizers or main dishes.

Jams and jellies are a good place for a novice canner to start. Canning low acid fruits and vegetables, on the other hand, requires much more care. Turn tomatoes into tomato sauce, tomato paste, salsa or pasta sauce, or just can them whole. Can dilly beans, beets, corn, pears, plums or peaches. Apples can easily be made into applesauce. Did you catch a big albacore or salmon? You can also can that for later use. *Always make sure to follow canning instructions very carefully to avoid food poisoning. Canning is a science, not an art.*

Drying and canning have a further ecological benefit: the food needs no refrigeration, so no additional energy is consumed for storage.

Chapter 3: Eating Locally on a Budget

We sometimes hear people say that eating locally is more expensive. We acknowledge that out-of-pocket costs for local, organic, sustainably-raised food is higher.

However, the price of industrial food is artificially low. Many costs are hidden, including those to our personal health and the health of the planet. More discussion on this enormous issue can be found in Chapter 1.

> Steve Suppan, Director of Research at the Institute for Agricultural and Trade Policy, says, "It's not that we really produce cheap food, just that by externalizing a lot of the cost, we've made it appear to be cheap."[1]

Much of our industrial, processed and fast food, with its high fat, salt and sugar content, contributes to obesity, high blood pressure, diabetes, and other illnesses. Health care costs related to those conditions are not reflected in the price per pound of the food we eat.

> A 2009 study published in *The Journal of Health Affairs* reveals, "We estimate that the medical costs of obesity could have risen to $147 billion per year by 2008."[2]

We price-shop for food in a way that we don't for many other products. You want a faster computer with more features? A TV with a bigger screen? An automobile with better performance or styling? You know you will pay more. Quality in food also costs more, but we have been well-trained for decades to consider price as the most important criteria for our selections. It may be time to reconsider our priorities.

What is the value of food that tastes really good? Would you feel okay about paying more for a tomato that actually tastes like a tomato or a peach that is juicy and sweet?

What is the value of food that is healthier for you? Is grass-fed beef, containing one-fourth the amount of fat of feed-lot beef (and better for your health) worth more money?

Is the better value a sugary soda or two eggs from a pasture-raised hen? Each option costs less than a dollar.

That said, many people have serious economic constraints that cause the one-dollar hamburger to seem attractive. Here are some ideas to help save money without sacrificing food quality. Many of the ideas involve spending time rather than money. Some involve changing habits.

Grow Your Own Food

Growing in a small space, even in containers, can produce a lot of food.

If you don't want to start a garden for all or most of your produce, start with an herb garden. If you like fresh herbs, you know how much they cost at the grocery. Many herbs are perennial, so you can plant once for several years of harvest. Plant a few fruit trees; they are easy to grow and can provide fruit for years.

If it's allowed in your neighborhood, raise a few chicken for the eggs and/ or meat.

Appendix H can help you get started growing some of your own food.

Join a Community Supported Agriculture (CSA) Farm Program

Overall, your share of the farm products will cost less than buying produce items individually. Your menu planning will naturally follow the seasons. You will start with the available food and then decide what to cook rather than deciding what to cook and then look for the ingredients regardless of season.

Barter

In exchange for food, provide a service at which you are good. This might be a computer service, running errands, babysitting, accounting, or whatever your skill might be. Volunteer to work on a farm in exchange for food. You'll gain skills and new friends.

Cook From Scratch

Home-cooked food is usually less expensive than processed food and healthier than fast food. Regardless of a person's income level, cooking at home provides healthier diets. Take a cooking class. Read some of the articles in the food section of the local newspaper. Food for People offers free cooking classes at the Eureka North Coast Co-op kitchen. Cook with your children—it is an enjoyable family activity that will teach your children healthy food habits.

Process Your Own

Most packaged foods are very expensive per ounce—consider the price of salsa or salad dressing. A five-dollar bottle of salad dressing can be made at home for less than a dollar, using oil and vinegar or lemon, fresh garlic plus herbs from the kitchen garden. Chop tomatoes, onions, peppers, garlic and cilantro—voila! you have an excellent low-cost salsa. Next time you need whipped cream, buy local heavy cream and whip it yourself instead of spending nearly double the cost for an aerosol can. As you examine out-of-pocket costs for processed, prepared foods at the grocer, you will begin to see the savings in homemade. Some homemade items can be made in bulk and frozen for future use, saving both time and money.

Don't Waste

Eat the food you buy. Don't throw it away.

> Timothy Jones, in a University of Arizona study, reports: "On average, households waste 14 percent of their food purchases. Fifteen per cent of that includes products still within their expiration date but never opened. Jones estimates an average family of four currently tosses out $590 per year, just in meat, fruits, vegetables and grain products."[3]

Be Creative

Keep the peelings and trimmings from vegetables to make a vegetable soup stock. Buy a whole chicken for a lower-per-pound price and roast it for a meal. After dinner, remove the remaining pieces of meat. It might be enough for a chicken salad, or add it to that vegetable stock for a wonderful soup (with a few added vegetables). The leftover bones can also be used to make the stock for the soup. You can have at least one more meal from that chicken—maybe two.

Downplay Meat

Most Americans eat more meat than necessary for a healthy diet and meat is expensive. Adding a few vegetable-based meals to your weekly diet can save money and promote better health. Vegetarians do well without meat.

If you use meat, use it as an ingredient rather than as a meal. Employ eggs or dairy products rather than red meat—it's less expensive. If you want to include meat in your meal plan, buy range- or grass-fed meat or poultry raised in pastures. With the money saved from not buying a larger quantity of feed-lot meat, you can enjoy the higher quality of range-raised and organic poultry in the amounts you actually need. The recipe chapter on vegetable-based entrées provides more information.

In-Season Equals On-Sale

In-season produce and fruit is less expensive at the grocery and at the farmers' markets. Negotiate with the farmer for bulk price for case-lots. Preserve some of that less expensive food for later use.

Forage

Gather, hunt and fish. It's out there, go find it. It also might be fun. *Make sure you know what to pick and where it is legal. Make sure you have proper fishing and hunting licenses and know the law.*

Assistance

Apply for WIC coupons from The Special Supplemental Nutrition Program for Women, Infants and Children. Use some of the WIC coupons to purchase good local food at our farmers' markets. Most farmers are happy to take the coupons.

Contact Food for People (FFP), our local food bank.

> Food for People is working to eliminate hunger and improve the health and well-being of our community through access to healthy and nutritious foods, community education and advocacy. Volunteers from FFP collect and distribute food gleaned from local farms, backyards and farmers' markets. FFP currently distributes food throughout our community by means of 16 area food pantries. Food is also distributed through the Children's Summer Lunch Program, Senior Brown Bag program and more. FFP now holds two People's Produce Markets (music an added attraction), during the summer and early fall in Eureka and Garberville.

Food for People, Inc.
The Food Bank for Humboldt County
307 W. 14th St.
Eureka CA 95501
707-445-3166 telephone 707-445-5946 fax
www.foodforpeople.org

If you can afford it, send a little money to Food for People to help our neighbors through tough times.

Food For People encourages more people who are eligible for Food Stamps to get them. Only 57 percent of eligible people apply. Changes to eligibility rules in 2009 make it easier for families with children under 18, primarily, to qualify, but others may also qualify. This government money can add tremendously to the local economy. Use the stamps at farmers' markets.

> In 2008, through Food for People's gleaning program, Humboldt farmers donated nearly 60,000 pounds of fresh, nutritious produce for community members in need.

Grace Good Shepherd Church in McKinleyville, like some other local churches, cultivates gardens specifically to produce fresh, organic food for low-income households in their community. The food goes to those who might not otherwise be able to afford organic vegetables. Do you belong to a local organization that might do the same?

Advocate for Policy Change

Our last suggestion will not save you money today but may help us all over the long term. Become aware of national legislation regarding government food policy and agricultural subsidies. Much legislation benefits large agri-business over the welfare of the consumer. If an issue is important to you, contact your government representatives and let them know your views. Two organizations can help you stay informed.

Signing up for e-mail notices from The Organic Consumers Association is an easy way to stay posted.

> The Organic Consumers Association (OCA) is an on-line and grass-roots non-profit 501(c)3 public interest organization campaigning for health, justice, and sustainability. The OCA deals with crucial issues of food safety, industrial agriculture, genetic engineering, children's health, corporate accountability, Fair Trade, environmental sustainability and other key topics. We are the only organization in the U.S. focused exclusively on promoting the views and interests of the nation's estimated 50 million organic and socially responsible consumers.[6]

Visit the The Cornucopia Institute's web site for information related to family-scale farming. Their mission is:

> Seeking economic justice for the family-scale farming community. Through research, advocacy, and economic development our goal is to empower farmers—partnered with consumers—in support of ecologically produced local, organic and authentic food.[7]

Chapter 4: History, Present and Future

Naysayers look at our existing globally-based industrial food system and say, "Re-localize our food system? It's not possible to produce that much food locally." Such a criticism, however, fails to recognize that not only can we produce that much food locally, but we already have. By examining the historical record of what First Nations' People relied on for sustenance, and what Euro-American immigrants produced locally, we can see that our region suits us perfectly for agricultural independence. Not only can we produce plenty of food, but thanks to our diverse elevations and maritime and inland zones, we can grow a wide variety of crops throughout a very long growing season.

Food is Sacred
Cheryl A. Seidner, Wiyot

Food is Sacred . . . it's not just for pleasure . . . but to sustain life.

The day begins with prayer. Food is gathered, prepared and prayed over once again, giving thanks to the Creator for the abundance of all that is gathered.

Everything has a season and it is no different for gathering indigenous crops. Whether it be salmon, abalone, mussels, eel, surf fish, clams, crabs, rabbit, deer, elk, acorns, hazel nuts, pepper nuts, berries, onions, potatoes and all the rest, we are patient—waiting for the right time to harvest.

When the time is right, we gather the family and off we go to those favorite spots that we have been tending for generations. A lunch is packed: smoked eel and salmon, Grandma's sand bread and a Mason jar filled with water. With buckets, sacks and baskets in hand, off we go. Never taking more than what we needed was always the rule.

Camping on the river bar in the willows or on the beach, watching Mama cooking over the open fire and sleeping on the ground under the starry nights; it was a fantastic adventure. Watching Dad surf fish and teaching us to do the same was great fun.

Today it is different; barbed-wire fences have stopped our comings and goings. "No Trespassing" signs have gone up where we once gathered. There was a time when the County sprayed the roadside where we would gather berries and such. We are all grateful that that has almost stopped. Today we look for new places to gather and we continue our search for the indigenous foods of yesterday.

We always remembered to gather enough to share—not forgetting those who could not come with us. Today is no different, and we remember those who can no longer gather.

The recipes have been handed down for generations. Rarely are these recipes in written form. Eel and water-fried potatoes, smoked salmon napes, fried potatoes and fresh eggs for breakfast, and clam chowder and oven bread are a few of those recipes. Nothing fancy here, just down-home cooking for the plain and simple life. This may be the case for the indigenous people of Humboldt County, the Yurok, Hupa, Mattole, Karuk, Bear River and Wiyot.

Life is sacred, as is the food of the indigenous people throughout the world. Up until 1860, the Wiyot had for centuries held a World Renewal ceremony where all the local tribes came together. The ceremony was to thank the Creator for all that had been provided in the previous year and to pray for the coming year, to set the world right and to begin the new year.

History from 1850

European settlers arrived in the early 1850s and found good land for crops and livestock. Three early reports verify the abundance and variety of the foods produced in the 19th century.

Product	1860[1] Acres	1860[1] Bushels	1880[1] Acres	1880[1] Bushels	1891[3] Acres	1890 Bushels
Wheat	1,564	40,564	3,705	86,600	1,504	350,000[2] 34,587[3]
Barley	58	1,991	3,289	54,418	2,244	250,000[2] 103,221[3]
Oats	542	15,723	7,193	260,774	7,805	600,000[2] 351,234[3]
Corn	63	1,990	364	10,223	572	100,000[2]
Peas	883	31,584	656	17,321	776	38,413[3]
Potatoes	744	56,632	1,706	9,428,000	1,434	221,934[3]
Butter in pounds		34,400		96,750		Estimated 2,023,720[3]
Cheese in pounds		6,800		1,400		n. a.
Apple trees		15,888		10,457		n. a.
Peach trees		2,330		2,550		n. a.
Pear trees		567		927		n. a.
Plum trees		508		1,223		n. a.
Horned cattle		19,205		26,623		n. a.
Cows		n. a.		n. a		13,638[3]
Cattle*		n. a		n. a		18,822[3]
Sheep		523		170,829		93,104[3]
Goats		18		372		142[3]
Hogs		8,194		7,267		5,304[3]

Table 4.1 Agriculture in Humboldt County in the 19th Century
*Stock cattle, beef cattle and calves

By 1881, Humboldt County was exporting potatoes, oats, wheat, peas, wool, barley, apples, cowhide, bacon, pork, lard, tallow, butter, leather, beef, fish, salmon, tanbark, charcoal and flax seed. In 1881, Humboldt County exported more than 21 million pounds total. In addition, the county exported poultry, eggs, horses, calves, sheep, hogs, pelts, skins, furs and many lumber products, the largest exports being wood products, potatoes, oats, wheat, peas, wool and butter.[1]

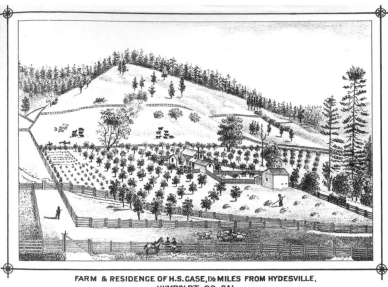

FARM & RESIDENCE OF H.S.CASE, 1½ MILES FROM HYDESVILLE, HUMBOLDT CO. CAL.

By 1892, there were 26 creameries. A salmon cannery was located at the mouth of the Eel River, and Fortuna had a fruit cannery.

The Fortuna fruit cannery was started in 1892 and by 1893, canned 25,000 cans of strawberries, prunes, plums, cherries, raspberries, currants, gooseberries, wild blackberries, huckleberries, pears and "pie fruits." The Humboldt Chamber of Commerce reported the fruit cannery " . . . has been of inestimable benefit to the surrounding country in stimulating fruit production, especially berries and small fruits for which the soil and climate of Humboldt are particularly adapted." In one season, this cannery established a reputation for excellence of its product and easily contracted the whole output for 1893 at profitable figures.[3]

By 1913, we have the following reports:

It should not be forgotten that one of the greatest apple experts in the world, George E. Rowe, vice-president of the American Pomological Society, has declared that Humboldt county contains some of the best apple-growing lands on the face of the earth.[4]

Albert E. Etter, Humboldt County's famous plant breeder and strawberry grower, predicts great things for the small fruits and berries. He sees many spots which are capable of being transformed into veritable gardens of Eden, this without any fear of frost or pests.[4]

By 1927 Humboldt County farmers were winning numerous awards at the California State Fair. Seven first prizes for apples, four for varieties of wheat, two for barley and three for oats. Sorghum and maize also won first prizes. Four varieties of beans, crisp head lettuce, Swiss chard, sweet corn, spinach and three varieties of potatoes also took first-place awards. Many gold medals and third awards were also won in a large number of categories.[5]

From 1951, Humboldt County's records show that agricultural output has been dominated by livestock and dairy products. Livestock and dairy products, which accounted for more than 90 percent of the dollar value in 1951, now account for more than 80 percent. Fruit, vegetable and grain crops have been a small proportion of the economic value of our agriculture since 1950. They peaked in the 1970s, reaching nearly ten percent, largely due to the success of the potato crops. Since then, fruit, grain and vegetable crops have represented about two to four percent of the economic value of agriculture in Humboldt.

> Potatoes were once a major export crop of Humboldt County. An article in the *Times-Standard,* May 9, 1971,[9] reports:
>
> > Old files of the *Humboldt Times* from the 1860s through the 1890s indicate the potato industry was a major item. However, the battle with plant diseases was never successful, and growers gave up until recent years, when science rescued the crop.
>
> The article further reports:
> > The potato crop from this area is highly desirable for potato chips, because of their excellent quality. The major buyers are Granny Goose, Laura Scudder and Eagle Foods.
>
> At the peak, farmers were converting dairy land to potato fields at Grizzly Bluff, Pleasant Point, Waddington Island, the Loleta Bottoms, Blue Lake and Carlotta areas.[9] Acreage may have exceeded 2,500 producing over 30,000 tons of potatoes.

A few other trends may be noted. In the 1950s through 1970s, Humboldt County produced a large volume of chickens, ducks, pigeons, geese and turkeys. In 1951, the county produced 832,149 dozen eggs. That's almost ten million eggs! But production of eggs or poultry for meat is not currently significant. Hog production in 1951 was almost 5,000 animals. The last figure available for hogs is 200, in 1995. Sheep and lamb production was at 90,000 head in 1951, down to 3,370 in 2007.[10] Grain, once an important crop in our region, has economic importance since the 1980s only for animal feed.

> The *Humboldt Standard* reported: Large producers of turkeys were located in McKinleyville, Glendale, Hoopa and Blue Lake. The turkey count was 1,600 in 1941[7] and more than 2,100 by 1950. Humboldt County produced over 370,000 pounds of chicken in that same year.[8]

Some parts of our agriculture may have declined, but this brief review demonstrates that local self-sufficiency is indeed possible.

Current State of Agriculture

Although we, like many American communities, have become reliant on non-local industrial food, many of the local crops are coming back. Del Norte, Humboldt and Trinity Counties are seeing a revival of local farms. The rise and growth of farmers' markets and CSAs, as well as restoration of our historic variety of food crops, is encouraging. Many small farmers are starting to raise chickens and geese for meat and eggs, as well as rabbits. There is the beginning of a pork business. Two new farmers are growing grains including wheat, oats, barley and other grains.

Table 4.2 provides a snapshot of agricultural land use in the Tri-County region. We have many farms and a substantial amount of land designated as agricultural with the vast majority of it being used for dairy and beef products.

	Del Norte	Humboldt	Trinity
Number of Acres	18,168	597,477	124,943
Number of Farms	85	852	181
Average Size	214	701	690
Cropland Acres	7,987	33,877	n.a.
Percent in Cropland	43.96	5.67	n.a.
Top Crops in Terms of Acreage	Forage, bulbs, corms, rhizomes, etc.	Forage, floriculture, vegetables, grapes	Forage, grapes, Christmas trees, apples, vegetables

Table 4.2 2007 Agricultural Statistics in 2007[12]

**Other categories from United States Department of Agriculture are "pasture," "woodland" and "other uses."

Organic production is now an important part of our agricultural economy. Organic practices are used on cattle and dairy ranches as well as farms that produce the food we eat directly. Humboldt County's organic crops include beef, feed for livestock, dairy products, fruits, vegetables, nuts and grains. Most of the fruits and vegetables that can be grown here are available in their organic form. Our options are many.[13]

Threats to Our Agricultural Future and What is Needed

A study by Susan Ornelas, an Arcata local-food advocate, has shown that the region can produce 3,000 calories per day for each of the current residents. The potential exists for us to once again be reliant on our local food base, but there are a number of threats facing our future agricultural sustainability.

The 2003 Farm Bureau's Humboldt County Agricultural Survey[14] reported the three largest threats to county agriculture as being:

1. limited/decreasing land availability;
2. regulations; and
3. marginal profits

Melanie Patrick, Market Development Coordinator for the Humboldt Chapter of Community Alliance with Family Farmers, reports that Humboldt

County lost 87,000 acres to "non-ag" between 1964 and 1982. An additional 100,000 acres were converted between 1982 and 2002. She estimates that only 50,000 acres remain. The USDA puts the estimate in 2007 at 33,877 acres for Humboldt County and 7,987 acres for Del Norte counties. Ms. Patrick further explains that her number of 50,000 is about the minimum acreage needed for us to be locally sustainable.

The Humboldt County Farm Bureau reinforces this point:

> The importance of agricultural land is unquestionable; yet, during the past several decades, nearly 100,000 acres of land has undergone land use changes due to subdivision activity. The County is currently attempting to slow down the agricultural land conversion process by supporting the Williamson Act Program[15]. Nearly 200,000 acres of land in the County is presently under this program. Humboldt County will continue to support the Williamson Act, as well as other measures to discourage the loss of agricultural land.
>
> Because there is a net importation of agricultural products into the county, a need exists to provide for the future production of essential food supplies; promote the continued presence of agriculture in Humboldt County; and conserve and utilize lands where agriculture is or can become economically viable. Many opportunities exist through non-traditional crops, intensive management and the operator's commitment to agriculture, to significantly contribute to the county's agricultural production. Much of the rural land in the county has the potential for a variety of agricultural uses.

The State of California has not provided money for the Williamson Act for the 2009-2010 budget year. Local governments are working to keep the program going, but it is difficult, given current economic conditions. This additionally threatens agricultural land.

> The California Land Conservation Act of 1965—commonly referred to as the Williamson Act—enables local governments to enter into contracts with private landowners for the purpose of restricting specific parcels of land to agricultural or related openspace use. In return, landowners receive property tax assessments which are much lower than normal because they are based upon farming and open space uses as opposed to full market value. Local governments receive an annual subvention of forgone property tax revenues from the state via the Open Space Subvention Act of 1971. (Williamson Act)

We can help protect our food future by advocating for agricultural land preservation. The County's General Plan and decisions made at the County Planning office and by city governments will affect our future. Aside from land scarcity, land cost is high, making it very difficult for young farmers to get started.

The basic infrastructure to support agriculture is broken. A broken infrastructure and regulations favoring large agricultural entities make it difficult for small farmers to make a living. We need central warehouses where farmers can take their fruit and vegetables for distribution to restaurants and grocery stores, as well as for export. We need local distributors who will coordinate between the farmers and the restaurants and groceries. We need processing facilities for poultry and produce. We need canning, freezing and drying facilities. Clearly a wide variety of business opportunities exists.

Hard work by many individuals and organizations is resulting in rebuilding parts of the infrastructure. Humboldt-CAFF has programs to connect farms with schools, restaurants and to the statewide CAFF warehouses to our south. In addition, two infrastructure projects are taking shape. A small group of people, including Sarah Brunner of Wild Chick Farm, Susan Ornelas of Arcata, and the Jacoby Creek Land Trust, has helped form the Humboldt Poultry Cooperative. A grant has been obtained for the construction of a mobile poultry processing unit. Farmers will be able to process their poultry and rabbits for sale on their farms and at farmers' markets. A project between the Yurok tribe and the Del Norte County economic development group is underway to create a fish cannery in the Klamath area.

We have made a start but there is much more work to be done to create a local food system that can fully sustain us.

The infrastructure will be put in place and the farmers will grow the crops and raise the animals if the market demand exists and if the community supports policies to make it possible. We can start by voting with our dollars. We can choose, three times a day, to support the local food economy and our community.

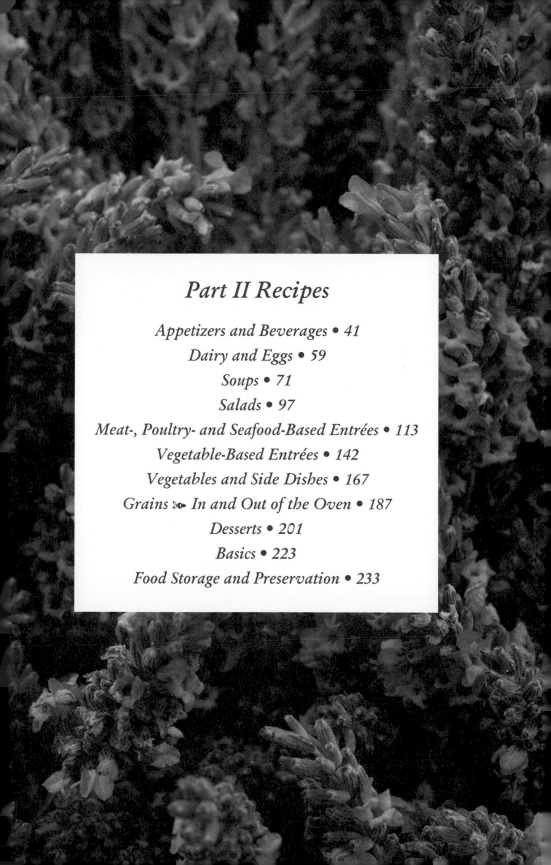

Part II Recipes

About the Recipes

The recipes in *Locally Delicious* focus on our local foods. Most of the ingredients are grown or raised within Del Norte, Humboldt and Trinity Counties. Olive oil, rice and some cheeses are from our extended area of approximately a 250-mile range.

Spices are included for the reasons described in Chapter 1. There are a few other minor "cheats" where a very small amount of a non-local ingredient is needed in a recipe that is overwhelmingly local.

Some ingredients are not commercially available but can be grown in our region and are grown in some personal gardens. By including them, we hope local farmers will be encouraged to grow them. These include bush cranberries, dent corn, garbanzo beans, Japanese winter greens, pomegranates, shallots, soy beans and sunflower seeds.

Appendix B lists farms and what they grow. Most ingredients are available from many local farmers; however, some are only grown by a few farmers. For some of these hard-to-find ingredients, we list the farm that produces them on the recipe page where they are used.

We list our contributors at the end of each recipe. We thank each one of them. All of the recipes were reformatted to fit the style chosen for the book. Some were altered to make them more local. Some were edited for number of servings. We hope we did not make any changes that will cause the authors of these recipes to be unhappy. If so, or if we made errors, we apologize in advance.

Please use the recipes and the seasonality charts on pages 248-251 to get started (or to continue) enjoying our local bounty. But first, a note from local cooks from our past:

1907
Eureka Cook Book,
The Ladies League of
the First Congregational
Church

PREFACE

TO to be a Good Cook means the knowledge of all Fruits, Herbs, Balms and Spices, and all that is healing and sweet in fields and groves, and savory in meats, means carefulness, inventiveness, watchfulness, willingness and readiness of appliance. It means the economy of your great grand mothers and the science of modern chemists. It means much tasting and no wasting. It means English thoroughness, French art and Arabian hospitality. It means in fine, that you are to be perfectly and always ladies (loaf-givers) and are to see that everyone has something nice to eat.

RUSKIN.

Appetizers and Beverages

Crunchy Baked Chevre

2-4 Servings

Serve on top of mixed greens, on garlic croutons, or top pasta with a tomato-based sauce and the baked chevre.

Preheat oven to 350°

6 ounces Cypress Grove chevre
Shape or cut chevre into 4 equal pieces about ½-inch thick. Set on paper towels for about 30 minutes to dry.

½ teaspoon dried thyme leaves, crumbled
2 tablespoons chopped fresh parsley
½ cup fresh bread, dried and rolled into crumbs
Combine herbs and crumbs.

¼ cup extra-virgin olive oil
Brush cheese with oil, then roll in crumb mix. Pour remaining oil into a shallow glass baking dish, then place coated chevre in dish. Bake 10 minutes.

Remove from oven and let cool about 5 minutes to firm.

Cypress Grove Chevre

Cypress Grove Chevre Olive Spread

4-6 Servings

The olives highlight the tangy chevre in this delightful cracker spread.

5 ounces Cypress Grove Purple Haze chevre
1 cup Kalamata or assorted olives, coarsely chopped by hand or in a food processor
Water crackers or toasted baguette rounds
Extra-virgin olive oil
Let cheese come to room temperature. Place on a serving plate and surround the chevre closely with the chopped olives. Drizzle liberally with olive oil and season with freshly ground pepper.

Cypress Grove Chevre

Lauren Cohn-Sarabia, Food Stylist
Chris Wisner, Photographer

Garlic and Sun-Dried Tomato Spread

4-6 Servings

Perched on a slice of a sweet baguette, this Mediterranean appetizer will have you wishing you had made a triple batch. Served with other antipasto dishes, this will be the star attraction.

Preheat oven to 350°

4 large garlic bulbs (or 1 elephant garlic), peeled and separated into cloves
1½ cups chicken broth
1 tablespoon olive oil

Place garlic cloves in baking dish. Cover with chicken broth and drizzle olive oil over top. Bake 45 minutes to an hour, until cloves are tender and soft. Mash the cooked garlic.

12 ounces sun-dried tomatoes in olive oil, julienned
16 ounces feta or goat cheese, crumbled

Pour tomatoes over garlic mixture and top with cheese. Bake another 15-20 minutes (until cheese melts).

1 baguette, sliced

Serve in a bowl alongside the bread slices.

Barbara Cohen

Stuffed Nasturtium Flowers

6 Servings

Naturally peppery, the bright flowers make a delicious appetizer and provide a colorful highlight to your table. This recipe makes filling for 12 flowers, but you may increase it to serve your party needs.

12 nasturtium flowers (in their prime)
½ cup soft chevre
¼ cup thinly sliced scallions
Optional: ⅛ cup diced sun-dried tomatoes

Mix the cheese, scallions and dried tomatoes together. With the back side of a spoon, spread into the cavity of the nasturtium flower.

Lauren Cohn-Sarabia
Comfort of Home Catering

Cucumber "Crackers" and Cheese

4-6 Servings

1 large cucumber
12 mixed cherry tomatoes, cut in halves
Small handful of fresh basil

Wash cucumber, tomatoes and basil in cool water. Pat dry. Cut cucumbers into ¼-inch thick chips. Place on plate and lightly blot top of cucumber with a towel.

4-ounce package goat cheese, at room temperature

Spread a dollop of goat cheese on top of each cucumber chip. Sprinkle small amount of chopped basil on the cheese. Place a cherry tomato half, cut side down, in the middle of each piece.

Cyndi Freitas

Los Bagels Pesto Spread

About 3-4 Cups

1¼ pounds cream cheese, softened

Whip cream cheese in a mixing bowl until soft.

½ cup basil
¼ cup walnuts
1 tablespoon garlic (or more to taste)
⅛ cup olive oil

Purée in food processor until smooth. Add to cream cheese. Mix until combined, scraping down sides of the bowl regularly to incorporate all cheese.

This spread should last about 2 weeks in the refrigerator.

Los Bagels

Editors note: Quantity adjusted from two quarts to one.

Check with the following farms for walnuts:
Sunny Slope Farm or Trident Lightning Farm and Orchard

Cypress Grove Chevre

Wanting a source of healthful milk for her children, Mary Keehn began raising Alpine goats in the 1970s. She quickly discovered that she had a natural talent for selectively breeding goats. Her herd began winning numerous awards and before she knew it, Mary was recognized as America's premier breeder of Alpine dairy goats.

As Mary's goat stock continued to improve, she was faced with an unexpected consequence: surplus milk from fifty goats! And so, armed with her kitchen stove and a knack for inventing unique and delicious recipes, Mary began dabbling with cheese making. It soon became clear that selective goat breeding was only one of Mary's many talents; she had a natural flair for cheese making as well. In 1983, with the help of family and friends, Mary made the move from kitchen hobbyist to cheese making entrepreneur.

Today, renowned for its innovative range of fresh, aged and ripened cheeses—many invented by Mary—and internationally awarded for excellence, Cypress Grove is a leader in the domestic goat cheese market.

Bean Dip for Pâté or Green Burritos

About 2 Cups as dip or pâté

4 Servings in burritos

This bean-based appetizer can be used as a dip with tortilla chips. Use it as you would a pâté on crackers or on a cucumber slice. For a meal, use it rolled in a tortilla or piece of lettuce with some added chopped vegetables.

1 cup dry beans
4 cups water

Soak beans overnight in about 4 cups of water. Pour off soaking water. Add about 3 cups of fresh water. Bring to a boil, lower heat and simmer until tender.

(If you forgot to soak the beans, put them in about 3-4 cups of water and simmer until tender—1½ to 2 hours.)

Drain the cooked beans thoroughly.

½ cup olive oil
¼ red bell pepper
2 teaspoons paprika
1 teaspoon ground cumin
1 green onion
1 teaspoon salt
½ jalapeño pepper, or ¼ teaspoon ground cayenne

Put all ingredients in a food processor. Process to a paste-like consistency.

If you want to use this as bean dip, thin with a bit of water, probably not more than ⅓ cup, but until the desired consistency is reached. Serve with tortilla chips.

For pâté, serve it on cucumber slices.

For a burrito, place about ½ cup of pâté on a lettuce leaf or flour tortilla. Add chopped tomato or other chopped fresh vegetables. Fold over ends of lettuce leaf or tortilla and roll into burrito shape. Eat whole, or slice across roll to create appetizers.

Ann Anderson

Beans from Warren Creek Farm

Savory Kale and Leek Flan

6 Servings

Preheat oven to 325°

2 large leeks
1 tablespoon butter
1 tablespoon olive oil

Coarsely chop the leeks, using both the white and green parts. In a large frying pan, sauté the leeks in the butter and olive oil over medium heat about 5 minutes, until they are soft.

¾ pound of kale, coarsely chopped

Stir in the kale and cook about 2 minutes more or until it is also soft. Purée the mixture in a blender or food processor and pour into a large mixing bowl.

3 eggs
1 cup vegetable or chicken broth (See pages 224 and 225)
Optional: 1½ ounces Parmesan or pecorino cheese

Whisk the eggs into the broth. Add the egg mixture and optional cheese to the bowl with the processed kale.

⅔ cup cream

In the same sauté pan that was used for the kale and leeks, bring the cream to a simmer. Pour the cream into the kale, leek and egg mixture slowly, whisking constantly as you do so.

Salt and pepper to taste

Add salt and pepper, then pour the mixture into 6 buttered ramekins or custard cups. Place them into a metal pan with hot water half way up the sides of the cups. Bake in pre-heated oven 30 to 35 minutes. To test to see if done, insert the tip of a knife into the center of one custard. The knife should come out clean.

When the ramekins are cool enough to handle, run a knife around the inside of each cup and turn the flan out onto individual plates. Serve with bread, crostini or bruschetta.

Patricia Cambianica
La Trattoria

Olivada

About 3 Cups

This is a simple but delicious spread for crackers or toast. (See pages 198 and 199 for crackers)

2 cups mild green olives, pitted
1 clove garlic
½ cup walnuts, lightly toasted
½ teaspoon rosemary

Finely chop the olives, garlic, walnuts and rosemary in a food processor.

About ½ cup extra-virgin olive oil

While processor motor is running, pour enough olive oil into mixture to form a smooth paste.

Henry Robertson
Henry's Olives

Muffaletta

6-8 Servings

This is a tasty local version of the olive salad used on the famous New Orleans sandwich of the same name.

1½ cups green olives, pitted
1 cup sun-dried tomatoes
1 red pepper, roasted
2 tablespoons capers
1 clove garlic
1 tablespoon red wine vinegar

Pulse ingredients in a food processor.

Extra-virgin olive oil

Drizzle in enough olive oil to make a spreadable paste.

This delectable mixture is traditionally spread on a crusty roll, along with salami, mortadella, provolone and havarti cheese. It also makes a delicious spread on toast, crackers or bruschetta.

Henry Robertson
Henry's Olives

Lauren Cohn-Sarabia, Food Stylist
Lauren Cohn-Sarabia, Photographer

Check with the following farms for walnuts:

Sunny Slope Farm
Trident Lightning Farm and Orchard

Henry's Olives

In 1993, Henry Robertson picked up a crate of raw, freshly picked olives at the North Coast Co-op in Arcata. He cured them, following a recipe in the crate. The result surprised Henry and the olives were well received by his family and friends. For a few years he continued to cure olives, altering the recipe, experimenting, and sharing them with his family and friends. Each year it seemed the demand would grow and grow. Co-workers and friends of friends began asking for them, buying them for themselves and as gifts. As the demand for his olives grew, so did the need for curing space. In 2003, Henry's woodworking shop was renovated and is now the home of Henry's Olives, a cottage industry that cures more than four tons of olives per year. The olives are cured in small batches and are never canned, resulting in the quality and freshness of Henry's Olives.

Stuffed Cherry Tomatoes

25-30 Stuffed tomatoes

Cherry tomatoes are bite-sized appetizers in their own right. They can also be delectable little containers for a variety of stuffings. Our recipe offers two stuffings.

The preparation of the tomatoes is the same for all versions. Wash and dry the tomatoes. Cut off the tops and scoop out the seeds. Lay them upside down on paper or cloth towels to drain.

Cheese Stuffing

Stuffing for 25-30 Tomatoes

16 ounces goat cheese
Milk
Parsley
Paprika

Let the cheese come to room temperature and blend it with enough milk so that it can be easily spooned into the tomatoes. If you want a fancy finish, fill tomatoes using a cake decorating or pastry bag. Garnish with parsley and/or sprinkle the tops with a little paprika. Refrigerate before serving.

Smoked Fish and Cheese Stuffing

Stuffing for 25-30 Tomatoes

8 ounces cream cheese
1 tablespoon lemon juice
1 teaspoon Worcestershire sauce

Mix lemon juice and Worcestershire sauce with cream cheese until it reaches a smooth consistency.

1 tablespoon finely chopped parsley
1 tablespoon finely chopped fresh basil
(for a different flavor, use fresh tarragon)

Mix in herbs.

1½ cups flaked smoked salmon, tuna or other smoked fish of your choice

Add fish and stir to mix well. Spoon into tomatoes. Cover and refrigerate before serving.

Ann Anderson

Toasted Kale

1 Large bowl

Toasted kale bits are crunchy and taste a bit like a veg etable chip—light and crispy and no fat!

Preheat oven to 400°

1 bunch kale
Wash kale, trim and tear into bite-size pieces.

Put kale on an ungreased cookie tray and cook 5-7 minutes, or until crunchy and browned. It needs nothing else.

Lynne Wells

Nutty Vegetable Crackers

About 2 dozen crackers

Vegetable crackers taste great with goat cheese.

2 cups mash from whatever vegetables you use to make vegetable juice. Try carrots, beets, celery, onion, garlic, arugula—be imaginative!
Process vegetables in a juicer. Keep the juice for drinking and the mash for making crackers.

½ cup ground walnuts
Your choice of spices
Optional: ½ cup soaked buckwheat or sun-flower seeds—be creative!
Mix the mash with spices and walnuts.

Roll out the mash mixture between sheets of wax paper or plastic. Cut into squares and place on dehydrating shelves. Set the dehydrator heat to about 105°. You can start the temperature at 120° for the first three hours, then lower the heat. Crackers take about 24 hours to become dry and crisp.

Store in airtight container.

Gail Coonin

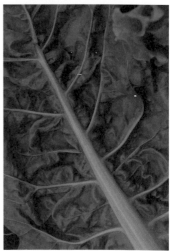

Check with the following farms for walnuts:

Sunny Slope Farm
Trident Lightning Farm and Orchard

Salsa

About 3 Cups

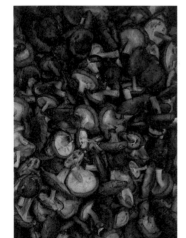

1 small onion
2-3 serrano or jalapeño peppers
2-4 cloves garlic, chopped
1 teaspoon olive oil

Add a very small amount of oil to a large frying pan and "dry-fry" the onion, chilies and garlic, turning with tongs, until evenly browned, about 5 minutes.

1 pound tomatillos

Broil the tomatillos, turning over a couple of times, until they start to soften and ooze juice.

½ cup chopped fresh cilantro
⅓ to ½ cup vegetarian broth or water (See page 224)
Salt and pepper

Use a blender to blend all ingredients well. Pour mixture into bowl. Add cilantro and broth to thin to desired consistency. It should have a more liquid consistency. Add salt and pepper to taste.

Debby Harrison

Marinated Mushrooms

8 Servings

These marinated mushrooms are so good they're habit forming, and easy to prepare too!

¼ cup lemon juice
½ teaspoon mustard
⅛ teaspoon pepper
½ teaspoon salt
¾ cup olive oil

Place marinade ingredients in a jar and shake to blend.

1 pound mushrooms, uncut if small, or cut into bite-size pieces
½ cup chives, chopped
½ cup parsley, chopped
Optional spices: dash of hot sauce, 2 teaspoons pressed garlic or ½ teaspoon tarragon

Combine and add to marinade. Marinate for at least one hour.

Ann Anderson

Roasted Bay Nuts

Gather nuts from the bay tree in the fall when they ripen but before the hulls rot.

Remove the hulls; dry the nuts in a low-humidity environment.

Roast the nuts in a 450° oven until they are creamy coffee colored. If they are too light or too dark, they taste bitter.

Clara Arndt

Gravlax (Cured Salmon)

About 8-16 Servings per pound of salmon fillet

Enjoy on bagels with cream cheese or on potato latkes with sour cream.

½ to ¾ cup kosher salt
½ cup coarsely ground black pepper
Sprinkle about ¼ cup salt and about ⅓ of the pepper onto the bottom of a glass baking dish.

1 salmon fillet, with or without skin
Zest of 1 orange
Fennel fronds, chopped, or fresh dill, chopped
Lay the fillet on the bed of salt and pepper, skin side down. Coat top of fish with the remaining salt and pepper. Sprinkle with the orange zest, then cover with the chopped fennel or fresh dill greens. Cover with plastic wrap and refrigerate 4-5 days.

Clean the salt, pepper and herbs off the fish and slice it thinly.

For lox:
If you have a cold smoker, you can smoke the prepared fish for 2-3 hours.

Henry Robertson
Henry's Olives

Fish Ceviche

6 Servings

This is usually served as an appetizer. Can be eaten with corn tortilla chips. (See page 203 for tortillas)

> **1 cup lemon juice**
> **1 cup lime juice**
> **2 cloves garlic, chopped**
> **1 small onion, chopped**
> **⅛ teaspoon crushed red pepper**

In a large bowl, combine lemon juice, lime juice, chopped garlic, onion and pepper.

> **2 pounds sole fillets, cut into tiny pieces, or substitute other local firm white fish**

Add the fish and stir.

> **2 tablespoons olive oil**
> **2 cups tomatoes, chopped**
> **½ cup (or to your taste) cilantro, chopped**

Add vegetables and oil. Cover; refrigerate 1 hour. Be sure liquid covers the fish so as to "cook" it. Add more juice if needed.

Add more vegetables if you like. You may determine the exact flavor and the amount of ingredients, but the cilantro is crucial.

> **Salt and pepper**

Refrigerate at least another hour to marinate. Test for salt and crushed pepper; adjust seasonings to your taste.

Patty Hoffman

Vegetable Tray

One of the easiest appetizers is to simply cut up fresh vegetables and arrange them on a tray. Add a cup of dipping sauce and you are finished. The Buttermilk Salad Dressing on page 112 is one to try.

Cut up sweet peppers—use a few colors—carrots, summer squash and celery. Add some radishes and cherry tomatoes for accents.

Lauren Cohn-Sarabia
Comfort of Home Catering

Barbecued Oysters

**6 Oysters per serving as an entrée;
2-3 as an appetizer**

Fresh oysters
Favorite topping

Place oysters on barbecue and heat until shells open up. Pull off top shell; put oysters in the bottom shell and back onto the barbecue. Add your favorite sauce on top. Cook until firm.

Simple sauce:
Lemon juice
Butter
Salt and pepper

See also watermelon sauce from Curley's (below), or use one of our local bottled barbecue sauces listed in Appendix F.

Catherine Peterson
North Bay Shellfish

Watermelon Barbecue Sauce for Oysters

Enough for 2 dozen oysters

½ sweet onion, diced (about 1 cup)
1 garlic clove, chopped
1 tablespoon olive oil

Sauté onions and garlic in oil until they are limp.

1 small ripe seedless watermelon (approximately 1 pound), rind removed, chopped

Add watermelon to pan and simmer 10 minutes.

4 tablespoons ketchup
1 teaspoon Worchestershire sauce
Juice from ½ lemon
1 teaspoon oil
Kosher salt to taste

Add remaining ingredients and simmer one hour.

Purée in a blender and season with kosher salt.

Curley's Grill
Ferndale CA

More than 70 percent of the fresh oysters consumed in California are grown in 450 acres of Arcata Bay, where the conditions are ideal.

Currently there are five companies raising both Pacific Oysters and Kumamoto oysters for export and the restaurant trade.

The Arcata Bay Oyster Festival is an Arcata Main Street event held annually. The festival began 15 years ago as a way to promote the area's local aquaculture industry. On average, 15,000 people attend each year.

Crab Dip

About 1 cup

**2 tablespoons mayonnaise or sour cream
 (See page 231 for sour cream)
1-2 tablespoons chili sauce (See page 227)
1 tablespoon lemon juice
Salt and pepper to taste**

Mix together mayonnaise (or sour cream), chili sauce, lemon juice and seasonings.

1 cup cooked crab meat, flaked

Add crab meat to sauce mixture. Serve on crackers or toast rounds.

Ann Anderson

Deviled Crab

4 Servings

Custardy, melt-in-your-mouth crab appetizer will delight your guests. A great recipe to start off the crab season!

Preheat broiler to 400°

**2 tablespoons butter
¼ cup onion, chopped
¼ cup bell pepper, chopped
¼ cup celery, chopped**

In a sauté pan, simmer all ingredients until onions are golden brown.

**¼ cup bread crumbs
¾ cup milk or cream**

Combine with sautéed vegetables and set aside.

**2 eggs
¼ teaspoon salt
1½ teaspoons Dijon-style mustard
Dash of hot sauce (try Weitchpec hot sauce)**

Stir together and add vegetables, bread, cream mixture. Cook on stove top until thickened.

1½ cups cooked crab meat, flaked

Add crab and mix. Pack into crab shells or ramekins. Brush with melted butter.

Broil until lightly browned.

Ann Anderson

Tomato Juice

4 Servings

This recipe can easily be modified. Change the amount and type of vegetables used, or add hot pepper for a snappier juice. Adjust herbs and spices to suit your own taste.

**About 12 medium-size tomatoes (use fewer
    if tomatoes are large) Use one type of
    tomato or a mixture of several types.**
½ cup water
1 or more slices of onion
2 ribs of celery
**3 sprigs of parsley (regular or Italian) or
    use watercress for a peppery flavor**
Optional:
**1 jalapeño pepper (I would not suggest
        using both watercress and jalapeño
        together)**
Cilantro to taste
1 tablespoon fresh tarragon leaves

Simmer for about 30 minutes. Strain mixture to remove seeds and skins.

1 teaspoon salt (or to your taste)
¼ teaspoon paprika
Optional:
Honey, to taste
Lemon, to taste
Horseradish, to taste
**¼ teaspoon cayenne pepper powder.
        (Do not use if you already used a
        fresh jalapeño.)**

Add other spices and mix. Chill and serve.

Ann Anderson

Kefir Culture

4 Servings

This kefir culture is a descendant of one originally brought to the U.S. from Russia, and has been passed down in one family for more than sixty years before making its way to me.

The kefir culture is a symbiosis between a bacteria and a yeast variety that forms a soft organism called a "scobie." This culture is different from the commonly purchased kefir drinks found at stores and has slightly different taste.

Suzanne Simpson

About 1 quart milk. You can start with either more or less, if you wish.
A few grains of Kefir culture*

Add the culture to a quart jar of the milk and cover with a cloth. Cheesecloth and muslin work well, although any cloth will do. Let the milk sit out for 1-3 days, depending upon room temperature and desired taste. Usually 24-36 hours is sufficient at room temperature. The longer it sits, the more sour it becomes. If you wish to speed up the culturing process, try stirring it occasionally and keeping it warm.

After 24 hours, try a bit of the kefir and check the consistency. When you feel like the kefir is done, take a spoon and scoop out the culture. If you are not going to use it again right away, wash the culture. Put it in a clean glass container with fresh milk in it to keep it alive. The culture may be stored, refrigerated, up to 3 weeks. The kefir is ready to drink as it is, or you may wish to sweeten it with honey, maple syrup or fruit. Store extra kefir in the refrigerator.

The kefir will thicken as it ferments and will eventually curdle and separate into curds and whey. If this happens, you can make a kind of soft cheese similar to chevre, allowing the curds to drain through a muslin cloth or several layers of cheesecloth.

Drinking a cup or so of kefir a day is great for replenishing pro-biotic bacteria.

Suzanne Simpson

*Ask your friends if they have some starter to share with you. Then keep it going and pass it on.

Eggs from Huckleberry Farm and Nursery
Chris Wisner, Photographer

Dairy and Eggs

Carrot Soufflé

4 Servings

A slightly sweet side dish. Serve as an accompaniment to a salad or a main dish.

Preheat oven to 350°

1 pound carrots, chopped
Steam carrots with a dash of salt until soft.

½ cup unsalted butter
In a large bowl, mash carrots. Add butter and mix.

3 eggs, separated into whites and yolks
1 teaspoon vanilla extract
Mix egg yolks and vanilla and add to carrots.

1 tablespoon flour
1 teaspoon baking powder
½ teaspoon salt
¾ cup sugar or ⅔ cup honey
Optional: dash of cinnamon or nutmeg
Sift flour and add salt, honey or sugar, and baking powder.

Blend all ingredients together until smooth, or of desired consistency; some small carrot chunks may be left.

Beat egg whites until they form peaks. Carefully fold eggs whites into mixture.

Place mixture into a buttered baking dish or soufflé cups. Bake 45 minutes. Serve warm or cold.

Jason Whitley
Earthly Edibles

Humboldt Times, June 24, 1865
WANTED, Fresh Butter and Eggs
by L. C. Schmidt & Co

Alexandre EcoDairy Family Farm
Photograph supplied by Alexandre EcoDairy Family Farm

Potato Frittata

8 Servings

This is an easy, delicious potato dish. Serve as a side dish or a hearty main-course meal.

Preheat oven to 375°

16 large eggs, beaten
Salt to taste

Combine eggs and salt in a bowl.

3 tablespoons melted butter

Coat a glass baking dish with melted butter. Dish must hold about 7-8 cups. A 13½-inch x 8¾-inch x 1¾-inch dish is about right.

3 large red potatoes, thinly sliced
1 large red onion, sliced into ⅛-inch thick slices
2 handfuls chopped basil

Put a thin layer of potatoes into baking dish. Then put in a layer of basil, a layer of onion and finally one more layer of potato. Pour eggs over all ingredients. Bake approximately 1 hour. Fritatta is done when an inserted knife comes out clean.

Suzanne Simpson

Warren Creek Farm
Chris Wisner, Photographer

Tortilla de Patatas

3 Servings as main dish
6 Servings as side dish

½ cup olive oil
1 pound fingerling potatoes, washed,
peeled and sliced ¼ inch thick
Salt to taste

Heat the oil in a skillet. Add the potatoes and salt and cook until the potatoes are browned. Be sure to stir so that the potatoes don't stick. If you want a lower calorie version, boil the potatoes until they are cooked; drain them, and just briefly sauté them in a very small quantity of oil. Drain the browned potatoes well or the resulting tortilla will be greasy.

4-6 eggs, well beaten

Add the cooked potatoes to the beaten eggs.

Optional additional ingredients (select one
or two):
¼ cup scallions, chopped
¼ cup red pepper, minced
¼ cup spinach, chopped
2 or 3 cloves garlic, minced

Optional ingredients can be slightly cooked in oil or left raw. Add them to the cooked potato and egg mixture.

Oil the sides and bottom of another skillet. Pour in all of the mixture. Shake the pan after a moment so that the mixture doesn't stick. When you see that it is congealed, put a plate over the pan and flip the tortilla onto the plate. Slide the tortilla back into the skillet and brown the other side. (An alternate method is to put it under the broiler in the oven).

Slice the tortilla into pie-shaped wedges. Serve warm, at room temperature, or refrigerate overnight.

Carol Moné

Egg Strata

4 Servings

A favorite lunch dish at Northcoast Preparatory and Performing Arts Academy (NPA) in Arcata. It's a tasty way to use up leftover bread of any kind.

Preheat oven to 350°

Butter, enough to coat a 3-quart baking dish
6 pieces of bread, cut into 1-inch cubes
Spread bread in buttered pan.

8 eggs, beaten
1 cup milk
1 cup grated cheese (more, if you want it cheesier). Any type of local cheese will do.
1 teaspoon chopped fresh basil
1 teaspoon chopped fresh oregano
1 teaspoon chopped fresh sage
Salt and pepper to taste
2 cups vegetables cut into 1-inch pieces. Any vegetables you like—onion, asparagus, peppers, mushrooms, zucchini, chard or spinach—all work well in this recipe.

Mix eggs, milk, cheese, seasonings and vegetables and pour over the bread cubes. Bake 30 minutes, or until eggs are firm to the touch.

Serve hot. Delicious with salsa on top.

Lauren Cohn-Sarabia
Comfort of Home Catering

Italian Tomato Cheese Strata

6 Servings

Makes a deliciously hearty breakfast, lunch or dinner.

Preheat oven to 375°

1 tablespoon olive oil
1 cup carrots, grated
4 large cloves, finely chopped

Heat oil, add carrot and garlic; cook 30 seconds.

28 ounces fresh tomatoes, chopped
1 teaspoon fresh thyme, chopped
¼ cup fresh basil, chopped

Add tomatoes, basil and thyme. Cook, stirring, until dry, 20-25 minutes.

2½ cups milk
16 slices white or wheat bread

Grease a 2-quart casserole. Soak bread slices in milk 3 minutes. Drain and save milk.

1 pound Cheddar cheese, shredded

Alternately layer bread, sauce and cheese.

5 large eggs
Salt and pepper to taste

Mix together eggs, reserved milk, and salt and pepper to taste. Pour egg over strata, poking with knife until liquid is absorbed.

Bake until puffed and golden and knife inserted in center comes out clean, about 45 minutes.

Glee Brandon
Loleta Bakery

Loleta Cheese Company

Bob and Carol Laffranchi founded Loleta Cheese Company in 1982. The idea started with Bob when he was teaching agriculture education at Eureka High School. He began to lead his students through the process of cheesemaking, and the rest, as they say, is history.

Bob and Carol decided cheesemaking was what they wanted to do with their lives.

They are committed to manufacturing superior quality cheese, and in the process, contributing to the economy of Humboldt County, California. Their factory is located in the historical 1919 Bertsch Building, which they purchased and remodeled as their cheesemaking factory, specialty food and wine shop, and lavish gardens.

California Summer Squash Quiche

4-6 Servings

This light quiche does not call for a baked crust; however, you may add the filling to a crust of your choice if preferred.

Preheat oven to 325°

**1 pound summer squash such as zucchini
    or crookneck, cut into ¼-inch rounds**
½ onion, chopped

Combine squash and onion and steam until soft. Mash them together, leaving mixture slightly chunky. Drain off juice and leave to cool. Save reserved juice and steaming water for soup at another time.

4 eggs, beaten
1½ to 2 cups hard cheese, grated

Combine eggs and cheese.

½ teaspoon basil
½ teaspoon oregano

Add egg mixture and herbs to squash and mix.

Pour mixture into a buttered deep-dish pie pan or other baking dish (about 1-quart) and bake, uncovered, 30-40 minutes, or until knife inserted in center comes out clean.

Lia Webb

Option: Cut a few extra pieces of zucchini and use to decorate top of quiche. Cut a few cherry tomatoes as additional garnish. Add to top of quiche before baking.

Lauren Cohn-Sarabia, Food Stylist
Lauren Cohn-Sarabia, Photographer

Potato Crust Quiche

4 Servings

A nutritious alternative to a flour-crusted quiche.

Preheat oven to 350°

**1 pound russet potatoes, boiled and
    mashed**
1 teaspoon salt
⅓ cup butter

Butter deep-dish pie pan. Combine mashed potatoes with salt and butter. Spoon potato mixture into pan and smooth with a spatula. Bake until potato crust is slightly firm. Remove from oven.

**½ medium size carrot, chopped into small
    pieces (about ½ cup)**
½ cup zucchini, chopped into small pieces
**½ cup green beans, chopped into small
    pieces**

Sauté carrots, green beans and zucchini in 1 tablespoon butter until crisp-tender.

Spread vegetables into pie shell.

1½ cups milk
2 eggs
**1 cup soft cheese, such as Brie, Camembert
    or cream cheese. You can mix various
    cheeses.**

In blender, blend milk, eggs and cheese. Pour over the vegetables.

¼ cup basil, chopped
Sprinkle basil on top of vegetables.

Bake about 45 minutes, or until knife inserted in center comes out clean.

Faith Eastwood

We have not found a commercially made Brie or Camembert in Humboldt, Trinity or Del Norte County. Some of our close neighboring areas do have some that are carried in local markets. Look for Marin Fresh Cheese, Rouge et Noir and Rogue Valley Cheese. Gina Marie has award-winning cream cheese from Willows.

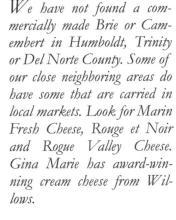

Humboldt Times, November 19, 1864

EGGS! EGGS! Until the arrival of the Steamer
I will pay sixty-five cents for EGGS.

W. J. Sweasey

Quiche with Kale Crust

4 Servings

Preheat oven to 350°

One bunch of kale or Swiss chard, steamed until very limp

Line an ungreated 9-inch pie pan with 3-4 layers of kale or Swiss chard.

6-8 eggs
1 tablespoon milk

Mix eggs and milk together.

1 medium onion, chopped
2-3 cloves garlic, minced
Zucchini or other in-season vegetables, chopped
1 tablespoon butter or olive oil

Sauté vegetables in butter or olive oil.

Note: When all the vegetables have been sautéed and the eggs have been added, the mixture should fill the pan. The editors suggests about a cup, total, of vegetables.

Let the vegetables cool, then add them to the eggs.

1 cup cheese, Monterey Jack or medium sharp cheese (get wild and add some slices of Humboldt Fog goat cheese)

Stir in the cheese.

Salt

Add salt to taste and pour mixture carefully into the kale crust.

Bake until set, about 25 minutes, or until a knife inserted in center comes out clean.

Jennifer Bell

When cooking with only local products, it can be tricky, for now, to make a crust with flour unless you belong to a grain CSA. Most quiche crusts are made with flour, but this one is made with large leaves of kale or Swiss chard.

Quiches aren't rocket science—experiment with any savory flavors. Add herbs from the garden—many grow here year around. Chives add an oniony flavor, thyme or winter savory are tasty additions. Many delicious vegetables are grown here, so your quiche can vary depending on the season. By the way, if you are calorie or fat conscious, the kale quiche is saving you about a zillion calories and grams of fat, is easier to prepare than the flour/butter crust, and I think you'll like it better.

Jennifer

*Mobile Chicken Coop
at Jacoby Creek Land Trust*

Clark Family Corn Pudding

6 Servings

This recipe was given to me more than 30 years ago by a co-worker in San Francisco named Frances Clark. I've made this recipe many times, with fond memories of working together and discussing old family recipes.

Preheat oven to 325°

Butter a lidded 2-quart casserole dish.

1½ cups milk
6 eggs, beaten
⅔ cup sugar or ½ cup honey
1½ teaspoon salt
2 teaspoons cornstarch

Beat together until fluffy.

2 pints fresh corn, cut from the cob
6 tablespoons butter, melted

Stir the corn and melted butter into the milk mixture.

Pour into the prepared dish, cover, and set dish inside a larger pan filled with water to about halfway up the side of the baking dish.

Bake 1 hour. Stir occasionally.

Lauren Cohn-Sarabia
Comfort of Home Catering

Dairy is the largest agricultural industry in Humboldt County and is also important in Del Norte County. Many dairies supply to Humboldt Creamery (now owned by Foster Farms Dairy) and some operate independently and sell under their own label. Alexandre EcoDairy Family Farm, in Crescent City, is one of the independents.

A more recent development has been the growth of the dairy goat industry. Much of this growth may be driven by the need for goat milk for our world-recognized goat cheeses, some produced by Cypress Grove Chevre, Inc.

Humboldt County also has several locally produced cow's milk cheeses, including those from the Humboldt Creamery and the Loleta Cheese Factory. Del Norte County is home to Rumiano cheese. If you extend the region we have Blue, Gorgonzola and TouVelle from the Rogue Creamery in Southern Oregon, and Brie and Camembert from Marin French Cheese Company in Mendocino County.

In 1951, Humboldt County produced almost 10 million eggs. We no longer have large-scale egg producers. However, you can buy eggs at farmers' markets, through at least one CSA, and from Alexandre Family Eco-Dairy at their farm or through some of our local grocery stores. Duck and goose eggs are also available from a few farms. Or you can keep a few chickens yourself.

Beets from Willow Creek Farms
Chris Wisner Photographer

Soups

Quick Oyster Stew • 72

Carrot Soup • 73

Delicious Barley Goose Soup • 74

Chanterelle Barley Soup • 75

Cream of Purslane Soup • 75

Rx: Chicken Soup • 77

Creamy Tomato Soup • 78

Nina's Borscht • 79

Leek and Potato Soup • 80

Super Zucchini Soup • 81

Easy Corn Chowder • 82

Clam Chowder • 83

Parsnip-Apple-Honey-Mustard Soup • 84

Portuguese Kale or Mustard Green Soup • 85

Gazpacho • 86

Caldo Gallego • 86

California Onion Soup • 88

Winter Harvest Soup • 89

Savory Croutons • 89

Cioppino • 90

Roasted Vegetable Soup • 92

Mushroom Soup with Paprika • 93

Cheddar Corn Chowder • 94

Quick Oyster Stew

8 Servings

¼ cup butter
Heat butter in soup kettle.

2 medium-size onions, peeled and chopped
1 stalk celery, chopped
Add vegetables to the pan and cook until onions are golden.

3 cups water
1 cup clam juice
1½ pounds potatoes, peeled and cut into ½-inch cubes
½ cup parsley, minced
½ teaspoon sugar
1 teaspoon salt
¼ teaspoon freshly ground pepper
Add to onion mixture, cover pot and cook at a low boil for 15 minutes.

2 cups fresh corn, cut from cob
Add the corn and simmer another 10 minutes.

2¼ cups milk
2 roasted red peppers, diced
1½ pints fresh oysters with liquor
Add to the pot and bring just to a boil. Lower heat and cook gently until oysters plump up and edges curl. Don't overcook or oysters will be tough. Adjust seasonings and serve immediately.

Martha Haynes

North Bay Shellfish
Scott Sterner

Carrot Soup

6-8 Servings

This is an old family recipe handed down from my mother, grandmother and aunt.

1 tablespoon oil
1 medium onion, chopped
Heat oil in 4-quart saucepan. Add chopped onions and sauté until tender and lightly browned.

8 medium carrots, cut into 1-inch lengths
6 cups chicken or vegetable broth (See page 224)
¾ teaspoon salt
Pepper to taste
Add carrots, chicken broth, salt and pepper. Reduce heat to low, cover, and simmer 15 minutes or until carrots are tender. Cool completely, then process soup in a blender, only filling blender ¾ full at a time. Blend until smooth.

Sour cream
2 teaspoons chopped fresh dill, plus a sprig of dill for garnish
Soup can be served warm or chilled. Before serving, stir in chopped dill. Garnish with dollop of sour cream and a sprig of fresh dill.

Nancy Sheen
Sheen Farms

Nothing beats a warming bowl of soup on a cold day! And it's an easy way to use leftover meat or poultry. A few beans and some rice or chopped vegetables are all you need for a meal. You can freeze premade stock in ice cube trays and store the cubes in plastic bags in the freezer, or freeze the stock in glass jars, leaving 3 inches of headroom. Your soups will go together in a snap.

Energy Saving

After the water has come to a boil, remove lidded pot from the stove, set it on a folded bath towel, and wrap it with a second towel. Then wrap it with a down comforter or a few layers of blankets. The soup will stay hot for about six hours. Unwrap it, put it on the stove and bring it back to a boil. Then rewrap it in the blankets for another six hours. This is an extremely energy-efficient "slow cooking" method.

Delicious Barley Goose Soup
About 4 Quarts

Goose bones, gizzard, heart and neck (feet are also excellent if available)

In a large soup pot, cover the goose parts with water. Put lid on pot and bring to a boil. Simmer goose for 3-4 hours on the stove. (See energy-saving tip in sidebar.)

Allow the liquid to cool and remove the bones from the meat. Chop the gizzard and heart into little bits and add to the preserved liquid with the rest of the meat.

4 cloves garlic, minced
3 large carrots, diced
¾ cup barley (Shakefork Community Farm)
1 cup chopped onion, lightly sautéed
4 stalks celery, finely chopped
1-2 cups wild mushrooms, if available
3 quarts water
3-5 skinned broccoli stalks, cubed
A handful of Solstice Soup Mix from Claudia's Herbs (about ⅛ cup)
Pepper to taste
3 tablespoons salt dried from local ocean water (See page 225)

Add to soup pot. Bring the soup to a boil and cook for about an hour, until vegetables are soft but toothsome instead of mushy.

1 bunch parsley, including stems, finely chopped
Optional: 3-5 kale leaves (Lacinate/Dinosaur variety is best)

Add parsley and kale. Cook about five minutes, until kale has turned a brighter green but before the parsley turns black.

Shail Pec-Crouse
Tule Fog Farm

Chanterelle Barley Soup

10-12 Servings

2 onions, chopped
¼ cup olive oil
8 cloves garlic, peeled and chopped

In a 5-quart soup pot, sauté the onion and garlic in oil.

2 tablespoons marjoram
¼ tablespoon thyme
1 tablespoon salt
½ tablespoon celery seed

Add seasonings.

2 quarts chanterelle mushrooms, carefully washed and chopped into ½-inch pieces

Add a bit more oil to the soup pot and sauté mushrooms until tender.

15 cups water
1 cup barley

Add water to mixture until the pot is almost full, then add barley. Bring to a boil, lower the heat, and simmer at least 45 minutes before serving. Add salt and pepper to taste.

The Beachcomber Café
Trinidad

Cream of Purslane Soup

4 Servings as a starter
2 Servings as a meal

1 cup chopped purslane
1 tablespoon butter

Wilt the purslane in the butter in a skillet over low heat.

4 cups cream or milk
½ cup white wine
Salt
Pepper
Paprika

Heat the milk or cream. Blend the purslane with the milk, return the mixture to a saucepan, add the wine and seasonings. Do not allow to boil.

Carol Moné

Farmer Paul Lohse sometimes sells verdolaga, or purslane (Portulaca oleracca), Gandhi's favorite vegetable. Purslane may even be growing wild in your yard. As another option, you can use Miner's Lettuce, which can be foraged from our region or try watercress, which is commercially available.

Caution: Be 100% positive about the identity of any wild plant before you use it.

Rx: Chicken Soup

We think this soup is just what the doctor would order! It is not only delicious, but it really makes you perk up if you are feeling under the weather or just want to wrap yourself up with a big bowl of comfort.

6 Servings for a hearty meal

1 whole chicken, cut up
4 cloves of garlic, peeled
1 large yellow onion, peeled and chopped
Water to cover the chicken completely in a pot
Dash of salt and pepper

Prepare the chicken and cover with water in a large cooking pot. Add the garlic, onion, salt and pepper. Boil until the chicken is cooked through and begins to fall off the bone.

Remove the chicken from the pot and separate out the bones, skin and fat from the meat.

Save the meat in a separate bowl.

2 carrots, peeled and sliced into ½-inch pieces
4 medium-sized ribs of celery, sliced into ¼- to ½-inch pieces
½ cup chopped parsley
Optional: 1 cup of small-size pasta, barley or rice

Put vegetables and the pasta or rice into the pot of soup and cook for 30 minutes.

If you have a separator, use it to skim off the chicken fat at the top of the pot. Otherwise, the best way to remove the chicken fat is to put the entire pot in the refrigerator for a few hours or overnight, then skim off the solid fat from the top of the pot.

Reheat the soup, add the cooked chicken, make any adjustments to the seasoning and serve hot.

Lauren Cohn-Sarabia
Comfort of Home Catering

Lauren Cohn-Sarabia, Food Stylist
Lauren Cohn-Sarabia, Photographer

Tip:

Skinning Tomatoes or Peaches

Drop whole tomato or peach into boiling water. Leave in for 20-30 seconds. Remove and let cool until it can be handled. Skin will slip off easily.

Creamy Tomato Soup

6-8 Servings

1 tablespoon olive oil
1 medium onion, diced
1 tablespoon chopped garlic

Sauté in soup pot until soft, about 10 minutes.

1 teaspoon salt
¼ teaspoon pepper
¼ teaspoon cayenne

Add spices and cook for 30 seconds.

About 4 pounds fresh tomatoes, skinned and diced
4 cups vegetable or chicken stock

Add to pot and bring to a boil. Reduce heat and let simmer until reduced by a quarter, 20-30 minutes. Allow to cool completely. Purée cooled mixture in a blender or food processor.

For the roux:
2 tablespoons flour
2 tablespoons butter
1 cup cream or milk

In a large saucepan, melt butter; whisk in flour, and incorporate cream or milk to create a roux.

Cook, stirring, for about five minutes. Slowly blend tomato mixture into the milk mixture, stirring to prevent lumps. Adjust seasonings. Reheat if necessary.

Martha Haynes

Nina's Borscht

8 Servings

4 cups cabbage (about half a head), sliced into long thin strips

2 medium-large beets, peeled (about 2 cups)

1 carrot, peeled and chopped

1 stalk celery, chopped

¼ green pepper, seeded, membranes removed, chopped

2 large tomatoes, peeled and chopped (about 2 cups)

1 clove garlic, chopped

1 bay leaf

Salt and pepper to taste

Cover vegetables with water and simmer about 2 hours.

2 boiling potatoes, diced

Add potatoes and cook about 30 minutes, depending on the size of the pieces.

Adjust seasonings.

Sauerkraut (See page 238)

Sour cream (See page 231)

Sauerkraut and sour cream may be served at the table to add to soup.

Rita Carlson

I met Nina more than 30 years ago while working in San Francisco. As a young girl, Nina and her family escaped Russia after the revolution by walking to China, where they lived for a while. From there, she and her family went to South America, then Canada, and finally the U.S.

Leek and Potato Soup

4-6 Servings

6 large leeks, peeled and trimmed
Split leeks in half lengthwise. Under running water, gently separate layers and wash to remove silt.

¼ cube butter (2 tablespoons)
Melt butter in soup pot. Sauté leeks until soft, 5-7 minutes.

1 pound potatoes, peeled and diced
Add potatoes and sauté until soft.

6 cups chicken or vegetable stock See page 224)

Salt and pepper to taste
Add 2 cups of the stock. Let simmer about 10 minutes, then allow to cool completely. Put mixture in blender a bit at a time and process until smooth.

Return mixture to pot and add remaining 4 cups of stock and salt and pepper to taste. Continue to simmer for about 15 minutes, or until it tastes done.

Note: This is a good basic soup recipe for using greens. This recipe works well with nettles, which can be picked in the spring. If using nettles, pick only the freshest leaves and tops. Be sure to always use gloves when handling nettles. Cooked nettles do not sting and they are a wonderful, cleansing spring tonic.

Suzanne Simpson

Redwood Roots Farm
Chris Wisner,
Photographer

Super Zucchini Soup

10-12 Servings

This is a nice luncheon or dinner soup. Serve hot, in 12-ounce bowls, with a dollop of sour cream and a sprinkle of fresh chopped chives. I serve it with crusty French bread or a sourdough baguette. This soup can be frozen.

2 medium white or yellow onions, diced
2 stalks fresh celery, diced small
3 tablespoons extra-virgin olive oil

In a 6-quart or larger soup pot, sauté onions and celery until tender.

4 cups of fresh zucchini, diced

Add zucchini. Cover with water and bring to a boil. Reduce heat and simmer 30 minutes. Cool completely.

Blend cooked vegetables, a small amount at a time, in an electric blender until smooth. Return to soup pot and warm over low heat. Stir as needed to prevent scorching.

For white sauce:
4 tablespoons butter
6 tablespoons flour

Melt butter in a large iron skillet over medium heat. Stir in flour.

2 cups milk

Slowly add milk, whisking constantly, until the mixture thickens.

4 cups chicken stock (See page 224)

Whisk in chicken stock about a cup at a time. If you like a thicker soup, do not to use all of the stock. The quantity of soup will be less with less stock.

Stir into the zucchini mixture. Season to taste with paprika, salt, pepper and fresh chopped parsley.

8 ounces cream cheese

Dice cheese and stir into the soup until it's melted.

Phyllis Geller

Editor's suggestion: For a bit more tang, add a tablespoon of lemon juice.

I got this recipe from a friend over 35 years ago. I have modified it to use products grown and produced in and around Humboldt County.

Phyllis

Easy Corn Chowder

5 Servings

This recipe makes a quick and delicious tummy-warmer.

¼ cup corn meal

Grind the corn meal in a food processor until very fine. Set cornmeal aside.

6 cups frozen sweet corn, defrosted or fresh corn cut from the cob (about 6 ears)
3 green onions, trimmed and halved
1 clove garlic, peeled

Drain the corn and put into a food processor with the scallions, garlic and corn meal. Blend until mixture is mushy. You may have to do this in two batches unless you have a big processor.

6 cups hot vegetable stock (See page 224)

Tip the corn mixture into a large saucepan; add the hot vegetable stock and bring to a boil. Turn down the heat and let the chowder simmer, partially covered, for 10 minutes.

Preheat oven to 400°

1 package (about 14 ounces) lightly salted tortilla chips (See page 203 for corn tortillas)
2 cups grated cheese

Meanwhile, spread the tortilla chips on a baking sheet. Sprinkle chips with cheese.

Warm in the hot oven 5 to 10 minutes, or until the cheese melts.

Optional: 2 long red chili peppers, de-seeded and finely chopped
Salt to taste

Ladle the soup into bowls and put a small mound of cheese-molten chips into the middle of each bowl. Top with some of the red chili.

Lauren Cohn-Sarabia
Comfort of Home Catering

Note: Corn can be frozen in the summer and used in winter for this soup.

Clam Chowder

4-6 Servings

6 pounds littleneck clams, rinsed well
Open clams, one at a time; place meat in a bowl. Strain juices and add sufficient water to equal 5 cups. Chop clams coarsely and set aside.

6 ounces pancetta bacon, diced
In large pot, sauté pancetta until crisp, about 5 minutes. Pour off fat, leaving 1 tablespoon.

3 tablespoons unsalted butter
Add butter and melt.

1 yellow onion, diced
2 celery stalks, diced
2 garlic cloves, minced
2 teaspoons chopped fresh thyme
Add onion, celery, garlic and thyme. Cook 3-5 minutes, until the onion is soft.

2 tablespoons flour
Add flour and cook for another minute.

2 pounds Yukon Gold potatoes, peeled and diced
2 bay leaves
Add potatoes, bay leaves and clam water. Once the liquid has begun to boil, reduce heat and simmer about 15 minutes, until potatoes are soft.

1 cup cream
2 teaspoons Worcestershire sauce
Salt and pepper to taste
Optional: cayenne, to taste
Stir in remaining ingredients.

With a fork, gently mash potatoes to thicken the soup. Add clams and cook for 2 minutes. Remove and discard bay leaves.

1 tablespoon fresh chives, chopped, for garnish
Serve soup warm, garnished with chives, if so desired.

Martha Haynes

Parsnip-Apple-Honey-Mustard Soup

4-6 Servings

Serve as an appetizer with whole-grain crackers or bread, or alongside your favorite sandwich or winter salad. An excellent prelude to a meal including dark leafy greens such as kale or chard.

**2 tablespoons olive oil or butter
4 cloves garlic, chopped**

In a 3-quart soup pot or larger, heat oil or butter over medium heat. Add garlic to butter and sauté briefly.

4-5 medium-sized parsnips (the size of a fat carrot), trimmed, peeled and diced

Add diced parsnips and sauté until golden, about 10 minutes.

**2 medium-sized tart apples, peeled, cored and diced
1 tablespoon ground coriander seed
2 tablespoons honey**

Add apples and coriander; stir to combine. Add honey and sauté 2-3 minutes more.

3 cups vegetable or chicken stock (See page 224)

Add the vegetable or chicken stock. Cover pot and bring to a boil; reduce heat to simmer.

When parsnips are very tender, remove pot from heat and let soup cool completely.

In a blender or food processor, purée soup in batches until the consistency is smooth and creamy. Return the soup to the pot and reheat over medium heat.

1 tablespoon prepared mustard (any kind will do, but Dijon-style or stoneground is best), or use 1 teaspoon dried mustard mixed into a paste with 1 tablespoon water

Stir mustard into the soup and mix well.

**Salt
Pepper
Apple cider vinegar to taste**

Taste soup and correct seasoning with salt, pepper, and a few dashes of apple cider vinegar until the taste suits you.

Variations: For a one-bowl meal, add chopped greens such as kale, chard, or spinach to the soup when you put the purée back on the heat. Use fresh or dried herbs (dill, tarragon, cilantro, rosemary, etc.) or dried chili powder (paprika, chipotle, etc.) in addition to or instead of the coriander. Substitute other root vegetables such as celeriac, rutabaga or turnip, for some of the parsnips.

Fawn Scheer

Portuguese Kale or Mustard Green Soup

4 to 6 Servings

2 large bunches of kale or mustard greens, well chopped
1 pound linguişa or bacon, cut in ½-inch slices

Sauté onion and linguişa or bacon in a large soup pot. Drain off excess oil.

3-4 boiling potatoes, peeled and cubed
1 large onion, chopped
1-2 cups fresh large older fava beans, shelled, with white covering removed

Add the potatoes, peeled fava beans and the greens and stir.

Water or vegetable broth to cover (See page 224)

Add the water or vegetable broth, salt and pepper to taste. Bring to a boil; lower heat and simmer until well cooked.

Anna Toste

I grew up with this soup. You can use just kale or just mustard greens, or a mixture of half and half. You may also cook a soup bone and make your own broth, saving the meat to add to the soup after it's cooked. It's yummy!

Anna

Gazpacho

4 Servings as a starter

Gazpacho is a Spanish cold soup from Andalucía. It is a "drinkable salad."

**4 large fresh tomatoes, peeled and seeded
4 cloves of garlic, minced
1 large cucumber, peeled, seeded and
    chopped
1 large green pepper, seeded and chopped
2 tablespoons good local olive oil
1 tablespoon lemon juice or vinegar to taste
Small piece of rustic bread, crust removed,
    broken into pieces**

Put all chopped ingredients into a blender and blend well.

Add salt to taste.

Carol Moné

Caldo Gallego

4 Servings as a main course

This is a hearty dish from Galicia in northern Spain. It is peasant food.

**2 large Yukon gold or yellow Finn pota-
    toes, or 4-6 fingerling potatoes**

Slice or cube potatoes and boil until nearly tender, then drain.

**Greens from 4 or 5 turnips (If turnip
    greens are not available, use kale.)**

Blanch the greens for 30 seconds, then chop them.

**4 large cabbage leaves, chopped
1 cup cooked dried canario or poblano
    (from Pueblo) beans
2 quarts broth (chicken, pork or vegetar-
    ian)(See page 224)
4 cloves garlic, chopped
Splash of sherry**

Assemble ingredients in pot with broth and cook until the potatoes are done but not falling apart. Add sherry to taste. Serve with bread.

Carol Moné

*Gazpacho, Lauren Cohn-Sarabia, Food Stylist
Chris Wisner, Photographer*

California Onion Soup

4 Servings

This is a perfect soup to warm you on a North Coast winter evening.

4 tablespoons (½ stick) unsalted butter
4 large onions, halved and thinly sliced

Melt the butter in a large soup pot. Add the onions and cook 20 minutes over medium heat, stirring occasionally.

¼ cup honey
¼ to ½ teaspoon salt
¼ to ½ teaspoon pepper

Drizzle honey over the onions. Cook, stirring occasionally, until onions are caramelized, about 10 minutes. Sprinkle with salt and pepper.

6 cups beef stock (See page 225)
2 tablespoons dry sherry

Add half the stock and simmer 15 minutes, uncovered, over medium heat. Add the remaining stock and the sherry; cook until the broth has a full, robust flavor, approximately 40 more minutes.

4 large thick slices French bread

Toast the French bread. Preheat the broiler or the oven to 350°.

1 cup grated Swiss cheese

Divide the soup among four ovenproof bowls. Place 1 piece of toast on top of soup in each bowl and sprinkle grated cheese on top, covering the entire piece of toast.

Place bowls under the broiler until cheese melts and soup is bubbly hot.

Lauren Cohn-Sarabia
Comfort of Home Catering

Winter Harvest Soup

4 Servings

A rich winter soup served with savory croutons.

- **1½ tablespoons butter**
- **3 cooking apples, peeled, cored and chopped**
- **½ cup diced celery**
- **1 large onion, chopped**

Melt butter in medium saucepan. Add the apples, celery and onions; sauté 5 minutes over medium heat.

- **1 cup chestnut purée, unsweetened (See tip in sidebar)**
- **2 cups chicken or vegetable stock (See page 224)**

Add to apple mixture and cook an additional 5 minutes. Remove from the stove and cool. Place well cooled mixture in a blender, a cupful or so at a time, and purée.

- **½ cup heavy cream**
- **Salt and pepper**

Return puréed mixture to the saucepan. Stir in the cream, adding more stock if the soup is too thick. Season to taste.

Heat gently and serve with croutons.

Savory Croutons

- **1 small loaf day-old French bread, cut into ¼- to ½-inch cubes**
- **½ cup olive oil**
- **4 cloves garlic, pressed**
- **¼ teaspoon salt**
- **1 tablespoon dried or 2½ tablespoons fresh herbs of your choice (rosemary, thyme or oregano are always good).**

Place bread cubes in a medium bowl. In a small bowl, combine olive oil, garlic, salt and herbs. Stir well. Pour over bread cubes and toss to coat well. Spread bread cubes into an ovenproof pan and bake at 325° for about 20 minutes, until cubes are toasted. Remove from pan and cool and store in air-tight container.

Lauren Cohn-Sarabia
Comfort of Home Catering

Tip:

Chestnut Purée
Preheat oven to 400°

Use a sharp knife and cut an 'X' into the flat side of each chestnut shell. The cut will provide a way for the steam to escape and make peeling easier.

Place chestnuts in a baking pan, single layered and roast for 15-20 minutes, stirring after about 10 minutes. Shells will peel back when thoroughly roasted.

Remove from oven and cool 10 minutes. Peel shells off nuts and place in a food processor. Puree until smooth and thick.

Check with the following farms for chestnuts:
Mcintosh Farms
Moonshadow Farms
Sunny Slope Farm

Cioppino

A local version of this classic seafood stew. Serve hot with fresh, crusty bread.

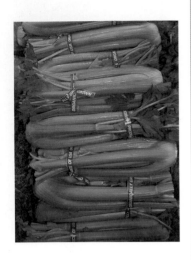

4 Servings as a main dish
6-8 as an appetizer

Traditionally, the shellfish are cooked in the soup base in their shells, which can make for rather messy eating, but also provides a deeper flavored base. An alternative is to make a stock from the shellfish, as described below.

If you prefer to serve the stew with the crab in-shell, first clean out the innards. You can break the legs into sections and/or pre-crack the shells with a nutcracker. Otherwise, remove the crab meat from the shells and set meat aside. In a pot large enough to hold any empty crab shells, bring an inch or two of water to boil. Add the shells, and reduce heat to low; let the shells simmer (do not boil) while you prepare the stew.

Add about an inch of water to a pot, add mussels/clams, then steam until the shells open. Discard any whose shells do not open. Set aside, saving the water for use in the stew. You can use canned clams as well, but be sure to add the juice from the can to the stew.

1 medium-sized fennel bulb, diced; or
halved and thinly sliced cross-wise
Olive oil

Heat a few tablespoons of olive oil in a large soup pot over medium-high heat. Sauté fennel for 5 minutes, until it starts to brown slightly.

1 onion, diced or thinly sliced
4 cloves garlic, minced

Add onions and garlic. Sauté 5 minutes.

3 ribs celery, chopped
1 small pimiento pepper (or red bell pepper), seeded and chopped
2 tablespoons chopped fresh parsley or 1 tablespoon dried parsley flakes
1 tablespoon chopped fresh dill or 1 teaspoon dried dill weed
1-2 teaspoons finely chopped fresh thyme

1 quart canned stewed tomatoes, chopped or puréed
3 cups water or stock

Add celery, bell pepper and herbs; stir in tomatoes, 1 cup of water, and the stock reserved from the cooked shellfish. Bring stew to a boil, then reduce heat and simmer briskly for 20-30 minutes, until fennel is tender.

½ cup white wine

Stir in the wine and cook a few minutes more.

1-2 pounds fresh seafood. Use 2 or 3 different types (mild white fish, mussels, crab, clams, etc.)
Salt and pepper

Strain the stock from the simmered crab shells, and add to the stew. Add chunks of fish and any raw seafood and cook 3-5 minutes. Add other pre-cooked seafood and remove from heat. Let sit a couple of minutes, season with salt and pepper to taste. Serve hot, including all varieties of seafood in each bowl.

Lydia Scheer

Charter Boat out of Trinidad

Roasted Vegetable Soup

3-4 Servings

If you make extra roasted vegetable as a side dish from the recipe on page 169, you can use them in this Roasted Vegetable Soup .

Preheat oven to 375°

1½ pounds ripe tomatoes, peeled, cored and halved
3 large yellow bell peppers
3 zucchini (each 4 to 6 inches long)
1 small eggplant
Olive oil

Put vegetables on a cookie sheet and drizzle with 2-3 tablespoons olive oil.

4 garlic cloves
2 onions, cut into eighths

Tuck in garlic and onion amongst the vegetables.

Pinch of dried thyme
Salt and pepper

Sprinkle vegetables with spices. Bake about 30-35 minutes, until soft and browned.

Cool the vegetables. Remove eggplant and pepper skins. Chop mixture in a food processor until it is salsa-like.

4 cups vegetable stock (See page 224)

Combine stock and vegetables. Simmer 20-30 minutes.

½ cup cream

Stir in cream. Adjust seasonings.

Martha Haynes

Mushroom Soup with Paprika

4 Servings

This is an outstanding soup—very rich. A crisp green salad would be a good accompaniment.

2 tablespoons butter
2 cups chopped onion
Sauté onion in butter.

12 ounces fresh mushrooms, sliced
1½ teaspoons dried dill weed or 1 table-
    spoon fresh
1 tablespoon Hungarian paprika
1 tablespoon tamari
1 teaspoon salt
½ cup vegetable stock (See page 224)
Add to onion mix. Cover and simmer 15 minutes.

To make a white sauce:
2 tablespoons butter
3 tablespoons flour
1 cup milk
In another saucepan, melt the butter and whisk in the flour, a bit at a time, keeping it smooth. Slowly add milk, whisking constantly. Cook over low heat, stirring frequently, until thick, about 10 minutes.

1½ cups vegetable stock
2 teaspoons lemon juice
¼ cup chopped fresh parsley
Fresh ground pepper to taste
½ cup sour cream
Stir into the white sauce; blend well. Stir in the mushroom mixture. Cover and simmer 10-15 minutes, stirring occasionally.

Martha Haynes

Lobster Mushroom

Cheddar Corn Chowder

10-12 Servings

8 ounces bacon
Sauté and drain on paper towels.

4 tablespoons unsalted butter
¼ cup olive oil
Warm in 5-quart Dutch oven.

6 cups chopped yellow onions (4 pounds)
Sauté about 15 minutes. Onions should show signs of caramelizing.

½ cup flour
2 teaspoons kosher salt
1 teaspoon pepper
½ teaspoon turmeric
Mix together dry ingredients.

12 cups chicken or vegetable stock (See page 224)
Whisk dry ingredients into stock.

2 pounds white boiling potatoes, cut into chunks
Add and cook for 15 minutes.

Using a fork, mash some of the potatoes against the side of the pot to make soup somewhat thicker.

10 cups fresh corn, cut from the cob (about 10 ears)
Add and simmer for 10 minutes.

2 cups half-and-half
Add to the soup.

Keep simmering long enough for it to warm up, but don't allow it to boil.

Garnish with:
½ pound sharp Cheddar cheese, grated
Bacon reserved from first step

Martha Haynes

Lauren Cohn-Sarabia, Photographer

Salads

Heirloom Tomato Platter

6 to 8 Servings

2 pounds heirloom tomatoes, choose any variety.

Slice tomatoes into ¼-inch thick rounds. Arrange on plate or platter.

1 clove garlic, pressed
⅛ cup vinegar
¼ cup olive oil
Salt and pepper to taste

Swirl together and pour gently over tomatoes. Optional: scatter chives, dill, chopped basil or thyme over entire platter. Serve at room temperature.

Lauren Cohn-Sarabia
Comfort of Home Catering

Barley Salad

8 Servings as a side dish

1 cup barley, hulled and cooked (See tip in sidebar)
5 green onion stalks, chopped
1 large carrot, grated
1 red, yellow, or orange bell pepper, chopped
½ cup sliced red radishes
¼ cup coarsely chopped parsley
¼ cup chopped lemon or garlic chives
¼ cup chopped fresh basil

Combine in a large bowl.

½ tablespoon Dijon-style mustard
1 large garlic clove, minced
⅓ cup red wine vinegar

Combine in a small bowl.

½ cup extra-virgin olive oil
Salt and pepper to taste

Drizzle into mustard mixture, whisking vigorously to emulsify.

¼ pound fresh arugula lettuce

Line the serving bowl with the arugula. Spoon the salad into the center and serve.

Scott W. Binder

Lauren Cohn-Sarabia, Food Stylist
Lauren Cohn-Sarabia, Photographer

Tip:

Preparing Barley

If your barley comes from a grain CSA, it will probably have hulls on it. To remove the hulls, soak the barley overnight in water, allowing 4 cups of water to 1 cup of barley. The next day, give the barley a stir and strain off the hulls that rise to the surface. Salt the water and bring to a boil over high heat. Reduce heat and simmer the barley 1½ hours, or until tender/al dente.

I made this recipe for the North Coast Co-op's Local Food Challenge Potluck on September 28, 2008. I used all local produce from the farmers' market and the last of Kevin Cunningham's Shakefork Community Farm barley harvest from last year. This recipe was one of the Taster's Choices, and I won a gift certificate at the potluck for it. This dish is best made ahead, as the flavors will blend overnight. Make sure that you take it out a few hours ahead of serving as it is best at room temperature.

Cooking Beets

Cut off root tails and leafy tops to within 1 inch of the beet. Wash beets. Place beets into a pot with enough water to cover. Cover pot and bring to a boil, then reduce heat to medium-low and cook until beets pierce easily with a fork or knife—about 45 minutes for medium-sized beets. When done, remove from heat, drain water, and let set a few minutes to cool. One at a time, squeeze each beet firmly between thumb and fingers; peels should slide right off. Any peels that don't come off easily can be trimmed with a knife.

Check with the following farms for walnuts:

Sunny Slope Farm

Trident Lightning Farm and Orchard

Beet and Berry Salad

4-6 Servings

This recipe is easily adaptable to the seasons. For a fall or wintertime salad, substitute chopped apples, Fuyu persimmons, or dried cranberries in place of the berries.

3 tablespoons balsamic, apple cider, or red wine vinegar
2 tablespoons extra-virgin olive oil
1 teaspoon Dijon-style mustard
Drizzle of honey
Dash of salt and pepper

Combine dressing ingredients in a small jar and shake well to mix.

6 medium-size beets, cooked and peeled (See tip for cooking beets in side bar)
1 pint basket of strawberries or a mixture of strawberries, raspberries and/or blueberries, sliced or chopped

Toss beets, berries and dressing together and let marinate 20 minutes or longer, tossing a few times while you wait.

1 large head of lettuce or ½ to 1 pound mixed salad greens, trimmed and washed
1 bunch of spinach or ½ pound loose spinach leaves, trimmed and washed

Mix together salad greens and spinach in a salad bowl; top with the beet-berry mixture. Serve with selected garnishes:

Toasted nuts or seeds (sunflower, flax, walnuts, etc.)
Chevre-style cheese, crumbled
Chives, chopped
Fresh herbs (mint, dill or fennel fronds, lemon balm, thyme, etc.), chopped
Edible flower petals (calendula, sunflower, borage, etc.)

For an alternate serving method, use large, cup-shaped lettuce leaves (such as butter lettuce or romaine) and place a scoop of the beet-berry mixture on top. Garnish as desired.

Fawn Scheer

Kale Salad

4 Servings

2-3 carrots, peeled and sliced into rounds
Steam for 2 minutes, until crisp-tender but not cooked through. Place in a salad bowl.

**1 large bunch of kale, washed, trimmed
and torn into bite-sized bits**
Lightly steam kale (about 2 minutes) and add to the salad bowl.

1-2 stalks celery, washed and chopped
1-2 cloves fresh garlic, peeled and minced
¼ cup good virgin olive oil
Juice of one lemon
Salt and pepper to taste
Optional: herbs of your choice
Add to the kale and carrot mixture and serve immediately. This salad does not hold up well for more than a few hours.

Lynne Wells

Marinated Beet Salad

12 Servings

**4 pounds beets, cooked, peeled and sliced
(See tip for preparing beets, page 98)**
⅔ cup red onions, julienned
Mix beets with red onions.

1 tablespoon minced garlic
¾ cup red wine vinegar
1 cup olive oil
½ teaspoon black pepper
2½ teaspoons salt
Combine dressing ingredients in a small bowl and mix. Pour dressing over beets and onions, mixing well.

4 ounces goat cheese
Add small chunks of goat cheese before serving.

Lindsey S. Byers
Community Alliance with Family Farmers
AmeriCORPS VISTA member

Corn and Black Bean Salad

6 Servings

Dried beans are available in the fall at the Farmers' Markets from Warren Creek Farms.

½ cup chopped red onion
2 cups cooked corn
2 cups cooked black beans
1 cup chopped bell pepper
2 cups chopped tomatoes
½ cup chopped cilantro
Optional: 1 jalapeño, seeded and minced

Mix together vegetables and toss with Cumin-Vinaigrette Dressing (below). Let marinate at least one hour.

Serve on individual plates on top of a lettuce leaf. Garnish as desired or try a sprig of cilantro and slice of lemon.

Tom and Kay O'Gorman
Trinity River Farm

Cumin-Vinaigrette Dressing

About ½ Cup

2 teaspoons Dijon-style mustard
2-3 garlic cloves, minced
2 tablespoons red wine vinegar
2 tablespoons lemon juice
⅓ cup olive oil
½ teaspoon coarsely ground black pepper
½ teaspoon cumin
¼ teaspoon salt

Mix ingredients and use for Corn and Black Bean Salad (above). Good on other salads, too.

Tom and Kay O'Gorman
Trinity River Farm

Coleslaw

8 Servings

6 cups shredded cabbage (about 2 small
heads or 1 large head. Use all green or
mix green and red cabbages)
½ sweet pepper, chopped
Optional: 1 large carrot, grated

Dressing:

½ cup mayonnaise
¼ cup finely chopped onion
2 teaspoons vinegar or lemon juice
⅛ teaspoon Worcestershire sauce
Salt and pepper to taste
½ teaspoon sugar or honey

Mix dressing ingredients well. Pour dressing onto
cabbage mix and toss well.

The Cookbook Team

Waldorf Salad

8 Servings

1 cup diced celery
2 cups diced apples
½ cup chopped walnuts
¾ cup mayonnaise

Place all ingredients in a bowl and toss well.

The Cookbook Team

*Check with the following farms
for walnuts:*

Sunny Slope Farm
*Trident Lightning Farm and
Orchard*

Mixed Green Salad

8 Servings

Lettuce, one or more heads. Choose your
favorite or use more than one type.

Add seasonal fresh vegetables. This is the time to
be creative, even a little bit wild. Try adding dried
cranberries, thin slices of jicama or daikon radish, seeds, edible flowers.

Toss your creation with the dressing of your
choice. Garnish with nasturtium flowers, goat
cheese or berries.

Lauren Cohn-Sarabia
Comfort of Home Catering

Persimmon, Pear and Apple Salad with Pomegranate

6 Servings

This mixed-fruit salad makes a colorful and delicious goodbye to summer!

2 Fuyu persimmons, peeled and diced into ½-inch pieces
2 large Asian pears, peeled, cored and diced into ½-inch pieces
½ cup chopped walnuts
¼ cup chopped parsley

In a salad bowl, toss the fruit with the nuts and parsley.

¼ cup olive oil
2 tablespoons lime juice

Whisk the oil and lime juice together until blended.

Add to the fruit in the bowl and toss to coat. Season with salt and pepper. Chill until serving time.

1 head butter lettuce, washed, dried, and separated into leaves
Seeds from 1 pomegranate

Arrange the lettuce leaves on a serving plate or individual plates. Mound the persimmon salad over the lettuce leaves and sprinkle with pomegranate seeds.

Lauren Cohn-Sarabia
Comfort of Home Catering

Tip:

Seeding a Pomegranate

Peel and seed the pomegranate under water in a bowl or dish-pan to avoid staining hands and surfaces.

Carol Moné

Check with the following farms for walnuts:

Sunny Slope Farm
Trident Lightning Farm and Orchard

Melon Blueberry Salad

4-6 Servings

This salad is a delicious addition to summertime potlucks or picnics.

1 large pale-fleshed melon such as honey-dew or crenshaw, peeled, seeded and cut into 1-inch pieces
1 pint blueberries, rinsed and patted dry
½ cup mint leaves (whole tiny ones or thinly sliced large ones)

In a large bowl, combine melon pieces, blueberries, and mint leaves.

¼ cup lime or lemon juice
2 tablespoons honey, warmed to dissolve well

To make the basic dressing, mix together lime juice and honey until honey dissolves. Pour dressing over fruit and toss to mix well.

To spruce up the dressing, make a syrup with one of the additional flavorings of your choice.

Warm lime juice and honey in a small pan over medium-high heat. Add small bits of one or a few of the following: cardamom pods or seeds, lavender flowers, vanilla bean or extract, scented geranium leaves, lemon verbena leaves, lemon balm leaves, fresh ginger root or dried powder, lemongrass leaves. Bring syrup to a boil and cook a few minutes over medium-low heat.

Remove from heat and let syrup cool. Strain out leaves and seeds. Pour over fruit and toss to mix well.

Lydia Scheer

German Potato Salad

6 Servings

This recipe comes from Great-Grandma Emma Rankin.

3 large slices bacon (about ½ cup)
Fry bacon until crisp. Remove from pan, cool and cut into small pieces.

½ cup minced onion
Add onion to pan and sauté until just tender, not brown.

1½ teaspoons flour
4 teaspoons sugar (or 3 teaspoons honey)
½ teaspoon pepper
Salt to taste
½ cup vinegar
½ cup water
Mix flour, sugar, salt and pepper and stir in the vinegar and water until smooth. Add to the bacon pan and simmer until slightly thickened.

2 pounds small white potatoes, boiled and sliced ¼-inch thick
Pour vinegar and sugar mixture over sliced cooked potatoes. Add in bacon pieces and stir carefully.

Eat right away if you like warm German potato salad, or refrigerate to allow flavors to meld.

Lia Webb

Zucchini Salad

6 Servings

2 pounds zucchini, grated
1 teaspoon salt
Mix zucchini and salt in a bowl and set aside for 1 hour. Squeeze out moisture and discard liquid, saving the grated zucchini.

3 tablespoons sour cream or yogurt
3 tablespoons mayonnaise
1½ tablespoons Dijon-style mustard
1 clove garlic, minced
Mix together sour cream, mayonnaise, mustard and garlic. Toss with zucchini.

Lettuce and tomato
Serve on lettuce with tomato.

Trinity River Farm

Savory Cauliflower Salad with Fresh Herbs

6-8 Servings

Sweet cauliflower is a natural partner to fresh herbs, chosen at their seasonal peak. Serve alongside chicken or fish, pasta or whole grains, or top your favorite salad greens.

- 1 large head cauliflower, trimmed and cut into bit-sized florets (about 4 cups of florets), use raw or cooked (See tip for cooking in sidebar)
- ¼-½ pound fresh seasonal vegetables (try sugar snap peas, carrots, or fennel bulb), trimmed and cut into ¼-inch slices
- 1 cup green onions or chives, trimmed and chopped
- 4 tablespoons fresh parsley, trimmed and chopped
- 1 tablespoon fresh tarragon, dill, or marjoram, trimmed and chopped
- Optional: ½ cup nuts or seeds

In a large bowl, combine cauliflower with vegetables, nuts and seeds, and herbs. Toss gently to mix.

- 1 tablespoon prepared mustard, Dijon-style or stone ground
- 2 tablespoons olive oil
- 2 tablespoons yogurt or fresh cream
- 4 tablespoons apple cider or wine vinegar
- A drizzle of honey
- 1 teaspoon salt
- 1 teaspoon pepper

Combine remaining ingredients in a jar or small bowl and shake or whisk until well mixed. Pour dressing over salad and toss again. Mix well. Let salad sit at least a half hour (longer is better) to marinate. If cauliflower is raw, marinate for longer. Toss salad occasionally to redistribute dressing.

Serve as is, or on a bed of lettuce.

Fawn Scheer

Tip:

Cooking Cauliflower

Place cauliflower florets into a pot with 1 inch of water in the bottom. Cover pot and bring to a boil over high heat. Steam cauliflower to desired tenderness, anywhere from 1 minute to 5 minutes or more. Cauliflower should be firm enough to hold its shape.

Remove from heat and run cold water over the cauliflower to stop its cooking. As a alternative, fill bowl with water and ice cubes and put florets in bowl to cool. Set aside.

Sweet Cauliflower Salad with Fresh Herbs

4 Servings

Cauliflower is a natural partner with fresh herbs, chosen at their seasonal peak. Serve with chicken or fish, pasta or whole grains, or on your favorite green salad.

- 1 head of cauliflower (white is fine, but purple or orange really shines), raw or cooked, trimmed and cut into bite-size florets (about 4 cups of florets) (See sidebar tip for cooking cauliflower on page 105)
- 2 large ripe peaches, nectarines, pears, or apples, peeled (if desired), pitted or cored, and cut into bite-size pieces
- ½ cup toasted nuts or seeds
- ½ cup chopped spring onions or chives, green part only
- Small bunch of fresh cilantro, mint, or basil, trimmed and chopped

In a large bowl, combine cauliflower with vegetables and fruit, nuts and seeds, and herbs. Toss gently to mix.

For dressing:
- 2 tablespoons olive oil
- 2 tablespoons yogurt or fresh cream
- 4 tablespoons apple cider or balsamic vinegar, or lemon juice and a drizzle of honey
- Optional: 1-2 teaspoons ground cardamom, coriander seed, or ginger
- 1 teaspoon salt
- 1 teaspoon pepper

Combine dressing ingredients in a jar or small bowl and shake or whisk until well mixed. Pour dressing over salad and toss again. Mix well. Let salad sit at least a half hour (longer is better) to marinate. If cauliflower is raw, marinate longer. Toss salad occasionally to redistribute dressing. Serve as is, or on a bed of lettuce.

Fawn Scheer

Lauren Cohn-Sarabia, Food Stylist
Lauren Cohn-Sarabia Photographer

Barley

Quinoa

Check with Shakefork Community Farm for local quinoa in the future.

Quinoa Tabouleh

6 Servings

This traditional Middle Eastern salad is usually made with bulgar or barley but quinoa is used in this version. The quinoa adds the light nutty flavor that makes this dish distinctive. Barley makes it hearty.

2 cups quinoa, bulgar or barley (See cooking directions for hulling barley on page 97)

Cooking directions for quinoa: Rinse the quinoa thoroughly (minimum of 2 minutes) in a fine-mesh strainer to remove the bitter outer shells. Drain and place in a heavy-based skillet. Heat (without oil), stirring constantly, until the grains turn golden and begin to separate. Add 3 cups water and 1 teaspoon salt and bring to a boil. Reduce heat and cook about 15 minutes, or until the liquid is absorbed. Transfer to a bowl and set aside to cool.

Juice of 2 lemons
½ cup olive oil

Whisk together the lemon juice and 1 tablespoon of the olive oil in a small bowl and set aside.

1 cucumber, peeled and chopped
1 red onion, peeled and chopped (about 1½ cups)
1 pint Sun Gold cherry tomatoes, sliced down the middle
1 pint Kalamata olives, pitted
2 cups cooked garbanzo beans
1 bunch Italian parsley, chopped
1 bunch mint, chopped

Place the remaining oil, the cucumber, onion, cherry tomatoes, olives, garbanzo beans, parsley and mint in a separate, larger bowl. Add the quinoa, bulgur or barley and the lemon and oil dressing, and toss.

8 ounces sheep feta or chevre cheese
Salt and pepper

Crumble the feta cheese and mix into the salad with a little salt and pepper.

Marnin Robbins

Grilled Albacore Salad

4-8 Servings

1-2 pounds fresh albacore loin
About ½ cup lemon juice
½ cup olive oil

Combine lemon juice and olive oil in a flat, non-reactive pan. Add the fish, turning to coat both sides. Marinate in juice and oil overnight, turning at least once.

Drain marinade from fish. Grill fish until just done. Allow to cool, then flake into bite-size pieces.

1 cup green olives, pitted and halved
1 jar marinated artichoke hearts
½ red onion, thinly sliced
1 head of romaine, coarsely chopped
15 arugula leaves, chopped

Gently mix fish and vegetables together in a large salad bowl.

2 tablespoons extra-virgin olive oil
1-2 fresh lemons
Salt and pepper to taste

Sprinkle with olive oil and a squeeze of fresh lemon. Add salt and pepper to taste.

Henry Robertson
Henry's Olives

Advertisement in:
Eureka Cook Book, 1907
The Ladies League of the First Congregational Church

This is my version of the classic Salade Niçoise with a dressing that is more like a caesar dressing except instead of anchovies. I use the oil from the tuna for a nice subtle fish flavor. For this reason, a tuna that is cooked in the can or home canned is preferable.

I like to use products that are seasonal and available locally. I use asparagus in this recipe but later in the summer you might try blanched green beans or roasted peppers. Ed at Libation said he would enjoy this salad with a Loire Valley white wine such as a Sancerre or a dry Vouvray. Closer to home, there are some nice local dry Sauvignon Blancs that would pair nicely.

Brett Shuler

North Coast Salad Niçoise
4 Servings

2 medium size yellow Finn potatoes (red or purple ones also work)

Put potatoes in a pot of cold water. Bring to a boil, reduce heat and simmer until just tender, about 15 minutes. Drop potatoes into an ice bath to chill. Slice into ¼-inch rounds.

½ pound organic mixed greens

Toss greens lightly but thoroughly in dressing (recipe below).

4 hard boiled eggs, peeled and quartered
16 asparagus spears, trimmed and grilled
1 cup locally-cured olives
½ red onion, thinly sliced
1 6-ounce can smoked albacore tuna or home-canned tuna. Reserve the oil.

Divide greens among four plates. Arrange vegetables and eggs around the greens, and top with tuna and olives.

For the dressing:
1 egg
1 clove garlic
¼ teaspoon ground mustard
⅛ teaspoon Worcestershire sauce
¼ cup grated Parmesan cheese
1 tablespoon lemon juice

Combine in a food processor.

Oil from tuna
¾ cup light olive oil

With the food processor running, slowly drizzle in the tuna oil; then drizzle in the olive oil. Season to taste with salt and pepper.

Brett Shuler
Brett Shuler Fine Catering

Roasted Chicken Salad

4 Servings

Preheat oven to 350°

4 chicken breasts, skin on
Coat a baking pan with olive oil. Place chicken in pan and roast 30 minutes, or until juice from the meat runs clear when tested with a fork.

For the vinaigrette:
2 teaspoons red wine vinegar
6 teapoons olive or canola oil
1-2 teaspoons Dijon-style mustard
Swirl vinaigrette ingredients together.

For the salad:
½ cup cherry tomatoes, halved
2 cups diced celery
½ medium red onion, diced
1 teaspoon chopped tarragon
Optional: ¼ cup chopped basil

Combine vegetables and herbs and stir into vinaigrette mixture.

Remove chicken from the oven and immediately cut into bite-sized pieces. Toss these with the vinaigrette while they're still warm to ensure the moisture stays in the chicken. Serve over a bed of crisp lettuce.

Karen Ovetz

Roasted Chicken Salad could also be called Leftover Chicken Salad. Just cut up leftovers or use those extra bits of meat from a roasted chicken for a delicious second meal.

Lemon Garlic Salad Dressing

5-6 ounces

This dressing is wonderful with goat cheese on a Greek salad.

½ cup olive oil
3-5 tablespoons lemon juice
3-5 cloves garlic, crushed or minced
Whisk together. Add additional lemon juice and garlic to suit your own taste.

Salt and pepper to taste
Store dressing in a small glass jelly jar. Give it a good shake before using.

Ann Anderson

Italian Vinaigrette Dressing

About 1 cup

½ cup olive oil
⅛ cup red wine vinegar
2 cloves garlic, crushed
1 teaspoon honey
¼ teaspoon each salt and pepper
1 tablespoon fresh herbs of your choice,
    such as basil, rosemary, sage, parsley,
    thyme or a combination of any Italian
    herbs

Combine all ingredients and whirl in a blender.

Tomato variation:
¼ cup sun-dried tomatoes or 1 fresh tomato
For a tomato vinaigrette, add sun-dried or fresh tomatoes to the above recipe and purée in food processor.

Lauren Cohn-Sarabia
Comfort of Home Catering

Buttermilk Salad Dressing

About 4 cups

Here's a salad dressing, made without oil or vinegar, that incorporates only local products. Once you get used to this basic recipe, it's easy to experiment by adding other herbs or vegetables.

3 cups buttermilk
1 cup fresh basil
4 tablespoons fresh chives
2 cloves garlic

Place all ingredients in a blender and blend until smooth. Chill at least 1 hour before using.

Megan Blodgett
North Coast Co-op's Original Locavore Challenger

Fish at Trinidad Pier
Ann Anderson, Photographer

Meat, Poultry and Seafood

Apple Spiced Brisket • 115

Sirloin and Roasted Vegetables • 116

*Chili • 117

*Tacos • 118

Sizzling Cilantro Burgers • 119

*Iranian-style Eggplant Stew • 120

Cross Rib Roast • 121

Argentine Puchero (Beef Stew) • 122

Nigerian Goat Stew • 123

Dilled Short Ribs • 124

Casa Chicken • 124

Roasted Lemon Chicken with
Green Beans and Potatoes • 125

*Mu Shu Chicken • 126

*Chinese Plum Sauce • 127

Moroccan Chicken with Green Olives • 128

*Stir Fry • 129

Slow Roasted Brined Goose • 130

Snake River Lamb Shanks • 131

Grilled Lamb Chops • 131

Lamb Meatballs with Yogurt Sauce • 132

Venison Stew • 133

Mustardy Braised Rabbit with Carrots • 134

Rabbit in Wine Sauce • 135

Poached Salmon Variations • 136

Baked White Fish in Buttermilk• 138

Sushi • 139

Crabmeat Crêpes • 140

* May be made as vegetable-based entrée

Apple-Spiced Brisket

6 to 8 Servings

Preheat oven to 325°

¼ cup flour
3 to 4 pounds beef brisket (first cut, flat half, boneless)
Put flour and brisket into paper bag and shake to coat meat. Place floured brisket into a 9 x 13 x 2-inch covered baking pan.

1 teaspoon salt
Prick brisket liberally on both sides with a fork; sprinkle with salt. Place brisket, fat side up, in lidded baking dish or Dutch oven.

1½ cups apple cider
¼ cup honey
1 teaspoon ground cinnamon
1 teaspoon ground ginger
1 teaspoon grated nutmeg
Combine apple juice, honey and spices; pour over brisket. Cover baking dish. Bake 2 to 2½ hours or until tender. Remove from the oven.

2 tablespoons flour
In medium saucepan, dissolve flour in small amount of cooking liquid from baking dish.

¼ cup raisins
1 baking apple, sliced
Stir in remaining cooking liquid, raisins and apple slices. Bring to a boil and stir 1-2 minutes to form a light gravy.

Optional: sour cream
Gravy may be enhanced with sour cream, if desired.

Thinly slice brisket diagonally across grain. Serve with apple-raisin gravy.

Susan Combes
Humboldt County Cattlewomen

Meat, eggs, and dairy products from pastured animals are ideal for your health. Compared with commercial products, they offer you more "good" fats and fewer "bad" fats. They are richer in antioxidants, including vitamins E and C, and beta-carotene. Furthermore, they do not contain traces of added hormones, antibiotics or other drugs.

www.eatwild.com

Matt Reed, North Coast Co-op
Ann Anderson, Photographer

Sirloin and Roasted Vegetables
6 Servings

The Humboldt County Cattlewomen was first organized in 1955 and was originally called the Humboldt County Cowbelles. Their purpose was to encourage camaraderie among ranch women and to promote public relations for the beef industry. The first members held annual dinner-dances, rode in parades and worked on many beef promotion projects. In 1956 they began awarding an outstanding 4H girl each year with the Jessie Hunt Award (named after their first president). In 1970 they awarded the first annual Dorothy Kerr Award to an exceptional Future Farmer of America girl. Girls are still honored each year with these awards. In 1964 the first "Cowbelle of the Year" was awarded for special member participation. In 1987 the name of the Cowbelles was changed to Cattlewomen, locally and nationwide. The Humboldt County Cattlewomen have continued supporting the beef industry and education. They now have a vitally active scholarship program, awarding scholarships each year to students in agriculture education programs.

Preheat oven to 425°

For roasted vegetables:
1 medium eggplant
8 large mushrooms
1 medium onion
1 medium red, yellow or green bell pepper
1 medium zucchini

Cut vegetables crosswise into 1-inch thick slices. Leave mushrooms whole. Place vegetables in shallow roasting pan.

½ tablespoon olive oil
1 tablespoon balsamic vinegar
1 clove garlic, minced
¾ teaspoon dried rosemary leaves, crushed
Salt and pepper to taste

Combine oil, vinegar, minced garlic and dried rosemary in small bowl. Drizzle over vegetables and stir to coat.

Roast the vegetables 25 minutes or until tender, stirring once. Cool slightly.

For sirloin:
1½ pounds boneless top sirloin

Heat large skillet over medium heat. Place steaks in hot skillet. Cook top sirloin steaks 12 to 15 minutes (tenderloin steaks, 10 to 13 minutes) for medium-rare to medium, turning occasionally. Do not overcook.

Salad greens
Fresh rosemary sprigs

Remove from skillet; let stand 5 minutes. Carve across the grain into thin slices. Arrange beef and vegetables evenly on individual plates. Garnish with greens and rosemary sprigs.

Susan Combes
Humboldt County Cattlewomen

Chili
(Meat- or vegetable-based)

4-6 Servings

2 cups dry beans
Water to cover, plus 1 inch
Soak beans for at least 8 hours or overnight in water; drain and rinse.

1 bay leaf
2 jalapeño peppers, chopped, seeds and all
Put rinsed beans and water, jalapeño and bay leaf in a pot and bring to boil. Reduce heat to simmer. Cover and cook 1 hour.

1 pound grass-fed ground beef
1 onion, diced
When beans are almost done, heat a large frying pan over medium heat, add ground beef and diced onion and allow to cook, covered, with frequent stirring, about 8 minutes. Uncover and cook another 5 minutes.

2 ears fresh corn, kernels cut from cob
5 tomatoes, diced
Add ground beef to beans, along with corn and diced tomatoes; cook another 15 minutes.

Cilantro
Homemade cheese
Use cilantro and homemade cheese for garnish.

Clara Arndt

You can use any kind of dried bean, but I like the Warren Creek Farm "Jacobs Cattle" variety.

I also like to garnish with Loleta Cheese Factory's "Queso Fresco," instead of the home-made cheese.

Clara

Tacos (Meat- or vegetable-based)
6 Servings

Use this versatile recipe with leftover meat, fish or tofu. Be creative and try different vegetables and cheeses.

Customize your own taco! Put each ingredient in a separate dish and let diners assemble their own taco by first putting in meat or beans, then adding other ingredients as they like.

If you are using beans, heat them and skip the steps for cooking meat. (See pages 46 and 162 for bean recipes)

Olive oil
2 cloves garlic

Heat oil in skillet. Add garlic and cook until softened.

1 pound meat (grass-fed ground beef, organic ground chicken or turkey, chicken meat cut into small pieces, or fish)
1 tablespoon mild chili powder
1 teaspoon ground cumin
1 teaspoon dry oregano (3 teaspoons fresh)

Add meat and seasonings. Stir and cook till done. For fish tacos, add seasoning to the olive oil-and-garlic mix. Gently cook whole pieces of fish with seasoning, use a fork to break the fish into bite-size pieces.

1 cup chopped lettuce
1 large or 2 medium tomatoes, chopped
1 medium onion, chopped
Cilantro, chopped
1 cup grated cheese
Salsa
Lime or Meyer lemon, especially good with the fish
Salt and pepper
Tortillas (corn or flour)
Optional:
    Black olives
    Sour cream

Fry corn tortillas in oil, drain on paper towels or recycled brown paper bags. Wrap flour tortillas in foil or put in covered baking dish and heat in a 350° oven 5-10 minutes. Serve immediately.

Ann Anderson

Sizzling Cilantro Burgers

4 Servings

Preheat grill to medium heat. Brush grill grate with oil.

1 pound grass-fed ground beef
1 cup barbecue sauce (See many local options starting on page 283 in Appendix F)
1 teaspoon minced garlic

In a medium bowl, mix together ground beef, barbecue sauce and minced garlic. Shape into 4 patties. Cook patties on the grill 5-7 minutes on each side, or until done.

4 slices Monterey Jack cheese

Place a slice of cheese on each burger patty and let melt for 1 minute.

1 cup chopped fresh cilantro, divided

Press ¼ cup chopped cilantro onto each slice of melted cheese.

8 slices sourdough bread, toasted
4 lettuce leaves
4 slices tomato

To serve, place each burger patty on a slice of sourdough bread and top with lettuce, tomato and another slice of bread.

Susan Combes
Humboldt County Cattlewomen

Iranian-style Eggplant Stew (Meat- or vegetable-based)

A Persian classic easily made vegetarian by omitting the meat and doubling the amount of lentils. Serve stew over rice or with polow (See page 174), pilaf or similar dish.

4 Servings

Oil for frying
1 pound cubed meat of your choice (beef, lamb, chicken, goat)
1 onion, sliced

Over high heat, add enough oil to just coat the bottom of a deep skillet or heavy-bottomed large pot (at least 3-quart size). When the oil starts to form a slight haze above it, add the cubed meat and sliced onion. Stir meat and onions frequently, cooking until both are browned.

3 cloves garlic, sliced or chopped
1 hot green or red pepper (serrano, jalape-ño or cayenne), chopped; remove seeds for less spice
½ teaspoon powdered turmeric
½ teaspoon dried coriander
½ teaspoon powdered cumin
½ teaspoon powdered cinnamon

Add garlic and spices and cook, stirring, a few seconds more.

3 medium-large tomatoes, seeded and diced
2 cups water

Add chopped tomatoes and water; mix to combine everything well.

½ cup lentils or split peas (1 cup for vegeta-ble-based dish)

If using lentils or split peas, add them now, along with an additional 1 cup of water. Cover pan and let it come to a boil. Reduce heat to a simmer and cook, covered, at least 1½ hours.

6-8 Italian eggplants, sliced lengthwise into 3 equal slices
Salt

While stew is simmering, sprinkle cut sides of eggplant pieces generously with salt and place in a colander or lay flat to drain. Let salted eggplant sit at least 20 minutes to remove bitterness. Lay the pieces on a clean towel and press gently to remove excess salt and water.

Heat a skillet over high heat with enough oil to coat pan bottom. When oil is hot (slightly hazy), add eggplant slices in a single layer. Reduce heat slightly and fry eggplant, turning once, until it softens slightly and begins to turn golden. Set cooked eggplant on a towel or paper bag to absorb some of the excess oil. Heat more oil in the skillet, and cook remaining eggplant in this way.

Cut each eggplant slice into 3 or 4 large pieces. Add eggplant to the simmering stew, mix in gently, and simmer another 15 minutes. If the stew is too dry, add a bit more water.

Lydia Scheer

Cross Rib Roast

8 Servings

Preheat oven to 450°

3-5 pounds grass fed beef Cross Rib roast
5 small cloves of garlic
2 tablespoons extra-virgin olive oil
1 teaspoon salt
1 teaspoon pepper
1 teaspoon dried rosemary
1 teaspoon dried thyme

Make several slits in top of meat. Put a piece of garlic in each. Drizzle meat with oil. Sprinkle on salt, pepper and herbs. Place in a heavy-bottomed roasting pan and put in oven.

After 15 minutes, turn oven temperature down to 350°. Roast approximately 20 minutes per pound. Use a meat thermometer to be sure things are on target: 130° rare to 140° medium. Remove from oven, tent, and let stand about 25 minutes.

Humboldt Grassfed Beef

Tip:

Cross Rib Roast

The secret to serving this flavorful roast is to slice it thinly, whether you serve it hot or cold.

The Cross Rib is the cut between the shoulder and the rib. It's not as expensive as a classic rib roast, but not tough either (such as a rump or blade roast). After it is cold, very thin slices of this roast make a delicious sandwich or an elegant addition to your meat-and-cheese tray.

Argentine Puchero (Beef Stew)

6 Servings

Pure comfort food on a cool foggy night.

The ingredients and quantities can be varied according to taste.

2 pounds lean grass-fed beef stew meat
1 onion, chopped
2 tablespoons olive oil
6 tomatoes, chopped (even better: 12 or more sun-dried tomato halves)
2 cloves garlic, chopped
½ cup red wine
1½ cups water or beef stock

Brown the onion and meat lightly in olive oil in a large stew-pot. Add tomatoes, garlic, wine and water or stock. Cover and simmer 1½ to 2 hours until meat is tender, but not falling apart.

About 1 cup of chopped fruit, (6 fresh apricots, or the equivalent dried, or approximately the same amount of peaches or apples)
½ cup raisins
4 potatoes, scrubbed, peeled and diced
2 ears fresh corn, shucked, cleaned and broken into 2-inch rounds
2-3 zucchini or summer squash, chopped, or 1 small winter squash, cut into chunks

Add the rest of the ingredients and enough liquid to almost cover. This is almost a soup. Cover and simmer until everything is tender, about 30 minutes. Best served in large soup bowls or soup plates. French or Italian bread makes a tasty addition.

Marilyn Benemann

Nigerian Goat Stew

4-6 Servings

Goat meat is absolutely perfect for stew. It's best when market fresh. The stew flavors continue to develop, so leftovers are fabulous as well—if there are any!

1½ pounds of goat meat, finely diced
2 large onions, peeled and diced
2 carrots, sliced
1 clove of garlic, crushed
3 tablespoons olive oil

In a 5-quart Dutch oven over medium heat, sauté onions, carrots and garlic in the oil until onions are translucent.

2 cups tomato purée
½ bay leaf
⅛ teaspoon ground cloves
⅛ teaspoon ground ginger
1 dash of cayenne, Weitchpec Hot Sauce or Scotch Bonnet chilies (if you are brave)
¼ teaspoon salt
⅛ teaspoon white pepper
1 tablespoon freshly squeezed lemon juice (may use vinegar as substitute)
2 cups stock (I prefer to use the frozen stock from our summer-pastured chickens). You can use beef, vegetable or chicken broth. (See page 224 and 225)

Add all of the above to the stew pot. Bring to a boil, reduce heat, cover and let simmer until meat is tender to your liking. (1½ to 2 hours on stove top or in a slow cooker for 4 hours at high heat or 6-8 hours at low heat.)

1 tablespoon peanut butter
2 tablespoons flour

Heat the peanut butter over medium heat, stirring constantly. Sprinkle flour into the heated peanut butter and stir well.

Add peanut butter/flour mix to stew and let simmer a few more minutes. Check seasonings.

Joan Crandell
Wild Iris Farm

Joan found this recipe in the Library of Congress archives some time ago. It originally called for Scotch Bonnet chilies, but she just couldn't handle that much heat.

Goat is thought to have been the earliest animal domesticated, besides sheep and dogs. Cave art 10,000 to 20,000 years ago indicates that goats were common and important then. At the present time, goats provide the principle source of animal protein in many North African and Middle Eastern nations. Goat is also important in the Caribbean, in Southeast Asia and in developing tropical countries.

United States Department of Agriculture

About 63% of the red meat consumed worldwide is goat.

www.boergoatshome.com

Dilled Short Ribs

4 Servings

2 tablespoons olive oil
**2-3 pounds grass-fed beef short ribs,
    trimmed of excess fat**

Using heavy covered skillet or 5-quart Dutch oven, brown short ribs in hot oil until well browned on all sides. Drain excess fat from skillet.

1 cup water
1 small onion, chopped
1 cup grated carrots
2 tablespoons cider vinegar
1 teaspoon salt
¼ teaspoon pepper

To the short ribs, add water, onion, carrots, vinegar, salt and pepper; heat to boiling. Reduce heat and simmer, covered, 1½ hours

**1 teaspoon dried dill weed or 2 tablespoons
    chopped fresh dill weed**

Add dill weed and cook for one more hour or until meat is tender.

Before serving, remove meat from bones and fat from the pan liquid. Serve over brown rice.

Allison Hooper

Casa Chicken

8 Servings

Preheat oven to 425°

Olive oil
2 bell peppers, sliced into ¼-inch strips
1 onion, thinly sliced

Coat roasting pan with olive oil. Toss vegetables in a bit of olive oil and arrange in pan. Roast 25 minutes at 425°. Remove pan from the oven.

4 boneless, skinless chicken breasts
Salt and pepper to taste
**15 ounces homemade enchilada sauce (See
    pages 227 and 228)**
1 chili pepper, diced

Sprinkle chicken with salt and pepper and lay on top of the onions and peppers. Pour sauce and diced chili peppers over all. Bake at 350° for 25-30 minutes or until chicken is thoroughly done.

Karen Ovetz

I think this recipe got its name because you probably already have everything needed for it in your home.

When finished, this dish can be made into fajitas by slicing the chicken into long strips and wrapping everything into a tortilla. You can also cover a bowl of pasta or rice with the chicken and vegetables.

Roasted Lemon Chicken with Green Beans and Potatoes

4 Servings

Preheat oven to 450°

4 tablespoons olive oil
Juice of 1 lemon
4 cloves garlic, sliced
1 teaspoon salt
½ teaspoon ground pepper

In large bowl combine olive oil, lemon juice, garlic, salt and pepper. Whisk together.

1 pound green beans (ends and strings removed)

Add green beans and toss to coat. Remove green beans and arrange them in bottom of a 13 x 9 x 2-inch baking dish.

20 or so tiny new potatoes (or 6-8 medium size Yellow Finns or Yukon golds, quartered)

Add potatoes to same olive oil mixture and toss to coat. Remove potatoes and arrange around outside edges of dish on top of the beans.

4 chicken breast halves (If breasts are large, two may be enough. Use about 4 ounces per serving.)

Place chicken in olive oil mixture and turn to coat well. Lay chicken on top of vegetables and pour in any remaining marinade. Roast 30 minutes at 450° and reduce temperature to 350° for final 20 minutes. Let stand about 5 minutes before serving.

Allison Hooper

Mu Shu Chicken
(Meat- or vegetable-based)

6 Servings

If you want a vegetable-based Mu Shu, simply leave out the chicken.

1 tablespoon oil
1 tablespoon sesame oil
1 clove garlic, minced
Cook garlic in a large skillet over medium heat until tender.

1½ pounds boneless, skinless chicken, cut into thin strips
Add chicken to skillet and cook until it is no longer pink. Remove to a separate dish.

1 cup chopped green onion
½ head cabbage or bok choy, thinly sliced
½ cup sliced mushrooms
½ cup shredded carrot
Options: substitute any combination of finely sliced sweet pepper, sliced broccoli or summer squash for some of the vegetables. Use about 2 cups total.
Add a bit more oil if needed. Add the vegetables to the hot pan. Stir-fry until softened. Return cooked chicken to skillet.

2 teaspoons cornstarch
¼ wine or water
¼ cup soy sauce
1 teaspoon ground ginger
Mix the wine into the cornstarch. Add to skillet, along with the soy sauce and ginger. Stir.

½ cup bean sprouts
Add bean sprouts and stir. Cover and cook a few more minutes, but don't let vegetables get soggy. Wrap tortillas in foil or put in covered baking dish and warm at 350° for about 5 minutes.

Mu Shu plum sauce (See page 127)
6 flour tortillas (See page 202)
or 6 large lettuce leaves
To serve, spread a teaspoon or two of plum sauce on flour tortilla or lettuce leaf. Add about ½ cup of vegetable/meat mixture. Fold up bottom of tortilla or lettuce and roll.

Ann Anderson

Chinese Plum Sauce

About 1½ cups

Use this tasty sauce for your own vegetable- or meat-based Mu Shu.

3 ripe plums (if plums aren't ripe, set them on counter for a few days until ripened)
Cut plums in half and remove stones, then cut again into quarters. Place plum pieces in a food processor and purée until there are small flecks of skin still visible. Pour the purée into a mixing bowl.

1 small clove garlic
Grate the garlic with a microplane, if you have one; otherwise, chop very fine and add to the plum purée.

¼ teaspoon hot chili sauce (See sidebar) or fresh or powdered hot peppers, to taste
½ teaspoon ground ginger, or equivalent amount of grated fresh ginger
1 teaspoon soy sauce
Add chili, ginger and soy sauce to plums.

1 tablespoon raw honey
1 tablespoon rice vinegar
In a separate container, mix the honey and vinegar together until the honey is dissolved. Then pour the mixture into the plum purée.

1 green onion, finely chopped (white and green parts)
Add the chopped green onions.

Stir and refrigerate at least an hour before serving. Flavors will mellow with time.

Debra Lynn Dadd
"The Queen of Green"
www.dld123.com

Yellow Plums

Weitchpec Chile Company hot sauces are available at local groceries.

Most of their peppers are grown in Hoopa.

Moroccan-Style Chicken with Green Olives

4 Servings

Bring Morocco to the Six Rivers region with this delicious chicken recipe from Henry Robertson, our local "olive guy." It's great served with couscous or basmati rice.

8 boneless chicken thighs
¼ cup olive oil
Brown chicken in olive oil and set aside.

1 teaspoon minced fresh ginger
3 cloves of garlic, minced
1 tablespoon ground cumin seed
Large pinch of saffron threads*
Add more oil if necessary and sauté for 1-2 minutes.

2 cups chicken stock
Add chicken stock and stir well.

Return the chicken to the pan and cook on each side for about 10 minutes.

2 cups shredded romaine lettuce
When done, remove chicken pieces to a platter of shredded romaine.

¼ cup lemon juice
Add lemon juice to the pan and reduce over high heat for 3-4 minutes.

1 cup roughly chopped green olives
Add the chopped olives and ladle sauce over chicken.

Grated zest of 1 lemon
Garnish with lemon zest and serve.

Henry Robertson
Henry's Olives

*Dried calendula flower petals can substitute for saffron

Stir-Fry
(Meat- or Vegetable-based)

2 Servings

Stir-frying vegetables, with or without meat, makes one of those dishes that utilizes almost any vegetables that may be in your refrigerator. However, don't use any that are old; the fresher the vegetables, the better the stir-fry.

1 tablespoon olive oil
½ teaspoon sesame oil
1 medium onion, chopped
1 clove garlic, finely chopped
Heat oils to high heat in a large skillet. Add onion and garlic and stir-fry until soft.

6 ounces chicken, chopped into small pieces
Add meat and continue to stir-fry until meat is cooked through.

2-3 cups fresh vegetables, chopped

Some suggested vegetables:

Longest cooking: carrots, cauliflower

Medium cooking: broccoli, broccoli rabe, bok choy, green beans

Quick cooking: cabbage, Chinese cabbage, summer squash, kale, mushrooms, bean sprouts

Add slower-cooking vegetables and cook until they are almost softened. Add medium-cooking vegetables and cook until almost softened.

1 teaspoon soy sauce
Optional: ½ teaspoon ground ginger
Stir in quick-cooking vegetables and seasonings. Cover skillet or wok with lid. Steam until all vegetables are cooked but still a little crisp. Add more soy sauce if desired.

Serve with brown or white rice.

Ann Anderson

Slow-Roasted Brined Goose
About 3 Servings per pound

Preheat oven to 375°

One 5- to 9-pound goose
Brine:
1 cup sugar per gallon of water
1 cup salt per gallon of water
Water (1-2 gallons is enough to cover the goose, depending on size)

In a large food-quality container, add sugar and salt to water. Submerge goose for 8-12 hours—the longer it brines, the sweeter the meat. You may need to weigh the goose down with a plate or a bowl with water in it.

Stuffing:
1 Japanese-variety sweet potato, cubed
Handful of Solstice Soup Mix from Claudia's Herbs (about ⅛ cup)
1 cup cranberries
3 cups bread, cubed and toasted in oil
1 onion, chopped and sautéed until translucent
½ cup chopped parsley
1 cup wild mushrooms, if available, coarsely chopped and sautéed until translucent and soft
1 apple, peeled, cored and cubed
1-2 tablespoons salt dried from local ocean water (See page 226).

Mix the stuffing and fill the cavity. Place the bird, breast side down, in the pan. Pile the rest of the stuffing around the bird. Roast uncovered at 375° for 30 minutes, then lower the heat to 225°. Cover the entire pan with roasting pan lid or aluminum foil and roast about 45 minutes per pound of bird. Goose is done when the drumstick wiggles loosely. A deep poke in the breast with a sharp knife point should release clear, hot juice.

After cutting off the meat, save the bones along with the gizzard, heart and neck for goose soup (See page 74).

Shail Pec-Crouse
Tule Fog Farm

"Why are you growing geese instead of chickens?" We've answered this question hundreds of times now, sometimes feeling like we are letting our most enthusiastic customers down with the switch. "Local grass is more sustainable than importing organic soy from slashed Brazilian rainforests, or Chinese farmland," we reply. "Chickens can only eat 20% pasture, but geese are like cows that produce poultry meat."

Then we drop another bombshell. "Even if the feed was domestic but conventionally farmed, we wouldn't buy it: farming practices are most of the carbon footprint of conventional food."

So we farm geese. Goose eggs taste almost like chicken eggs, but are three times the size, with rich sunset-orange yolks. The meat is all toothsome dark meat with fantastic flavor, especially when brined and slow roasted. . . . we think it's the most appropriate poultry for our local foodshed.

Shail Pec-Crouse
Tule Fog Farm

Snake River Lamb Shanks

4 Servings

Preheat oven to 300°

4 large lamb shanks
2 tablespoons olive oil
3 large cloves garlic, pressed
Rub lamb shanks with oil, then rub garlic evenly over meat.

1½ teaspoons crushed dried rosemary
leaves, or 1 tablespoon chopped fresh
½ teaspoon freshly ground black pepper
½ cup dried cranberries (or raisins or dried cherries)
Arrange lamb in covered baking pan and sprinkle with rosemary, pepper and cranberries.

10 ounces beef stock or broth (See page 225)
½ cup red wine
Pour in broth and wine. Cover and bake 3 hours.

Let rest 5 minutes before serving. Serve with brown rice or polenta.

Allison Hooper

Grilled Lamb Chops

4 Servings

Great on their own, or served with a condiment such as mustard dill sauce or wine jelly.

8 lamb chops
Juice of one lemon
1 tablespoon dried oregano, or 2 tablespoons fresh
1 large clove garlic, minced
¼ cup olive oil
Salt and pepper to taste
Marinate lamb chops in lemon juice, oregano, garlic, oil, salt and pepper for one hour.

After 45 minutes, preheat grill to about 400°.

Place chops on grill. Turn over after 3 minutes and again after another 3 minutes. Continue until chops are done to your liking.

Henry Robertson
Henry's Olive

Lamb (and Beef) Meatballs with Yogurt Sauce

6 Servings

Preheat oven to 425°

For yogurt sauce:
**1 cup plain yogurt
1 clove garlic, chopped
¼ cup chopped parsley**
Combine in bowl.

For meatballs:
**1 pound lean ground beef
½ pound lean ground lamb*
1½ teaspoons finely chopped fresh mint
½ cup soft bread crumbs
2 eggs
1 medium onion, finely chopped
1¼ teaspoons salt
⅛ teaspoon pepper**
In a large bowl, mix ingredients well and shape into 18 meatballs, about 2 inches in diameter.

Place in a shallow 9 x 13-inch baking dish. Bake, uncovered, 20 minutes. Remove pan from oven; drain off fat. Reduce oven temperature to 400°.

**½ teaspoon dried basil, or 1½ teaspoons
fresh, chopped
2 cups tomato sauce (See page 228), or 2
cups chopped fresh tomatoes**
Stir basil (and salt and pepper, if fresh tomatoes are used) into tomato sauce and spoon over the meatballs. Cover pan and return to oven for 10 to 20 minutes, or until sauce is bubbly and meatballs are done to your taste. Serve with rice or couscous. Pass the yogurt sauce at the table.

Marilyn Benemann

*Humboldt County lamb is usually lean enough that you do not need the beef, or you can vary the proportions. Even better is ground Humboldt County goat—very light and lean.

Venison Stew

If you don't have access to venison, grass-fed beef works very well instead.

2-3 pounds venison, cubed
2 large onions, peeled and sliced
2 heads of garlic, peeled and diced
1 bottle red wine

Put venison, onions and garlic in large bowl. Pour a bottle of red wine over it and cover. Marinate 12-24 hours. If using beef, marinate for 6 hours.

With slotted spoon, remove venison pieces, garlic and onions from the wine. Save the marinade to use for cooking the venison.

1-2 cups flour

Dredge the venison pieces in flour; shake off excess.

½ cup olive oil

Put oil in a large cast iron kettle and brown the venison, about six minutes. Remove the venison to a plate and reserve. Add a little more oil, if needed, and brown the onions and garlic a few minutes.

6-8 carrots, cut into ¼-inch thick rounds
3 bay leaves
2 tablespoons chopped thyme
2 tablespoons chopped fresh parsley
Salt and pepper to taste

Put venison and the rest of the ingredients into the kettle, then add the reserved marinade. The stew should be covered with about 2 inches of liquid. If more liquid is needed, add water or more wine, according to your taste.

Bring to boil, then reduce heat to simmer. Cover and simmer 3-4 hours, until juices have been reduced. Stir 2 or 3 times an hour to make sure the stew is not burning.

Serve with oven-roasted potatoes with garlic and rosemary.

Suzanne Simpson

Here is a recipe for the hunters. Appendix I provides information on Foraging, Fishing and Hunting.

Mustardy Braised Rabbit with Carrots

4 Servings

Preheat oven to 325°

2 thyme sprigs
1 rosemary sprig
1 whole clove

Tie thyme, rosemary, clove in spice sachet or square of cheesecloth.

One 2-pound rabbit, cut into 8 pieces, rinsed and patted dry
1 teaspoon kosher salt
1 teaspoon ground black pepper
2 tablespoons flour

Place the salt, pepper and flour in a small bag. Add rabbit pieces, a few at a time, shaking bag well to coat the meat. Tap off excess.

4 tablespoons extra-virgin olive oil

Heat 3 tablespoons of the oil (reserve remaining oil) in a large Dutch oven over medium-high heat. Sear floured rabbit in batches, until browned all over, 5 to 6 minutes a side. Remove seared rabbit to a plate.

4 large leeks, halved lengthwise, cleaned well and thinly sliced crosswise
3 tablespoons chopped fresh sage

Transfer to paper towel–lined plate. Add remaining tablespoon of oil to pot; reduce heat to medium. Add leeks and 2 tablespoons of the sage and cook, stirring, until softened, about 2 minutes.

1 pound carrots, peeled, trimmed, and cut into 1-inch chunks
1 celery stick, diced
3 garlic cloves, thinly sliced
2 teaspoons whole coriander seeds
Salt and pepper to taste

Stir in carrots, celery, garlic, coriander, salt and pepper. Cook, stirring, until vegetables begin to color, about 5 minutes.

1 cup dry white wine

Add wine and increase heat to high. Cook, stirring, scraping up browned bits from bottom of pot until liquid is reduced by half, about 5 minutes. Return rabbit to pot.

About 2 cups chicken stock

Add stock (it should come almost halfway up the sides of rabbit) and herb sachet. Transfer pot to oven and cook, partially covered, until meat is fork tender, about 2 hours.

1-2 tablespoons Dijon-style mustard, to taste

Stir in mustard. Transfer rabbit pieces to serving platter. If liquid seems too thin, place pot over medium-high heat and simmer until it thickens slightly. Discard sachet.

2 tablespoons chopped fresh parsley, for garnish

Spoon sauce and vegetables over rabbit. Garnish with parsley and remaining sage. Serve with buttered noodles or rice, if desired.

Joan Crandell
Wild Iris Farm

Rabbit in Wine

4 Servings

1 rabbit (about 2 pounds)

Cut the rabbit into serving-size pieces.

2 onions, chopped
4 garlic cloves, minced
¼ cup oil, enough to fry the rabbit

In a heavy covered fry-pan or Dutch oven, sauté the onion and garlic slowly in 2 tablespoons of olive oil over medium heat for about 5 minutes. Remove from pan and reserve.

Add remaining olive oil; add rabbit pieces and brown, 5-6 minutes on each side.

2 cups red wine

Add onions, garlic and wine to the rabbit and simmer over low heat about 30 minutes or until the rabbit is tender, basting with copious quantities of wine.

Salt immediately before putting it on the table.

Adapted from a traditional Spanish recipe

Locally pasture-raised beef and lamb are available commercially in our region. Several farmers have started raising rabbits. Chicken and goose may be found from time to time. The Mobile Poultry Processing Unit (coming soon) will make the locally raised rabbit and chicken more available next year. Pasture-raised pork is available in Crescent City, and one farmer has started raising totally pasture-fed pigs (no purchased grain) in Arcata. Local fish is commercially available, as are oysters, clams and crab—that perennial mid-winter treat.

Poached Salmon Variations

6 Servings

½ cup dry white wine
1½ cups water
1 bay leaf

Combine wine, water and bay leaf in a medium sized skillet and bring to a simmer.

2 pounds of salmon filet or salmon steak

Gently add the salmon. Cover the pan and simmer over low heat 10-15 minutes. The fish is done when it fork-flakes easily.

If you wish to serve the salmon hot, place it on serving dish and garnish with lemon and dill. Serve with dill or fruit sauce (recipes below). To serve the salmon cold, carefully remove it from the liquid and drain. Refrigerate until ready to use. Can be served on a green salad or alone, with either the dill, the fruit or the cucumber sauce (See below and page 138)

Dill Sauce

About 1 cup

¾ cup sour cream
¼ cup mayonnaise
1 tablespoon chopped fresh dill
1 tablespoon horseradish
1 teaspoon grated lemon zest
1 hard-boiled egg, finely chopped
Salt and pepper to taste

Mix all ingredients in a mixing bowl. Refrigerate. Use with hot or cold poached salmon.

Fruit Sauce

About 1 cup

1 peach, 2-3 plums or 1 large Fuyu persimmon (peeled), finely chopped
1 whole lemon or lime, finely chopped, including skin
½ teaspoon chili powder

Mix all ingredients together. Use with either hot or cold poached salmon.

Kim Burns , Wildberries Market
Karen Wehrstein, Photographer

Cucumber Sauce
(for Salmon)

About 2 cups

1 large cucumber, peeled and finely chopped
½ teaspoon salt
1 cup sour cream
½ cup mayonnaise
1 tablespoon horseradish
2 teaspoons vinegar
1 teaspoon chopped fresh tarragon
1 teaspoon grated onion
Salt and pepper to taste

Combine all ingredients. Let stand for a few hours or overnight. Serve chilled with cold poached salmon.

Ann Anderson

Baked White Fish in Buttermilk
6 Servings

Preheat oven to 350°

1½ pounds white fish fillets (local rock fish or halibut)

Place fish in shallow baking dish.

1 small onion, thinly sliced
2 celery stalks, chopped

Arrange onion slices and celery on top of fish.

2 cups buttermilk
Salt and pepper

Pour the buttermilk over the fish. Sprinkle with salt and pepper to taste.

Bake about 30 minutes, or until fish flakes easily with a fork.

Ann Anderson

Sushi (Meat- or vegetable-based)

4-6 Servings

For the rice:

1½ cups short-grain white rice
1½ cups water

Wash and drain rice twice; soak rice in 1½ cups water for 30 minutes or more before cooking. Cover and cook about 20 minutes. Let it steam (covered) for another 15 minutes.

⅓ cup rice vinegar
3 tablespoons sugar
1 teaspoon salt

Mix the rice vinegar, sugar, and salt in a saucepan. Heat until the sugar dissolves; remove pan from heat and cool.

Spread the hot steamed rice into a large non-re-active, heat-proof container. Sprinkle the vinegar mixture over the rice and fold quickly but gently, using a wooden spatula. Fanning the rice as you mix it will help cool it and remove moisture. Once rice is cooked, use it right away.

Making the sushi rolls:

Nori (roasted seaweed)
Your choice of vegetable sliced into long narrow strips (Suggestions: carrots, red pepper, cucumber, very young zucchini, green onion, sweet potato, cilantro)
Cooked crab or smoked tuna, salmon or other fish (delete for vegetable-based sushi)

Lay a nori wrapper on a bamboo rolling mat (preferred) or waxed paper. Spread about ⅔ cup of rice in a thin layer on the nori. Add your choice of vegetables and fish. Add sesame seeds if desired. Roll tightly, using the bamboo mat. Be careful not to roll the mat into your sushi roll. Place completed rolls on a cutting surface; cut into 1-inch rounds, using a clean, very sharp knife.

Soy sauce
Wasabi mustard paste

Serve with soy sauce and wasabi.

Ann Anderson

Crab Meat Crêpes

Filling for 12 crêpes

Preheat oven to 400°

See crêpe recipe on page 204

For filling:

2 tablespoons butter
¼ cup minced green onions
1 pound crab meat, flaked
Salt and pepper to taste

Melt butter in large skillet Add onion, then crab. Sauté, stirring gently, 2-3 minutes. Add salt and pepper.

¼ cup dry white wine

Add and boil gently until liquid is all but evaporated. Place mixture in a bowl.

For sauce:

⅓ cup dry white wine

Add to same skillet and boil until reduced to just one tablespoon; remove from heat.

2 tablespoons cornstarch
2 tablespoons milk

Mix in small bowl, whisk into wine and return to heat.

2 cups heavy cream
Salt and pepper to taste

Add cream slowly to skillet; cook gently until thickened. Do not let the mixture boil. Season with salt and pepper.

¼ cup grated Swiss cheese

Add to mixture; stir until melted. Remove from heat.

Mix half of sauce with crab mixture. Check seasoning. Place a tablespoon of crab on each crêpe. Roll and place, seam side down, in baking dish.

1 cup grated Swiss cheese

Spoon reserved sauce over crêpes. Spread cheese over top. Refrigerate crêpes 30 minutes. Bake until bubbling, about 20 minutes. Can be frozen before or after crêpes have been baked.

Martha Haynes

Vegetable-Based Entrées

Many of the recipes in the chapters on Eggs and Cheese and Salads are suitable for the main course. Many of the recipes in the Meat, Poultry and Fish chapter can be vegetable-based entrées and are marked in the list of recipes on page 113.

Why and How to Eat a More Plant-Based Diet
by Karen Wehrstein, Nutrionist, with Ann Anderson

Eat all your colors! Add a fruit or vegetable to your daily diet. Eventually you may get up to 7 servings a day—it's easy to count: that's a piece of fruit (one that will fit in your hand); one handful (½ cup) of cooked vegetables or canned fruit; 6 ounces of juice or 1 cup (two handfuls) of leafy greens.

Plants provide energy, vitamins and minerals. They have additional positive health effects. Flavonoids, found in dark chocolate, black tea, blueberries, roasted soy beans, apples, oranges, purple grape juice and red wine (just to name a few sources) can help prevent and control cholesterol levels, blood pressure, diabetes and colon cancer risk. Flavonoids help prevent chronic diseases. Phytochemicals are pigment related and can be found in foods with strong distinctive coloring such as melons, broccoli, dark leafy greens, tomatoes, carrots, oranges and blueberries. Phytochemicals act as protective substances. Antioxidants, found in foods rich in Vitamin A, Vitamin C and Vitamin E, and the mineral selenium reduce the adverse effect of substances called "free radicals" that can damage cells.

If you plan to eat a plant-based diet, remember that no single plant contains all the essential amino acids needed to build proteins in your body. By combining different plant food sources, it is possible to get all the essential amino acids, thus creating a complete source for protein.

Many years ago, Frances Moore Lappé, in *A Diet for a Small Planet*[1], provided some easy guidelines for creating complete-protein meals. Complementary proteins do not need to be eaten in the same meal to obtain the benefits. Three examples of combinations that provide complete protein are:

> Grains (rice, corn, wheat, barley, etc.) + legumes (peas, beans, lentils)
> Grains + milk products
> Seeds (sesame or sunflower) + legumes

Traditional foods of most cultures have examples of this concept: corn tortillas and refried beans, stir-fry tofu with rice, chili beans and corn bread, Creole red beans and rice, pasta fasuli (spaghetti with beans).

Non-meat foods high in protein include eggs, milk, cheese, yogurt, soybeans, mung and broad beans, peas, black beans, black-eyed peas, kidney beans, garbanzos, lima beans, tofu, lentils, nuts and seeds. Vegetables higher in protein include watercress, kale, broccoli, collard, cauliflower, mushroom, lettuce (iceberg), okra, radish, cucumber, squash, cabbage, celery, eggplant, green onions, corn, beets, pumpkin and turnip. Many are also high in water content, making it difficult to consume enough to obtain adequate protein.

How much protein do you really need to eat? Healthy adults need 0.4 grams per pound of body weight per day. If you weigh 100 pounds, then you need 40 grams of protein. A three-ounce serving of animal protein is roughly equal to 21 grams of protein; ⅔ cup of beans and rice equals about 15 grams.

An average American's current per-capita meat consumption is more than 10 ounces per day[2]—almost twice the total amount of protein required. Furthermore, meat is not the only available protein source. In fact, according to the United States Department of Agriculture, we don't need any meat in our diet.

Protein has many important functions in the body and is essential for growth and maintenance. Protein needs can easily be met by eating a variety of plant-based foods. Combining different protein sources in the same meal is not necessary. Sources of protein for vegetarians include beans, nuts, nut butters, peas, and soy products (tofu, tempeh, veggie burgers). Milk products and eggs are also good protein sources for lacto-ovo vegetarians.[3]

As the world population grows it will become more difficult to sustain current levels of meat consumption. Meat production is also hard on the environment.

Demand for more a meat-centric diet is increasing as many nations achieve a higher standard of living. The current rate of consumption of red meat in the United States is not sustainable as people in other nations increase their meat consumption and the world population increases from 6 billion currently to an estimated 9.5 billion by 2050. And meat (especially beef) is a poor converter of plant energy into protein. In the feedlot, it takes 20 pounds of grain to produce 1 pound of beef. Pork requires 7.3 pounds and poultry 4.5 pounds of grain, per pound of meat produced.[4] A pound of beef can provide five people one serving of protein. The twenty pounds of grain (if it were wheat) needed to produce that pound of beef could provide 55 people with a serving of protein.

More land, water and energy are exhausted to produce meat-based protein than a plant-based protein. It takes about 5.75 acres to raise a steer to maturity. An average animal will produce about 1,000 servings. The same resources could produce 26,000 servings of tofu. In terms of water use, the beef would consume up to 13 times more water than the soy.[5]

While it takes 20,000 calories of fossil fuel to produce a pound of steak, only 500 calories of food energy result. Twenty-two to forty times less energy is consumed in grain and legume production.[6] In addition, corn-fed livestock contribute 18 percent of total greenhouse gas emissions.[7]

Not surprisingly, it is well documented that people who eat meat-heavy meals (particularly processed meats) are more likely to have heart disease and an increased risk of colon cancer. If you eat beef, choose 100 percent grass-fed beef. It has lower levels of cholesterol and saturated fats and more of the good omega fats and vitamin E. In addition, grass-fed beef uses one-eighth the energy of feedlot beef.[8]

Does this mean we have to stop eating meat altogether? No. It means cutting back on the quantity, changing the type of meat we eat, and supplying more of our protein needs from plant foods.

Eating a more plant-based diet just makes good sense, both for personal health and the long-term health of our planet. Here's to our health!

Butternut Squash and Fontina Risotto

10-12 Servings

8 cups broth, chicken or vegetable

Bring broth to a boil in a large pot. Turn down heat to keep it at a low simmer.

1 medium yellow onion, finely chopped
2 tablespoons butter
2 teaspoons olive oil

In a large heavy-bottomed casserole or Dutch oven, sauté the onions in the butter and olive oil until lightly golden.

2 pounds butternut squash, peeled, seeded and cut into 1-inch cubes

Add the cubed squash to the onions. Sauté together over medium heat about 2 minutes.

3 cups Arborio rice

Add the rice, stirring well as the rice "toasts," or becomes slightly translucent.

1 cup dry white wine

Add the wine and turn the heat down low. When the wine has evaporated, add about 1 cup of the warm broth, stirring constantly. Let simmer until liquid is almost completely absorbed. Add another cup of the broth and simmer it down. Keep adding 1 cup of broth at a time, reducing the liquid each time before adding another. Taste the rice after 15 minutes. You may not need to use all the broth.

Fontina cheese is available from the Loleta Cheese Factory

1 pinch nutmeg
⅓ pound fontina cheese, cubed
3 tablespoons chopped parsley

Traditionally, the rice should have a slight firmness to each grain. When the rice and squash tastes done, add the nutmeg, fontina and parsley and stir to incorporate.

Taste and correct seasonings. The addition of salt will be determined by how much was in the broth initially.

Patricia Cambianica
La Trattoria

Stuffed Delicata Squash

8 Servings

Serve this with turkey at Thanksgiving or at other winter feasts. It can also be the main course.

Preheat oven to 350°.

4 delicata squashes, each about 1 pound
Cut squashes in half and remove seeds. Bake until they test soft when pricked with a fork.

¼ cup wild rice
1¾ cup short-grain brown rice
4 cups water
Cook rice in gently boiling water, uncovered, about 45 minutes.

1 medium onion, chopped
2 tablespoons olive oil
Sauté onion in olive oil until softened.

3 cloves garlic, chopped
Add garlic and continue to sauté until garlic is soft.

1 pound bolete mushrooms, chanterelles, black chanterelles, or other mushrooms
Add mushrooms and continue to sauté. As an option, you can sear the mushrooms before adding them to the sauté so that they have a slightly chewy texture.

½ teaspoon sage
½ teaspoon thyme
½ teaspoon marjoram
½ teaspoon oregano
Black pepper to taste
Dried cranberries (can be soaked in wine)
Add cooked rice and add more oil if needed. Add spices.

¼ cup white wine (or sherry)
At end of frying, add wine.

Mound the rice mixture into the squash halves. Keep hot in oven until ready to serve.

Optional: top with grated Parmesan cheese
Debby Harrison

Tip:

Cooking Delicata Squash

Place squash cut-side down in a baking dish. Add about ½ inch water and cover. Squash will cook by steam heat and be done sooner.

Roasted Red Pepper Corn Tart
6-8 Servings

Cut this colorful tart into small pieces to use as an appetizer. It is also perfect as the main dish for dinner, paired with a crisp green salad. To roast one pepper, I use the toaster oven, although I usually roast several peppers at one time, saving the extras for other purposes.

Preheat oven to 400°

1 8-inch pie crust (See page 201)
In an 8-inch tart or pie pan, bake the crust according to the directions provided with type of crust used. Set aside to cool.

1 red bell pepper
Roast pepper. When browned, place pepper in a bowl and cover with clear plastic wrap to sweat and cool down. Once cool enough to handle, peppers peel easily. Use a knife to loosen the last little bits of skin. Dice pepper.

Reduce oven heat to 375°

1 tablespoon butter
2 tablespoons minced shallots
1 cup corn
In a frying pan, melt the butter. Add the shallots and corn and sauté until the shallots are translucent, 1-2 minutes. Remove from heat and set aside. Drain off as much liquid as possible.

2 eggs
1 cup whole milk
1 teaspoon kosher salt
½ teaspoon black pepper
Combine the eggs, milk, salt, and pepper in a bowl. Whisk to blend.

2 tablespoons chopped fresh oregano or marjoram
In a bowl, add egg mixture, herbs, the shallot/corn mixture and the diced pepper. Pour into tart- or pie-pan and bake until slightly puffed and a knife inserted in middle comes out clean, 25-30 minutes.

Remove from oven and let rest 15-20 minutes before serving.
Martha Haynes

Roasting the Pepper

If you have a direct flame, you can hold pepper in the flame until the skin turns brown and blisters. Cool in covered bowl and remove skin. If you are using a broiler, cut the pepper in half and remove seeds and membranes. Broil until skin browns and blisters and proceed as above.

Cauliflower-Cheese Pie

6-8 Servings

Preheat oven to 400°

For crust:

**2 cups (packed) raw potato, peeled and
grated**

Set the freshly grated potato in a colander over a bowl, salt it and leave it for 10 minutes. Squeeze out moisture.

½ teaspoon salt
1 egg, beaten
¼ teaspoon grated onion

Add potatoes to the ingredients above. Pat mixture into a well-greased 9-inch pie pan, building up the sides of the crust with lightly floured fingers. Bake 40-45 minutes, until browned. After the first 30 minutes, brush the crust with a little oil to crisp it. Remove crust from oven. Reduce oven heat to 375°.

For filling:

1 medium glove garlic, crushed
1 cup chopped onion
2 tablespoons butter

Sauté onions and garlic in butter for 5 minutes. Salt lightly.

**1 medium cauliflower, broken into small
florets**
¼ teaspoon dried thyme
½ teaspoon dried basil
½ teaspoon salt

Add herbs and cauliflower. Stirring occasionally, cook covered for 10 minutes.

2 eggs
¼ cup milk

Beat together.

1½ cups grated Cheddar cheese
Paprika

Spread half the cheese into the baked crust. Add the sautéed cauliflower, then the rest of the cheese. Pour the egg-milk mixture over all and dust with paprika. Bake 35-40 minutes, until set.

Martha Haynes

Truffredo (Truffle Tremor Alfredo)

2 - 4 Servings

1 tablespoon kosher salt
8 ounces fresh fettuccine pasta
Bring a large pot of water to a rolling boil. Add kosher salt and fettuccine.

Cook fettuccine until "al dente," about 7 to 8 minutes. Drain, reserving ¼ cup of the hot water.

¼ cup olive oil
½ cup finely chopped mushrooms
Heat olive oil in a skillet over low heat. Sauté mushrooms until tender.

3 cloves garlic, pressed
1 tablespoon chopped chives
1 tablespoon chopped fresh Italian parsley
Add garlic, chives and parsley to skillet. Sauté for one minute and remove from heat.

½ cup heavy cream
4 ounces "Truffle Tremor" chevre, rind
    removed
Heat the cream in a small saucepan over low heat. Stir in chevre until it is barely dissolved with just a few solid pillows remaining (until you can smell the truffle).

⅛ cup finely grated Parmesan cheese
1 pinch nutmeg
White pepper, to taste
Add Parmesan cheese, nutmeg and white pepper. Remove from heat; fold in the olive oil mixture.

⅛ cup pine nuts, toasted
Put fettuccine back in the pot and add the cheese, mushroom and herb mixture. Stir until blended well. Stir in the reserved water in small increments, until sauce is creamy but not dry.

Turn pasta onto a serving plate, top with chopped Italian parsley, extra Parmesan cheese and toasted pine nuts. Drizzle with olive oil.

Steve Brackenbury
Cypress Grove Chevre

Root Vegetable Gratin

12-15 Servings

Preheat oven to 400°

Butter a 3-quart covered baking dish.

For creamed mixture:
1 tablespoon unsalted butter
3 garlic cloves, minced
In large saucepan, over medium heat, melt butter. Add garlic; cook 1 minute.

3 cups heavy cream
Salt and pepper to taste
¼ teaspoon freshly grated nutmeg
Add cream, salt, pepper and nutmeg; heat just until bubbles form around edges of pan, about 5 minutes. Remove from heat; let stand 10 minutes.

1 pound parsnips, peeled and sliced ⅛-inch thick
1 pound sweet potatoes, peeled and sliced ⅛-inch thick
1 pound celery root, peeled and sliced ⅛-inch thick
8 ounces Swiss cheese, shredded
1 tablespoon minced fresh thyme
3 tablespoons minced fresh Italian parsley
In the buttered baking dish, arrange a layer of parsnips, slightly overlapping. Arrange a layer of sweet potatoes on top, then a layer of celery root. Pour half of cream mixture over all; sprinkle half of cheese, thyme and parsley on top. Repeat with remaining ingredients. Cover dish, place on baking sheet and bake 1 hour. Remove cover; lightly press gratin down with spatula. Continue baking until vegetables are tender and top is golden brown, 15 to 30 minutes more. Let stand 15 minutes before serving.

This takes about 2 hours, so leave plenty of time for it to cook. Not too much effort, but worth every minute. It would not be difficult to cut this recipe in half.

Martha Haynes

Be creative with this recipe. Substitute other root vegetables for the parsnips—try rutabaga or turnips. If you don't have sweet potatoes, use whatever potatoes you have on hand. A few carrots will add some color if you use white potatoes.

Parsnips

Rutabagas

Turnips

Colache (Aztec Stir-Fry)

6 Servings

Colache is essentially an Aztec stir-fry. It does use the three sisters (squash, beans and corn), especially that prolific sister, Zucchini, which we generally wish to use up. If you take this to the potluck in a large, hollowed-out squash, you will not need to worry about leaving your bowl there. The recipe can also be concocted in mid-winter from things you have canned or frozen, but, of course, it holds no candle to the fresh version.

3 tablespoons of oil (or lard, to make the taste more authentic)
Chopped onion to taste
Garlic to taste
About 1 pound zucchini, sliced
About 1 cup scarlet runner beans (fresh) or similar shell beans and/or snap beans, cut up
2 red, yellow or green peppers, hot or mild

Proceed as for stir fry: Heat the oil in a wok or large skillet and add the vegetables. Stir to brown, adding a bit of water to prevent scorching.

Cover and cook until tender, about 15 minutes.

2 or 3 large fresh tomatoes, skinned and chopped, (seeded, if you are highly motivated)
8 ears of fresh corn, kernels scraped from the cobs
1 tablespoon chopped fresh oregano
¼ cup chopped fresh cilantro
Salt to taste
Optional: ground coriander or cumin seed for additional flavor

Add the corn and tomatoes and cook 5 to 10 minutes more. Season to taste.

Carol Moné

Paul Lohse Farm
Chris Wisner, Photographer

Lauren Cohn-Sarabia, Food Stylist
Lauren Cohn-Sarabia, Photographer

Southwestern Vegetable Stew

6-8 Servings

The recipe adapts well to a slow-cooker. Add corn bread and a green salad for a complete meal.

1¼ cups dried beans, soaked overnight and drained
1 teaspoon salt
1 bay leaf
1 teaspoon dried oregano

Place drained beans in a large saucepan. Cover with water plus 1 inch; add salt, bay leaf, and oregano. Bring water to a boil, reduce heat, and simmer, partly covered, about 1½ hours. Remove beans from stove when they are cooked soft but not mushy. Drain the beans and save the broth.

1 pound tomatoes, fresh or canned, peeled, seeded, and chopped; juice reserved

Prepare the tomatoes, or use puréed charcoal-grilled tomatoes from a can.

2 tablespoons olive oil
2 yellow onions, cut into chunks

Heat the oil in a large skillet over high heat and sauté the onions 1 to 2 minutes.

4 cloves garlic, finely chopped
1 tablespoon chili powder (or more, to taste)
1½ teaspoons ground cumin seeds
½ teaspoon ground coriander seeds

Lower heat, add the garlic, chili powder, cumin, and coriander, and combine well. Add a little bean broth, so the chili doesn't scorch. Cook until the onions have begun to soften, about 4 minutes. Add the tomatoes and simmer 5 minutes.

1 pound mixed summer squash, cut into ½-inch pieces
4 ears corn, kernels removed from the cob (about 2 cups)
8 ounces green beans, cut into 1-inch lengths
2 ancho chilies, seeded, de-veined, and cut into narrow strips

Stir in the squash, corn, green beans, and chili

strips, along with the cooked beans and enough broth to make a fairly wet stew. Cook slowly until the vegetables are done, about 15 to 20 minutes.

4 ounces grated Monterey Jack cheese
½ bunch coarsely chopped cilantro or
**   parsley leaves (reserve some for garnish)**
Taste the stew and adjust the seasoning. Stir in the cheese and chopped cilantro. Garnish with the whole leaves of cilantro.

Make this early in the day or the day before, as the flavors are much richer over time. Try making it in your slow cooker. In the winter months, use fresh beans and corn frozen the summer before. Sprinkle the cheese on top, or allow folks to add their own as garnish. Left-overs can be served for breakfast the next morning. Put together a toasted English muffin, a fried or poached egg, heated stew, and grated cheese. Assemble in a pleasing order. *¡Buen provecho!*

Martha Haynes

Marinara Sauce

About 2 Cups

2 cloves garlic, minced
3 tablespoons olive oil
Sauté garlic in olive oil until soft but not browned.

1 teaspoon fresh oregano (or ½ teaspoon
**   dried)**
Optional:
1 teaspoon fresh rosemary (or ½ teaspoon
**   dried)**
2 teaspoons fresh basil (or ½ teaspoon dried)
⅛ teaspoon cayenne pepper
Add herbs to garlic and oil and sauté about 1 minute.

2 cups tomato sauce (See page 228)
Stir in the tomato sauce; simmer about 15 minutes. Serve over pasta. Top with Parmesan cheese.

Suzanne Simpson

As an option, sauté some fresh vegetables and add to the Marinara sauce to make a Pasta Primavera. Suggested vegetables are: carrots, zucchini or other summer squash, broccoli, cauliflower, sweet peppers, onion, or green beans.

Cornmeal is not yet readily available in our area. It can be grown in your garden as dent-corn, although it takes a huge amount of space. Dent corn stalks can reach 15 feet in height. We hope some of our local farmers will start growing it in the Willow Creek, Orleans or Southern Humboldt areas.

Polenta Pie

An easy deep-dish pizza with a thick and crunchy crust.

4 Servings

Preheat oven to 375°

Oil a 10-inch pie pan.

For crust:
1½ cups coarse cornmeal
1 teaspoon salt
1½ cups cold water
Combine cornmeal, salt, and cold water in a small bowl.

1 cup boiling water
Have the boiling water on the stove in a saucepan; whisk in the cornmeal mixture. Cook about 10 minutes over low heat, stirring frequently. It will get very thick. Remove polenta from heat and it let cool until it can be handled. Spread the polenta into a smooth, thick crust over the bottom and sides of the pan, using a spatula and wet hands.

Olive oil
Brush the surface with olive oil and bake, uncovered, 45 minutes.

For filling:
1 tablespoon olive oil
Heat oil in a medium-size skillet

1 small onion, thinly sliced
Add the onion to oil and sauté 5 to 8 minutes, or until it begins to soften.

½ cup thinly sliced bell pepper
10 mushrooms, sliced
1 small zucchini, thinly sliced
Add bell pepper, mushrooms and zucchini; sauté until everything is tender.

5-6 medium cloves garlic, sliced
1 teaspoon dried basil (or 2 teaspoons minced fresh)
½ teaspoon dried oregano (or 1 teaspoon minced fresh)
Freshly ground black pepper
Stir in the garlic and herbs and sauté a few minutes more.

¼ pound mozzarella cheese, grated
1 medium or 2 small ripe tomatoes, sliced

Increase oven heat to broiling temperature. Sprinkle half the cheese onto the baked crust, then add the tomato slices. Spread the sautéed mixture over the tomatoes, and sprinkle the remaining cheese on top. Broil until brown (about 5 minutes) and serve hot.

Laura Litzky-Hoberecht

Pasta

4-6 Servings

Making pasta is a delightfully tactile activity. It makes a great afternoon project for children.

1 pound flour
4-5 eggs
4 tablespoons olive oil

Mix together flour and eggs, as follows:

Mound the flour on a clean board or counter top. Make a well in the center of the flour. Crack the eggs into a separate bowl. Then pour the eggs into the well in the flour. Incorporate eggs into flour with your hands. Add another egg, if needed. Add a bit of olive oil. Knead dough on a lightly floured surface until it is shiny and not too sticky.

Roll the dough out very thin, using a pasta machine or a rolling pin. Cut into strips with a sharp knife, or use your pasta machine. Cut narrow noodles for fettucini or wide ones for lasagna. Do not boil lasagna noodles, but use them fresh in your lasagna recipe.

Drop the pasta into fully boiling water. Use about a gallon of water per pound of pasta. If you salt the water, only do so when the water is at a full boil. Stir once, gently. Cook until done "al dente," about 5 minutes. Drain well (but do not rinse) and top with a sauce of your choice.

Lauren Cohn-Sarabia
Comfort of Home Catering

Pesto alla Genovese

1½ Cups

This pesto works well for pizza or pasta and freezes well. Make large batches and freeze in small containers that are the right amount for one meal.

2 cups fresh basil
1 cup grated Parmesan or Romano cheese
3 cloves of garlic
1 cup olive oil
½ cup walnuts
Pinch salt

Combine olive oil and garlic in blender; blend briefly.

Add basil and walnuts. Blend briefly, but leave the mixture lumpy.

Blend in cheese by hand.

Some people prefer to leave the cheese out before freezing it, and add it when they use the pesto later.

A recipe for pasta is on page 155.

Note: An alternative to using basil in pesto is to use the greens from your garden. Gather some broccoli leaves, chard, pea greens, kale and a few sorrel leaves to make a bit heartier pesto than the more popular basil pesto. You can also include some basil leaves with the other greens.

Lauren Cohn-Sarabia
Comfort of Home Catering

Layered Vegetable Enchilada Casserole

6 Servings

Preheat oven to 350°

> **2 tablespoons oil**
> **2 cups (or a bit more) zucchini, diced**
> **1 cup chopped onion**

Sauté zucchini and onion together for 5 minutes.

> **2 cups or more spinach or coarsely shredded chard**
> **1 cup whole-kernel corn**

Add spinach and corn. Cook until spinach is wilted.

> **3½ cups enchilada sauce (See pages 227 or 228)**
> **12 corn tortillas (See page 203)**
> **2 cups shredded cheese**
> **Cilantro, finely chopped**

Spread ½ cup of enchilada sauce in a 3-quart baking pan. Mix in the cilantro. Arrange 6 tortillas, overlapping as needed, to cover bottom of dish.

Spread half of remaining enchilada sauce on top. Add and spread vegetable mixture and half the cheese. Top with remaining tortillas, then sauce. Bake 20 minutes; top with remaining cheese and bake 5 or 6 minutes more.

Patty Hoffman

Butternut Squash and Hazelnut Lasagna

6 Servings

Both the sauce and the filling can be made a day ahead.

Preheat oven to 425°

For filling:
1 large onion, chopped
3 tablespoons unsalted butter

Cook onion in butter in a 12-inch heavy skillet over medium heat, stirring occasionally, until golden, about 10 minutes.

3 pounds butternut squash, peeled, seeded, and cut into ½-inch pieces
1 teaspoon minced garlic
1 teaspoon salt
¼ teaspoon white pepper

Add squash, garlic, salt and white pepper and cook over medium-low heat, stirring occasionally, until squash is just tender, about 15 minutes. Meanwhile, make the sauce.

For the sauce:
1 teaspoon garlic, minced
3 tablespoons unsalted butter

Sauté garlic in butter in a 3-quart heavy saucepan 1 minute over moderately low heat, stirring.

5 tablespoons flour

Slowly whisk in flour and cook into a roux, whisking, 3 minutes.

5 cups milk, warmed slightly

Add milk in a slow stream, whisking constantly. Bring to a boil, stir, then reduce heat and simmer 10 minutes, whisking occasionally.

1 teaspoon salt
⅛ teaspoon white pepper

Whisk in salt and white pepper and remove from heat. Cover surface of sauce with wax paper if not using immediately.

2 tablespoons chopped fresh parsley
1 cup hazelnuts (4 ounces), toasted and chopped
1 teaspoon fresh sage

Remove cooked squash from heat and stir in parsley, sage, and nuts. Cool.

To assemble:

2 cups (½ pound) grated fresh mozzarella
1 cup finely grated Parmesan

Toss cheeses together.

12 sheets homemade fresh lasagna (See page 155)

Spread ½ cup of sauce in a buttered 9 x 13 x 2-inch baking dish and cover with 3 pasta sheets. Spread ⅔ cup sauce and ⅓ of filling across pasta sheets. Sprinkle with ½ cup cheese. Repeat two more times. Cover pan tightly with lid or buttered foil. Bake 30 minutes. Remove lid or foil; bake another 10-15 minutes.

Martha Haynes

Vegetable Casserole

4 Servings

A complete vegetarian meal.

Preheat oven to 325°

1-2 cups marinara sauce (See page 153)

Pour sauce into 2-quart casserole dish.

2 cups broccoli, chopped and steamed
2 cups cauliflower, chopped and steamed

Stir broccoli and cauliflower into the marinara sauce.

4 eggs, hard cooked and chopped

Top the vegetables with the chopped eggs.

1-2 cups white sauce (See page 229)
½ cup grated cheese
Dash Worcestershire sauce

Mix together and add to casserole dish; warm in a 325° oven.

Serve with carrots cooked with dill or orange, and brown rice pilaf, made to suit your fancy.

Karen Werhstein

Eggplant Tomato Stacks

8 Servings

Preheat oven to 425°

For onion mixture:
4 tablespoons olive oil
4 yellow onions, diced
1 tablespoon salt, or to taste
½ teaspoon pepper, or to taste
In large sauté pan, over medium-high heat, warm the olive oil. Add onions, salt and pepper, stirring occasionally, until onions are soft, about 10 minutes.

4-6 garlic cloves, minced (depending on your taste for garlic)
10 fresh basil leaves, cut into thin strips
1 tablespoon chopped fresh oregano
¼ cup chopped fresh Italian parsley
Add and cook 2 more minutes. Remove pan from heat.

About 1 tablespoon olive oil
Rub bottom and sides of a 12-inch cast-iron fry pan, or a spring-form pan, with olive oil.

1 eggplant, 2½ to 3 inches in diameter, sliced ⅛-inch thick
5 tomatoes, sliced ¼-inch thick
4 zucchini, halved crosswise and sliced lengthwise ¼-inch thick
Salt
Olive oil
Place 8 eggplant slices in a single layer in the pan and season with salt. Top each with 1 teaspoon onion mixture and 2 zucchini slices; season with salt. Add a single layer of tomato slices. Repeat the layering two more times, ending with the zucchini. Drizzle each stack with 1 teaspoon olive oil.

Bake until vegetables are tender, about 40 minutes.

½ cup Parmesan cheese
Sprinkle each stack with 1 tablespoon cheese. Bake another 10 minutes. Let vegetables rest 5 minutes before serving.

Martha Haynes

Ghanian-style Jollof Rice

4 Servings

This recipe is a liberal translation of a Ghanian recipe. West African foods tend to be very spicy; adjust spices to your taste toleration.

¼ cup cooking oil
½ cup tomato paste (See page 299)
1 large onion, sliced

In a medium-size saucepan over medium heat, sauté sliced onions about 5 minutes. Add tomato paste and stir. (For a smoother consistency, mix the tomato paste with considerable amount of water)

Salt to taste
½ teaspoon ground ginger
¼ teaspoon cayenne pepper

Add any seasonings of your choice (spicy seasonings optional).

2 carrots, sliced
1 bell pepper, diced
¼ pound green beans, diced
Optional additions: 1 cup fried or cooked meat and/or ½ cup of cooked beans of your choice

Leave to stand a few minutes, then stir in carrots, green beans and bell pepper. Add meat or cooked beans, if using.

1 cup of rice, rinsed well
1½ cups of water

Add rice and water to the sauce and stir. Cover and allow to cook, stir occasionally.

Rice is ready when finally soft.

Transcribed from Maureen Bansah,
by Lauren Cohn-Sarabia
Comfort of Home Catering

This is a traditional West African dish, served in many countries, all made a little differently. Our 2009-2010 AFS exchange student, Maureen Bansah from Ghana, taught us this one.

Purple Green Beans

Frijoles De la Olla (beans in a pot)

About 2 cups

Use as a side dish or as filling for tacos (See page 118).

1 cup dried beans
4 cups water

Wash beans thoroughly and carefully; remove any dirt or stones. Soak beans overnight in water to cover; drain. Alternatively, put beans in 3-4 cups of water and simmer until almost tender, about 1½ hours. Drain the cooked beans thoroughly.

1 tablespoon olive oil
1 onion, chopped
2 garlic cloves, minced
1 teaspoon salt

In a large pot, sauté onion and garlic until soft. Add beans, water to cover plus an inch, and salt. Simmer beans about an hour, or until tender.

Ann Anderson

Okonomiyaki
(Japanese vegetable griddle cakes)

4 Servings

½ cup Napa cabbage, shredded
1 or 2 green onions, minced
½ cup bean sprouts
Other grated vegetables such as sweet potatoes, winter squash, turnips or carrots, for a total of 2 cups of vegetables.
¼ cup flour
4-5 eggs, beaten

Combine all ingredients. Sauté on a lightly oiled griddle, over medium heat. Okonomiyaki should be crunchy on the outside and moist inside. Can be served plain or sauced with soy sauce or a light brown sauce to taste.

Chopped mushrooms, bay shrimp, ground or thinly sliced pork or squid can also be added.

Carol Moné

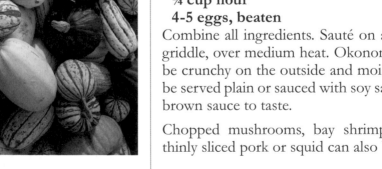

Ann Anderson and Suzanne Simpson, Food Stylists
Ann Anderson, Photographer

Vegetarian Cassoulet

6 Servings

Wanting to eat less meat and fat doesn't mean you have to give up some of your favorite dishes. Signature spices juxtaposed with the right combination of ingredients will often satisfy a craving for a certain food. Here, the combination of the traditional quatre épices seasonings (a traditional spice mixture of France), bread crumbs, garlic, and beans still tastes "cassoulet" without all the meat and preserved duck. It's not necessary to serve bread with this; it's filling enough by itself.

Preheat oven to 325° when you begin to cook the chard.

2 cups dried navy or small white beans
Soak beans in cold water to cover 4 to 6 hours or overnight. Drain, reserving two cups of bean liquid for use later in the recipe.

1 tablespoon quatre épices (recipe follows)
3 garlic cloves, minced, plus one head of garlic, cloves peeled
2 tablespoons salt
Put soaked beans in a large saucepan with the quatre epices, minced garlic and salt. Bring to a boil, lower heat and simmer, uncovered, 1 hour or until just tender.

2 large white onions, cut top to bottom into ½-inch slices
2½ cups vegetable stock (See page 224)
While the beans are cooking, place the peeled onions in a large saucepan with the stock. Simmer, uncovered, 15 minutes. Add ½ cup of the bean liquid to the broth and cook 15 minutes more, or until the onions are just tender. With a slotted spoon, remove onions to a platter.

12 baby carrots
Cook the carrots in the same broth 10 to 15 minutes, or until barely tender.

1 bunch Swiss chard, ribs removed, leaves chopped
Add the Swiss chard to the broth and simmer, uncovered, 5 minutes. With a slotted spoon, remove vegetables to a platter.

Oil for dish
¼ cup fresh bread crumbs
¼ cup olive oil or melted unsalted butter

To assemble the cassoulet, oil a 4- or 5-quart casserole dish. Add the cooked beans and the broth in which you have cooked the vegetables. Add the cooked vegetables and peeled garlic cloves, tucking the garlic in among the beans. Sprinkle the bread crumbs on top and drizzle with the oil. Bake 1½ hours or until the crust is golden, the broth evaporated, and the beans enveloped in a thick, creamy sauce.

For Quatre Epices:
Quatre épices literally means "4 spices." There's really no set-in-stone recipe for it, though this version has more than 4 spices. It's one of the secrets of great French patés and cassoulets.

1 teaspoon ground cumin
1 teaspoon ground coriander
1 teaspoon ground cinnamon
¾ teaspoon ground allspice
¼ teaspoon ground cloves
½ teaspoon ground cardamom
½ teaspoon ground ginger
½ teaspoon grated nutmeg
1 bay leaf, crumbled
¾ teaspoon dried thyme

Mix spices and dried herbs together in a blender until you have a fine powder. Store in a small jar with a tight-fitting lid.

Martha Haynes

Maggie May Farm
Chris Wisner, Photographer

Brown Rice and Summer Squash

4 Servings

Select a large enough covered pot to accommodate all of the ingredients.

1 cup short-grain brown rice
2 cups water or broth
Half a large onion, finely chopped

In a 4-quart saucepan, bring the water to a boil over medium-high heat. Add rice and chopped onion. Bring water back to a boil, cover the pan and lower the heat. Simmer about 30 minutes.

2 medium zucchini squash, sliced in
½-inch rounds
2 medium crookneck squash, sliced or
cubed ½-inch thick
2 medium pattypan squash, sliced or
cubed ½-inch thick

Add all of the chopped squash, right on top of the rice. Cover pot and continue cooking for 10 minutes.

2 or 3 large fresh tomatoes, chopped
2 cups grated Cheddar cheese

Add chopped tomato and cheese; cook until rice is done, about 5 more minutes.

⅓ cup soy sauce
⅓ cup chopped fresh basil

Remove rice mixture from heat and keep covered for approximately 5 minutes. Uncover; add soy sauce and fresh basil. Serve with green salad and garlic bread.

Barbara Rincon

Pole Beans, Paul Lohse Farm
Chris Wisner, Photographer

Vegetables and Side Dishes

Roasted Vegetables

I make this dish mostly during the cooler months of the year. Roasted vegetables are a delicious accompaniment to roasted meats, grilled sausage or chicken, or used as the main dish and served over a grain for a vegetarian meal.

The apples, added for a hint of sweetness, are an option. The vegetables listed are just a start; use any vegetables and any combination you like, as long as they are not too soft.

4-6 Servings

Preheat oven to 375°

4 bell peppers of any color, washed, seeded and cut into 1½-inch slices

2 onions, peeled and cut in half and with the bottom still intact. Slice again vertically to make two parts, or 4 quarters that will be in two parts. If the bottom becomes detached, it's okay; the onion just stays together better if the bottom is attached.

2 carrots, peeled
2 small rutabagas
2 small turnips
3 apples
2 zucchinis
¼ cup olive oil

Wash all vegetables. Cut carrots into 5 pieces, rutabagas, turnips and zucchinis into 6 pieces. Core apples and cut into wedges.
Oil baking pan with a thin layer of olive oil. In the baking pan, toss all the prepared vegetables in the olive oil, coating well.

1 bulb of garlic. Cut ⅛ inch off the top to reveal the garlic under the skin.

Pour a bit of olive oil directly over the top of the garlic bulb and place it in the pan with the vegetables and apples.

Bake 45 minutes to an hour. Vegetables will appear shrunken and a bit wrinkled when finished.

Lauren Cohn-Sarabia
Comfort of Home Catering

T Griffin and Ed Mata, Potawat Community Food Garden
Lauren Cohn-Sarabia, Photographer

If you have leftover roasted vegetables, puree them with some soup stock for a hearty soup. Recipe is on page 92.

Spicy Roasted Beets

4-6 Servings

Preheat oven to 375°

This recipe introduces a surprising and delicious complement to the natural sweetness of the beets.

4 each red, gold and chioga beets, cut into ½-inch cubes
1 Walla Walla onion, sliced
8-10 cloves garlic, finely chopped
3-4 tablespoons olive oil
Weitchpec Red Pepper Sauce to taste

In a shallow roasting pan, combine beets, onion and garlic; toss together in olive oil and pepper sauce. Bake one hour.

David Lippman
North Coast Co-op

Grilled Vegetables

The greatest thing about grilling vegetables is that they cook so quickly and easily.

Some favorite local vegetables for the barbecue are bell peppers, onions, corn-on-the-cob, eggplant, zucchini or other summer squashes, mushrooms, fennel and just about any softer veggie you like to eat.

Wash and dry vegetables. Slice into 2-inch or larger pieces. Onions can be cut in half or smaller and grilled. Eggplant and squashes can also be cut in half.

Brush the entire vegetable with olive oil or a combination of olive oil and herbs such as thyme, oregano, rosemary and salt and pepper. You may also wish to crush some garlic into the mixture.

Lay vegetable halves and slices onto the hot grill. Turn them over as soon as the pieces appear softer and a light grill mark has been left on the surface.

Repeat process for second side and remove when done.

Lauren Cohn-Sarabia
Comfort of Home Catering

Option:

Put vegetables on bamboo sticks and grill as a shish kebob.

Black-Eyed Pea Fritters

6 Servings

This dish, called "Akara," originally came from western and central Africa, then traveled with slaves to the Caribbean and also to South America.

A food processor is useful in making this dish.

1½ cups dried black-eyed peas
Soak the dried peas in a large bowl, covered with at least 5 inches of water, for about 16 hours.

Drain the peas, and put back into the bowl with fresh water. Rub the peas in your hands to release some of the pea skins, and skim them off. Don't worry if some stubborn skins don't come off.

1 small onion, peeled and coarsely chopped
1 teaspoon salt, or to taste
Ground black pepper
Ground cayenne to taste, usually ¼ to ½
    teaspoon
Optional:
    1 teaspoon ground cumin and/or
    ¼ bunch fresh cilantro

Drain the peas and put them in food processor with onion, salt, pepper, and cayenne; add optional ingredients if you use them. Process the peas until you have a grainy paste.

5 tablespoons hot water
Slowly add 5 tablespoons of hot water to the mixture to make the paste a bit thinner. It should be a little thicker than a pancake mix.

Olive oil for frying
In a frying pan, heat about ½ inch of olive oil over medium heat. Stir the batter, then drop by tablespoonsful into the hot pan until the frying pan is full. The fritters will be about 1½ inches in diameter. Turn the fritters over as they darken. Remove when done and put them on paper bags to drain off excess oil. Depending on your stove, they can take about 7 minutes to cook. Continue the process until the batter is used up.

Serve hot, topped with yogurt and tomato chutney, mango chutney or applesauce.

Suzanne Simpson

Carrot Casserole

6 Servings

For a spicier version, add 1 tablespoon of chervil, ½ tea-spoon salt and ⅛ teaspoon pepper. A dash of lemon juice would add a bit more tang.

Preheat oven to 350°

1 pound fresh carrots
Cook and mash the carrots.

2 eggs, beaten
1½ cups milk
1 cup shredded cheese, your choice
1 cup cracker crumbs (28 to 30 crackers) (See cracker recipes on pages 198 and 199)
Optional: Chopped crisp bacon or similar garnish, either stirred in or sprinkled on top.
Mix with the carrots.

2 tablespoons butter
Grease an 8- or 9-inch square baking dish. Pour mixture into baking dish.

Bake 40-45 minutes, or until a knife inserted in center comes out clean.

Patty Hoffman

Broccoli and Cheese

4 Servings

A sure way to get most kids to eat broccoli!

2 pounds broccoli, cleaned and cut into flowerets
Steam broccoli until just al dente.

½ cup to 1 cup shredded cheese of your choice
Remove broccoli from the steamer basket and cover broccoli with shredded cheese. Re-cover and heat until cheese is melted.

Lauren Cohn-Sarabia
Comfort of Home Cooking

Eddie Tanner, Deep Seeded Community Farm
Chris Wisner, Photographer

Barley Polow

4 Servings

Typically made with rice and served with saffron chicken or another stewed meat dish, this recipe is adapted for ingredients largely obtainable from local sources. Try it with curried lentils or chickpeas, seasonal vegetables, stewed or roasted meat, or other fragrantly spiced dishes.

Preheat oven to 300°

3 tablespoons butter or olive oil
1 large onion, thinly sliced
Heat a skillet over medium-high heat. Add butter or olive oil and sauté onions for several minutes, until onions begin to color.

¾ cup water or broth (See page 224)
Add water or broth, reduce heat to medium, and cook a few minutes more. Remove from heat.

3 cups cooked barley
1 large carrot, diced
½ cup plain yogurt
2-3 tablespoons dried currants or cranberries (or use fresh pomegranate seeds, if available)
Several pinches of fresh or dried calendula flower petals (a saffron substitute)
1 tablespoon pomegranate molasses (See page 175), or honey plus 1 teaspoon lemon juice
Optional: 1 teaspoon turmeric
In a large bowl, mix together cooked barley, diced carrots, half of the cooked onions, turmeric, yogurt, currants, calendula petals, and pomegranate molasses or honey and lemon. Lightly coat a 2- or 3-quart baking dish with oil or butter. Spoon barley mixture into the pan and press slightly to flatten. Spoon remaining onions and cooking water evenly across the top of the barley. Cover pan tightly and bake 45 minutes. Let rest a few minutes before serving.

Fawn Scheer

Pomegranate Molasses

To make your own pomegranate molasses, combine 2½ cups pomegranate juice (requires several pomegranates), ½ cup honey, and ¼ cup lemon juice. Simmer until mixture is reduced by about ⅔ the original volume. The result should be about the consistency of maple syrup, dark blood-red, and have a sweet taste with a rather tart kick. Pomegranate molasses is an excellent addition to both sweet and savory dishes.

Fawn Scheer

Beet Casserole

4-6 Servings

Even people who don't like beets will enjoy this dish. You can add some local goat cheese as well.

Preheat oven to 350°

5-7 beets
Trim all but 2 inches of greens (save these to eat later). Bake or boil the beets until fork tender (about ½ hour for small ones, 45 minutes to 1 hour for larger ones). Run cooked beets under cold water; slip skins and stems off and set beets aside to cool.

2 tablespoons vegetable oil
1-1½ onions, coarsely chopped
Sauté slowly until onions are almost caramelized (about 20 minutes, or for more crunch, sauté just 5-10 minutes).

Beets, cooled and grated
1-1½ cups Cheddar cheese, grated
Salt and pepper to taste
Grate beets into a medium bowl. Add cheese, onions, salt and pepper, and toss to mix thoroughly.

Pour mixture into baking dish. Bake 45 minutes or until bubbly and hot throughout and cheese has melted. Serve with lightly steamed or stir-fried washed beet greens, topped with a little lemon juice, for a complete mineral- and vitamin-rich use of the whole beet.

Lynne Wells

My name is Lynne Wells and I live in Bayside. I grow many of my own organic vegetables and fruit but shop religiously at the Arcata Farmers' Market in the summer and at the Co-op and Wildberries year round, using organic and locally-grown food as much as possible.

Here is one of my favorite recipes. I have not been known to be precise about measurements, but here is a close approximation of my improvisational nature. . . .

Editors note: We have quantified Lynne's recipe but you can vary the amounts to suit your own taste. This comment applies to most recipes, except for baked goods.

Portuguese Fava Beans

About 16 Servings

1 large onion, chopped
4-6 cloves garlic, chopped
1 pound linguişa or bacon, chopped or
    sliced

Sauté onion and garlic with the linguişa or bacon until the onion is limp. Pour off the excess grease.

Salt and pepper to taste
8 cups tender fava beans, shelled and
    washed well

Add salt and pepper. Add the beans to the onion mixture. Add a small amount of water; cover and cook until done, 25 to 30 minutes.

Optional:
    2 cups chopped tomatoes
    Hot sauce to taste

Anna Toste

Fava Beans with Yogurt

4 Servings

2 pounds fresh fava beans, shelled and
    washed well

Bring a pot of water to a boil. Add the beans. When water begins to boil again, reduce heat and simmer the beans until tender, 2-5 minutes.

Drain and rinse immediately with cold water. Slit the bean covering and lightly pinch beans to release them from the skins.

8 ounces plain low-fat yogurt
1 teaspoon honey
1 teaspoon fresh lemon juice
1 teaspoon dry mustard
Pinch ground nutmeg
1 clove garlic, peeled and crushed
1 teaspoon fresh mint, finely chopped
½ teaspoon freshly ground pepper
Salt to taste

Mix together remaining ingredients in a medium bowl. Add beans and stir.

Suzanne Simpson

Glazed Mushrooms and Chestnuts
4 Servings as a side dish or topping

Wild mushrooms, oyster mushrooms, or shiitakes are excellent cooked this way, but criminis, portabellos, or brown/white mushrooms benefit from some additional seasoning, such as tamari, herbs (rosemary, thyme), or spices (cayenne, caraway, fennel seed). This dish pairs nicely with steamed or lightly sautéed in-season vegetables, winter squash, potatoes, whole grains, or pasta.

½-1 cup chestnuts, cooked, peeled, and quartered (See tip in sidebar for preparing chestnuts)

In a medium-size dry skillet over medium heat, toast chestnut pieces lightly, about 1-2 minutes. Set chestnuts aside.

2 tablespoons olive oil or butter
1 shallot, peeled and thinly sliced

Heat olive oil or butter in the skillet. Add shallots and cook, stirring, for several minutes until shallots become very soft and begin to brown. Lower heat to keep from scorching the shallots.

2 cups mushrooms, trimmed, cleaned, and halved or quartered, depending on size

Add mushrooms to the pan and sauté a few minutes, until mushrooms begin to soften at the edges.

Add toasted chestnuts. Cook a few minutes more, stirring often.

1 tablespoons honey (omit if using apple juice, below)

Drizzle honey over the mixture and cook, stirring, 1-2 minutes.

¼ to ⅓ cup dry white wine or apple juice
Salt and pepper taste

Add wine or apple juice and stir to loosen stickiness. Reduce heat slightly and cook over medium-low heat until liquid is mostly evaporated, about 3-5 minutes.

Season as desired.

Fawn Scheer

Tip:

Preparing Chestnuts

Cut whole raw chestnuts in half with a sharp knife. In small batches, drop into boiling water and cook 5-7 minutes. Remove with a slotted spoon. While still warm, use a paring knife or nut picker to pry nut meat out of the shell. Pick or peel off inner skin (this is the trickiest part, and not totally necessary, but it's a good idea to remove as much as possible—the skins can leave a not-so-pleasant bitter or tannic taste in your mouth). Cleaned chestnuts freeze well and keep for several months.

Check with the following farms for chestnuts:
Mcintosh Farms
Moonshadow Farms
Sunny Slope Farm

For tip on roasting chestnuts and making chestnut purée, see page 89.

Sweet and Spicy Cabbage with Cranberries

6-8 Servings as a side dish

A flavorsome accompaniment to whole grains, potatoes, winter squash, or just about any roasted meat. Add cooked, sliced beets, slices of roasted fennel bulb, or sliced carrots for even more interest. Use leftovers in a potato salad or as you would sauerkraut on a Rueben sandwich.

2 tablespoons olive oil or butter
1 medium-size onion, thinly sliced
Sauté onions in oil or butter.

4 cloves garlic, minced
1 apple, peeled, cored and chopped
1 teaspoon each salt and pepper
Add garlic and apple to onions and sauté 10 minutes.

5-6 cups cabbage (about a 1-pound head)
Core, trim, and shred cabbage. Add cabbage to onion mixture in two batches. Cabbage is bulky and will shrink as it cooks—two batches makes it manageable. Sauté until all cabbage has wilted.

1½ cups whole cranberries
⅓ cup dry red wine or cranberry juice
¼ cup red wine vinegar or 3 tablespoons balsamic vinegar
1 teaspoon caraway or dill seeds
Add cranberries, wine, vinegar and spice to mixture. Cover and cook until mixture comes to a boil, then reduce heat and simmer for 15 minutes (longer if you like more tender cabbage). Stir occasionally to distribute juices and keep vegetables cooking evenly.

1 tablespoon prepared horseradish, or to taste
Additional salt and pepper to taste
Mix in horseradish just before serving.

Note: Cooking horseradish destroys its spiciness, so it is important to add it after cooking is complete.

Fawn Scheer

Au Gratin Potatoes

6 Servings

This is a local rendition of the classic potato recipe. Yellow Finns, red-skinned, and white or purple potatoes are excellent choices for this dish.

Preheat oven to 375°

Coat a 1½-quart oval or round baking pan with butter or oil.

2 pounds potatoes, peeled and thinly sliced
3 tablespoons flour

Sprinkle flour over potato slices and toss with hands to coat.

2 green onions, trimmed and sliced, or 2
    tablespoons diced onion
6 ounces shredded Swiss, or your own
    favorite cheese
2 cups half-and-half or whole milk
Pinch ground nutmeg

Combine the half-and-half and nutmeg. Bring to simmer, then remove from heat.

To layer the ingredients, spread a third of the potato slices over the bottom of the prepared pan, then sprinkle with half the green onions. Top with a third of the cheese. Repeat with more potatoes, the remaining green onions and about ½ cup of cheese. Top with the rest of the potatoes and remaining cheese.

Pour the milk mixture over the potato, onion and cheese mixture. Cover pan tightly with foil or lid. Bake 30 minutes.

4 tablespoons Parmesan cheese, shredded

Remove foil; sprinkle the Parmesan cheese over the top. Add more liquid if necessary. Re-cover pan and return to oven for another 30 minutes.

Patty Hoffman

Oven Roasted Potatoes with Fresh Fennel and Olives

4-6 Servings

Preheat oven to 350°

This is a rustic dish that partners nicely with chicken or lamb.

4 large russet potatoes, cut into ¾-inch cubes
4-6 cloves garlic, minced
1 fennel bulb, cut in half and thinly sliced
1 cup pitted green olives or oil-cured black ripe olives
⅓ cup extra-virgin olive oil
Salt and pepper to taste

Combine all ingredients in a large bowl. Toss to coat all food surfaces.

Roast in a shallow oven pan until potatoes are done; about 35-40 minutes. Turn once during cooking.

Henry Robertson
Henry's Olives

Oven Roasted Rosemary Potatoes

4-6 Servings

Preheat oven to 350°

4 large red potatoes, cut into 1½-inch pieces
⅓ cup extra-virgin olive oil
1 tablespoon chopped fresh rosemary
Salt and pepper to taste

Combine all ingredients in a large bowl. Toss to coat all surfaces.

Roast in a shallow oven pan or rimmed cookie sheet until potatoes are done; about 25-30 minutes. Turn once during cooking.

From Estelle (Bubbie) Raider
Interpreted by Ann Anderson

Greek 'Taters and Greens

4-6 Servings

For vinaigrette: (Prepare this first)
- **¼ cup lemon juice (Meyer lemon is best)**
- **1 tablespoon finely chopped fresh thyme**
- **1 tablespoon finely chopped fresh oregano**
- **2 tablespoons finely chopped fresh rosemary**
- **½ teaspoon red pepper flakes or 1½ teaspoons hot red pepper, seeded and finely diced**
- **2 tablespoons apple juice**
- **1 teaspoon salt**
- **Freshly ground black pepper to taste**
- **½ cup olive oil**

Mix the vinaigrette well in a large bowl and set aside.

For potatoes:
- **10-12 small potatoes (red, Yukon gold or Yellow Finn), cut in 1-inch pieces**

Steam potatoes in large pot 10-15 minutes, until only slightly firm.

- **1 large bunch of collards or kale, de-veined and coarsely chopped**
- **2 cloves garlic, pressed or finely chopped**

Put chopped greens and garlic on top of potatoes; steam 5-10 more minutes.

- **1 red bell or sweet pepper, seeded, roasted, skinned and coarsely chopped**

During the last minute of cooking, add the roasted red pepper.

When potatoes are cooked and greens tender, turn vegetables out into the bowl and thoroughly mix the hot vegetables with the vinaigrette.

- **½ cup Cypress Grove goat cheese, feta (or other firm goat cheese), coarsely crumbled**
- **¼ cup coarsely chopped toasted walnuts**

Top potato mixture with goat cheese and nuts and serve immediately.

Harriet Hill

Harriet uses Meyer Lemons from her garden. Walnuts can be purchased from Sunny Slope Farms at Southern Humboldt Farmers' Markets.

Check with the following farms for walnuts:

Sunny Slope Farm

Trident Lightning Farm and Orchard

Rye Pilaf

4 Servings

Pilaf is excellent served warm or piping hot, with yogurt or sour cream, alongside your favorite meal. It also makes an excellent cold salad. To serve as a salad, add a bit more vinegar, a spoonful of yogurt, and let sit overnight to marinate.

1 cup rye berries, cleaned of rocks and chaff

3 cups water or stock (slightly less for chewier berries)

In a 2½-quart or larger pot, combine rye berries and water; add a few shakes of salt. Cover pot, bring to a boil, and reduce heat. Simmer 30-60 minutes, until rye berries are chewy-tender. Don't start next step until rye is done. Once the rye has finished cooking, drain excess water, reserving some in a bowl or measuring cup. Save the rest of the rye cooking water for use in soups or bread making.

1 tablespoon olive oil or butter
½ cup chopped onion

Heat a large, heavy-bottomed skillet over medium-high heat. Add oil or butter, then the onion. Sauté onion 3-5 minutes, until it begins to soften.

1 medium-sized beet, peeled and diced
2 small carrots, scrubbed and diced

Add beets and carrots and sauté until vegetables begin to get tender. Add a few tablespoons of rye water to the skillet, stir and continue cooking until vegetables are tender.

1 tablespoon fresh dill weed or 1 teaspoon dried dill weed
1 tablespoon vinegar, or to taste
Salt and pepper to taste

Add a couple of cups of the cooked rye (make sure you have enough room to stir), dried dill, and vinegar. Mix well and continue cooking a few minutes more.

Fawn Scheer

Tip:

Converting Between Fresh and Dried Herbs

You can substitute ⅓ teaspoon of powdered herb or ½ teaspoon of crushed herb for 1 teaspoon of fresh chopped herb.

Fennel with Raisins and Cilantro

2-4 Servings

¼ cup extra-virgin olive oil
Heat oil in a heavy 12-inch skillet over medium heat until the oil shimmers.

2 fennel bulbs, stalks discarded, and sliced lengthwise ¼-inch thick
10 cloves garlic, finely chopped
½ teaspoon salt
½ teaspoon pepper
Sauté fennel, garlic, salt and pepper until tender but still crisp, about 6 minutes.

¼ cup raisins or ½ cup chopped apples
2 teaspoons whole coriander seeds
½ teaspoon orange zest*
¼ cup orange juice*
Stir in the raisins, coriander, zest and juice and sauté until raisins are plump, about 2 minutes.

½ cup chopped cilantro
Stir in cilantro just before serving. Garnish with fennel fronds and serve at room temperature.

* For a more local version, use zest and juice from Meyer lemon. Add a little honey to sweeten.

Lauren Cohn-Sarabia
Comfort of Home Catering

Fried Green Tomatoes

4 Servings

1 cup corn meal
1 cup flour
Mix in a paper bag or bowl.

4 large green tomatoes cut in ½-inch thick slices
Dredge tomatoes in flour mixture.

2 tablespoons olive oil
For each batch of tomatoes, first heat 2 tablespoons of oil and fry tomatoes quickly until coating is golden.

Drain on recycled brown paper bags. Serve immediately.

Boyd Smith
EcoGardening Sustainable Environment Co. & Farm

Lemon Beans

6 Servings

With summer's bounty, this is a refreshing way to prepare your green beans. Use as a salad or side dish.

1½ pounds fresh green beans, pre-cooked crisp-tender (about 3-4 minutes)
4 teaspoon freshly-squeezed lemon juice
3 cloves garlic, pressed
1 tablespoon olive oil
Optional:
   Chopped onion
   Bacon grease

Cook the beans. Drain beans and sauté with onions in garlic and olive oil (or bacon grease) for 2 minutes. Drizzle with lemon juice.

Patty Hoffman

Substitute asparagus for green beans in the spring or summer squash in the summer.

Zucchini Gratin

3-4 Servings

Preheat oven to 375°

6 medium zucchini, cut into half-rounds
1 cup chopped onion
3-4 garlic cloves, minced
¼ teaspoon pepper
¼ cup water
2-3 tablespoons olive oil

Cook zucchini, onions, garlic, pepper, water in oil in big frying pan at medium heat. Stir occasionally until zucchini is tender. Remove and let rest.

1½ cups shredded cheese

Combine half the cheese with vegetable mixture. Pour into a 9-inch pie pan.

1½ cups fresh bread crumbs
2 tablespoons butter, melted butter

Moisten bread crumbs with melted butter and mix in the remaining cheese. Sprinkle crumb mix over the top of pie. Bake for 20-25 minutes until golden and bubbling.

Patty Hoffman

Vegetable Cakes

6 Half-cup sized cakes

This is a great recipe for leftover vegetables. Use the suggested vegetables or try cauliflower, celery or broccoli.

Grate and chop vegetables separately, placing zucchini and carrots in different bowls.

2 tablespoons olive oil
¼ pound onions, diced (about 1 small onion)

Heat oil in a 12-inch frying pan. Add onion and sauté over medium heat until the onion begins to brown, 5-7 minutes.

½ pound carrots, grated
2 garlic cloves, diced

Add carrots and garlic; cook until carrots begin to soften.

1 teaspoon salt
⅛ teaspoon pepper
Cayenne to taste
A sprinkling of nutmeg

Add spices to the vegetable mixture and cook 2-3 minutes. Remove from stove and let cool for a few minutes.

2 eggs, beaten
½ cup cornmeal
1 pound zucchini, grated
¼ cup fresh parsley, chopped

Add cooked vegetables, beaten egg, cornmeal and parsley to zucchini.

2 tablespoons olive oil

Wipe out pan used for carrots. Add 2 more tablespoons olive oil, and heat. Using a ½-cup measure, make three vegetable cakes, add to pan, mash down with back of cup, and cook about 4 minutes per side. Keep the first cakes warm while cooking the second ones.

Serve with brown rice and tamari sauce. Freeze leftovers. Try serving tablespoon-size portions as appetizers.

Martha Haynes

Tip:

How to Pearl Barley

If you are using raw barley: put dry barley kernels into blender. Whiz a few times. Pour into a sifter. The "flour" will fall through and the remaining kernels will be pearled.

1 pound wild mushrooms, sliced thin

Pan fry mushrooms in dry pan. Remove and save for later.

6 tablespoons butter
2 cloves garlic, chopped
2 onions, chopped

Melt butter in skillet, add onion and garlic and cook until soft. Add mushrooms, cook two minutes.

1 cup pearled barley (or available local grain) (See tip in sidebar.)
1 tablespoon fresh basil, chopped or ½ teaspoon dried basil
⅓ to ⅔ cup stock
¼ cup fresh parsley
Salt and pepper to taste

(Use the higher quantity of stock on your first try. Quantity of stock depends on your specific local grain. If grain is too wet the first time than you can use less liquid, but if too little liquid is used, your grains won't cook fully.)

Add uncooked grain, basil, broth, salt, pepper and parsley. Bring to a boil.

Pour into casserole dish. Cover and bake at 325° for 45-50 minutes or until grains are cooked.

Optional: a bit of sherry and thyme, if available.

Lia Webb

Barley at Shakefork Community Farm
Chris Wisner, Photographer

Grain ❧ In and Out of the Oven

Grain in Humboldt County
by Kevin Cunningham, Shakefork Community Farm

Grain was grown in Humboldt County prior to the mass transportation of agricultural products and the centralization of grain farming in the Midwest. We can't boast the massive land base of the Great Plains or even the Central Valley, but Humboldt County is blessed with a good climate and good soils. Humboldt was not the main source of wheat or other grains for California, but we did actually export some of our product to San Francisco at a time when ships were the best form of transit. Our agricultural history is rich and varied and we are in the midst of a renaissance for the small farmer, including the rebirth of grain production.

One of the main features of our varied landscape is its many micro-climates that facilitate a broad range of crops. Our varied landscapes create one of the best and most diverse farming regions in the state.

In our past, various grain types were grown in the areas for which they were best suited. Places like Hoopa, Carlotta, and parts of southern Humboldt grew wheat. Grain from Hoopa won an award for wheat at a World's Fair. The bottom lands of both Ferndale and especially Arcata were renowned for their oats. Oats are one of the best cool weather grain crops and thrive in the moist environment of the bottoms. Today, many farmers continue to grow oats for hay and feed. Oats are now also being grown for food. Barley is another grain that can grow in a short season, and it was an important crop.

Our soils and climate are ideal for dry farming, meaning growing crops without providing irrigation. Corn can easily be dry farmed in most of the county. We no longer grow the specialized short season varieties that can mature seed here but corn is planted for silage. Dry beans like the Speckled Bayo and others have a long local history and were important within the Italian and Portuguese immigrant community. Dry beans are a staple crop that were once grown in quantity in Humboldt.

The rich landscape of Humboldt County still supports many local, small-scale farming operations. Farming will change as the market changes. As "local" becomes important to more people, we see opportunities for more farmers to grow grains. And ideally we won't simply have "grain farmers" but rather farmers that grow and raise many different crops and livestock, including grains on integrated farms. Our diversity is and will be our strength.

Kevin Cunningham, Shakefork Community Farm
Chris Wisner, Photographer

Barley Pancakes

Ten 3½- to 4-inch pancakes

"Barley—Nearly all the land in Humboldt Country not covered by redwood is well adapted to the raising of barley. As the lands are very prolific its cultivation has generally proved a good investment. The larger part sold is used at home by the mill men, this is generally ground before feeding."

History of Humboldt County, 1882

2 large eggs
¾ cup milk, kefir or yogurt
½ cup orange juice*
1 teaspoon vanilla extract
3 tablespoons unsalted butter, melted
2 tablespoons honey
¾ teaspoon salt

Whisk together the eggs, milk, orange juice, vanilla, melted butter, honey and salt.

1½ cups whole Shakefork barley flour

Stir in the barley flour. Allow the mixture to rest at room temperature while you thoroughly preheat your griddle or cast iron pan. Electric griddles can be set at 300°.

2 teaspoons baking powder

When you are ready to cook the pancakes, add the baking powder, stirring the batter for about 15 seconds, until the leavening is completely dispersed throughout. Pour the batter onto the hot griddle, using ¼ cup for each pancake.

Cook the cakes until they are golden brown underneath, about 3 to 3½ minutes. You may not see as many bubbles forming as you would with white flour pancakes. Instead, gauge readiness by when the cakes are golden brown. Gently flip the cakes over and cook until they're golden brown on the bottom, 2 to 2½ minutes more. Serve piping hot.

* Editor's note: To use totally local ingredients, substitute local Meyer lemon juice and add a little more honey. If you add honey, omit the vanilla.

Melanie Olstad
Shakefork Community Farm

Traditional Scones

8 Servings

For oven baking, preheat oven to 400°

Scones are traditionally made from oats or barley flour and are cooked on a griddle. That is the dictionary definition. The texture is improved greatly by the addition of some wheat flour, however, and oven-baking is easier.

2½ cups of flour of your choice (any combination of wheat, buckwheat, kamut, rye, cornmeal, oats and/or barley. Keep at least half of the measure wheat, for fewer crumbs. Go easy on the rye; use only 1 tablespoon flax seed)
⅓ cup sugar or ¼ honey
2 tablespoons baking powder
½ teaspoon salt
1 tablespoon grated lemon zest

Sift together. If using honey, add with wet ingredients.

½ cup chopped nuts
Berries, about ¾ cup (fresh, frozen or dried blueberries, huckleberries, currants, or chopped dried fruit)

Mix into dry ingredients.

¾ stick of butter, melted
1¼ cup buttermilk or runny yogurt, such as Strauss European style

Add and mix completely. Form dough into a ball and flatten to about 1½ inches thick. Cut into eighths and bake on a buttered sheet until done.

Or use the oiled griddle method. It is time-consuming and you need to watch closely. Covering the griddle works better, but then why not use the oven? Cooking time will vary with type of flour and fruit used.

Cool scones on a rack and store in an airtight container. They may keep for a week, but they have never lasted long enough to test this theory.

Carol Moné

*O*ats—*All the bottom lands in Humboldt County will produce 100 bushels per acre of this grain. The many new mills and other enterprises which have been added to the industries of the county during the past years, have created a home market for oats, so as to cut off exports considerably. The climate appears peculiarly adapted to the production of oats. The heavy fogs near the coast which have deleterious influence on wheat for flour-making purposes, appear to be just what is needed to make a good crop of oats. Oats will do well on any of the land, but the hill land will not produce as the bottom lands, but they will produce more than any of the States east of the Rocky Mountains. They are a good paying crop in the county.*

History of Humboldt County, 1882

Locavore Broonie

This recipe really benefits from an overnight rest. Mix up the batter at night and bake it in the morning.

Grease an 8½- by 4½-inch loaf pan.

1½ cup Shakefork cracked oats
1½ cup Shakefork whole barley flour
½ cup other flour, your choice (we use whole wheat or pastry flour)
1½ teaspoon baking powder
½ teaspoon salt

Whisk together the cracked oats, flours, baking powder, and salt in a large bowl.

½ cup unsalted butter

With a fork, two knives, or your fingers, cut in the butter until the mixture resembles coarse cornmeal.

3 large eggs, beaten
1 cup buttermilk, or use 1 cup whole milk plus 1 teaspoon apple cider vinegar to sour it
½ cup honey
1 to 2 apples, grated, or a cup of any seasonal fruit

In a separate bowl, combine eggs, buttermilk, and honey, then whatever fruit you are using. Add this mixture into the dry ingredients, stirring until the batter is evenly moistened. Spoon the batter into the prepared pan.

We recommend storing your raw batter, covered, in the refrigerator overnight.

In the morning, preheat the oven to 350°. Bake your broonie about 50-60 minutes, or until a toothpick inserted in the center comes out clean. Remove from the oven and cool on a rack. After cooling, remove from the pan and wrap well to store. It will remain moist for several days.

Melanie Olstad
Shakefork Community Farm

Kevin Cunningham and Melanie Olstad,
Shakefork Community Farm
Chris Wisner, Photographer

Lemon Barley Scones

16 Scones

Lemon lovers will be thrilled with the light, sunny flavor of these scones. Barley flour creates a tender scone with just a bit of crunch on top and the lemon glaze adds its cheerful touch to the whole.

Preheat oven to 375°

Lightly grease a baking sheet, or line it with parchment paper.

For scones:
  2 cups whole barley flour
  1 cup wheat flour
  ½ cup sugar (¼ cup regular, ¼ cup brown sugar) or ¼ cup of honey
  1 teaspoon baking soda
  1 teaspoon baking powder
  ½ teaspoon salt
  ½ cup cold unsalted butter

In a large bowl, mix together the flours, sugar (honey), baking soda, baking powder and salt. If using honey, add it with wet ingredients. Using a fork or pastry blender, cut the butter into the dry ingredients until the mixture resembles bread crumbs.

  1 large egg
  ¾ cup buttermilk
  ½ cup fresh lemon juice
  1 tablespoon grated lemon zest

In a separate bowl or large measuring cup, whisk together the egg, buttermilk, lemon juice and lemon zest. Add, all at once, to the dry ingredients and stir lightly and quickly with a fork until the dough is evenly moistened.

Turn the dough out onto a floured work surface and knead 2-3 times. The dough is really sticky; do the best you can. Divide dough in half and make 2 circles, each about ½-inch thick and 6 inches wide; divide each circle in to 8 wedges. If dough is wet and sticky, just drop by generous spoonfuls onto the baking sheet and lightly flatten. Bake until puffed and golden brown, about 20-25 minutes. Remove from the oven and place on a rack to cool for 15 minutes.

For lemon glaze:

½ cup powdered sugar
2 tablespoon fresh lemon juice
1 teaspoon lemon zest

While the scones are cooling, whisk together the sugar, lemon juice and lemon zest until smooth. Brush the glaze over the tops of the warm scones. Serve warm, or cool completely to be served later.

Anonymous

Barley Flour Drop Biscuits

About 8-10 biscuits

Preheat oven to 400°

1 cup Shakefork barley flour
½ teaspoon salt
2 teaspoons baking powder
2 teaspoons brown sugar

Mix the dry ingredients.

2 tablespoons cold butter

Cut the butter into the flour mixture with a wire pastry cutter or two knives.

1 egg, beaten
½ cup buttermilk
Optional: ½ cup fruit

Add the egg with half of the buttermilk. Add enough buttermilk to make a soft dough, but one that is thick enough to drop from a spoon onto a greased pan. Add fruit if you are using it.

Bake 7 minutes at 400°. Lower oven heat to 375° and bake 6-8 minutes more.

Judy Goucher

Some of biscuits with blueberries

Swedish Pancakes (Swedishes)
4 to 6 Large thin pancakes

Swedishes are mildly sweet, thin, and similar to crêpes. However, our family recipe is egg-based rather than the more commonly flour-based ones. For breakfast or dessert, they can be topped with butter and honey, jam, or fresh fruit and whipped cream. For brunch or a light meal, you can top with more savory items such as goat cheese, herbs, tomatoes or bacon.

Because Swedishes are so thin and delicate, you will need a quality flipper for cooking them—by "quality," I mean thin and flexible, not expensive.

½ cup wheat or barley flour
1½ cups milk

Mix flour and milk until the lumps disappear.

2 goose eggs (or 6 eggs from pasture-raised chickens)
1 tablespoon honey

Whisk in eggs and honey by hand until thoroughly mixed.

Heat a well-seasoned cast-iron skillet until a drop of water flicked onto it sizzles. Oil the skillet with a tiny amount of butter, just enough to keep the Swedishes from sticking but not so much that it ends up in a pool.

Pour ⅓ to ½ cup batter on the pan and tilt the pan in a circular motion or shake it to spread the batter very thinly. Cook over medium-high heat for about 30 seconds, until the outer edges are cooked solid but the very center is still viscous. Flip and cook for another 10 seconds or so. The goal is to have a soft, foldable pancake, not a stiff, crispy one. When properly cooked, the Swedishes should barely be browned on each side. Remove cooked Swedishes from skillet and serve hot. Top as desired.

Shail Pec-Crouse
Tule Fog Farm

Finnish Pancakes

1 Serving

This versatile recipe makes a delightful breakfast, or a light supper when served with a green salad. It could also be a dessert. It is a good beginning recipe for a child - the drama of the puffed pancake is exciting.

Preheat oven to 375°

3 tablespoons butter
In a pie pan, or a pan with sloping sides, sizzle the butter in the oven,

½ cup milk
½ cup flour
1 teaspoon salt
2 eggs
Mix the rest of the ingredients in a blender. Pour into the sizzling butter and set the pan back into the hot oven for 15 minutes. Remove from the oven.

½ cup grated Monterey Jack or Swiss
   cheese
or 1 cup sliced fruit
If using the cheese, place cheese into center of puffed pancake. Return it to the oven and bake just until cheese is melted—watch carefully. Cut into wedges and serve. If using the fruit, remove the pancake from the oven. It will deflate, but place the sliced fruit in the center, sprinkle with powdered sugar, cut into wedges, and serve.

Martha Haynes

Barley Flour Pancakes

4 Pancakes

1 egg, beaten
¾ cup buttermilk (or ½ cup plain yogurt
    and ¼ cup milk)
1 cup barley flour
2 teaspoons baking powder
½ teaspoon salt
1 tablespoon honey
Optional: ½ cup berries or ¼ to ½ cup
    chopped nuts

Mix the dry ingredients and combine with the liquids. Let stand 2 minutes. Fry on a greased 400° griddle until light brown and puffy.

Judy Goucher

Rye Crackers

About 40 crackers

Preheat over to 350°

1 cup rye flour
1 cup plus 3 tablespoons water

Place the flour in a bowl and gradually add the water, mixing well with a fork.

2 tablespoons olive oil
½ teaspoon salt

Mix in the olive oil and salt. Drop the batter a teaspoon at a time onto well-oiled cookie sheet, spacing the rounds about 2 inches apart.

If you bake the crackers in two batches, you may need to add 1 to 2 teaspoons of extra water to the second batch as the batter thickens after standing.

Caraway seeds
Additional salt, to taste

Sprinkle the crackers with caraway seeds and additional salt, if desired. Bake 20-30 minutes, or until the crackers are lightly browned and crisp around the edges.

Remove them from the baking sheet at once. As they cool, the center of the crackers will become crisp. When the crackers are cold, pack them in an airtight container.

Suzanne Simpson

Basic Crackers

About 36 crackers

Preheat oven to 400°

2 cups all-purpose flour
½ teaspoon salt
¼ teaspoon baking powder
1 teaspoon sugar or ¾ teaspoon honey

Mix dry ingredients together in a bowl. If using honey, add with egg and milk.

4 tablespoons butter

Using a pastry blender, cut the butter in until mixture resembles cornmeal.

1 egg
½ cup milk

Beat the egg into the milk and, using a fork, stir half of it into the flour mixture. Add the second half of the mixture, stirring quickly to incorporate.

Turn the cracker dough onto a floured surface. Knead carefully, just until it holds together. Then give the dough about an hour to rest. Use a rolling pin to roll the dough out until very thin, as for a pie crust.

Shape the crackers, using a floured cookie cutter. Press straight down, being careful not to twist the cutter, or cut into squares with a sharp knife. Place the crackers on a greased cookie sheet and allow to rest 5-10 minutes. Prick the crackers with a fork two or three times, as for a pie crust.

Coarse salt, herbs or herbal salt to sprinkle on top

Sprinkle crackers with the salt, herbs or herbal salt. Bake 5-6 minutes. Turn over and bake another 5 minutes, until crackers are nicely browned and crispy. Remove to a rack to cool. If they haven't all been eaten, store in an air-tight containers.

Martha Haynes

"*Wheat*—There is considerable wheat being grown throughout every agricultural portion of the county. But it is not the chief crop, as in most other counties of the State. All the county susceptible of cultivation will produce wheat. The bottom land near the bay will grow larger crops of wheat, even ninety to 100 bushels to the acre, but on account of the fogs the yield of flour is small, and that of bran, large. It does not present that hard, flinty appearance, such as give character and notoriety to California wheat.

As a wheat-growing section, this county is a decided success, but it has never been cultivated up to its capacity, and perhaps never will be. The yield per acre is greater than in any other portion of the State. More attention is given to this crop each year."

History or Humboldt County
1882

Mariah's Oat Cakes

8 Servings

These little cakes make a great quick breakfast when you're in a hurry. They last 5 days in a sealed container or freeze well.

Preheat oven to 350°

¾ cup unbleached flour
¾ cup whole wheat flour
1¼ cups rolled oats
¼ cup bran
¼ cup honey
1 tablespoon baking powder
¼ teaspoon salt

Combine flours, oats, bran, honey, baking powder and salt in a mixing bowl.

⅓ cup butter, cut into tablespoon-size pieces

Cut the butter into the dry mixture until it resembles tiny crumbs.

1⅓ cup diced dried fruit
½ cup milk
1 egg, slightly beaten

Stir the dried fruit, the milk and the egg into the dry mixture. Stir until everything is moistened.

Form the dough into a ball. Turn out on a lightly floured surface. Knead gently about 8 times and divide the ball into 8 small balls. Place the dough balls in an 8-inch square buttered pan. Flatten the balls slightly in the pan.

1 teaspoon honey
⅛ teaspoon cinnamon

Spread the honey on the surface of each ball and sprinkle with the cinnamon. Bake 20 to 25 minutes until golden brown.

Mariah Sarabia

Flaky Pie Crust

2 One-crust pies or 1 Two-crust pie

Preheat oven to 425°
2 cups sifted flour
1 teaspoon salt
Combine dry ingredients in a bowl.

¾ cup vegetable shortening or lard
Using a pastry blender, cut in the shortening until the mixture resembles coarse corn meal or tiny peas.

4-5 tablespoons cold water
Sprinkle on cold water, one tablespoon at a time, tossing the mixture lightly and stirring with a fork. Always add next tablespoon of water to the driest part. The dough should be moist enough to hold together when you press it with the fork.

Shape into a ball; wrap in wax paper. Refrigerate at least 30 minutes.

For a 1-crust pie:

When ready to bake, preheat the oven. Divide dough into two equal parts. Shape each half into a flat ball; smooth the edges so there are no breaks.

Use your hand to press one ball of dough into a flat circle on a lightly floured surface. Roll it lightly with short strokes outward from the center in all directions, until dough is ⅛-inch thick. It should make a 10- to 11-inch circle. Fold the rolled dough in half and lay in the pan. Unfold and fit into the pan. Be very careful not to stretch the dough. Gently press out any air pockets and make certain there are no openings into which pie filling could escape. Trim edge of dough.

Prick the dough with a fork so it doesn't shrink during baking, or line the dough with parchment and fill with pie weights.

Bake 12 minutes.

Martha Haynes

Flour Tortillas

8 Tortillas (8 inches round)

2 cups all-purpose flour, (low gluten content) or 1 cup all-purpose flour and 1 cup whole wheat flour
1½ teaspoons baking powder

Into a large mixing bowl, sift together the flour and baking powder.

1 teaspoon salt
2 teaspoons vegetable oil
¾ cup lukewarm milk or water

Whisk together the salt, vegetable oil and milk. Add to flour mixture, a little at a time, and mix. Keep adding liquid until the mixture is a workable but sticky dough.

Put the dough on a floured surface and knead for about 2 minutes or more until the dough is "elastic." Return the dough to the bowl, cover with a damp cloth, and let rest 15 minutes. Break the dough into 8 balls and place on a flat surface so they will not touch each other. Cover and let rest for another 20 minutes.

One dough ball at a time, place the ball onto a flat, floured surface and hand-shape into a 5-inch circle. Use a floured rolling pin to roll the dough into an 8-inch circle. Cook the dough circle on a hot, dry griddle or cast-iron frying pan. Let it cook about 30 seconds (it will blister), turn and cook for another 30 seconds. Place cooked tortilla in basket or dish and cover. Continue until all the tortillas are cooked.

Ann Anderson

Grist-Mill of Early Settlers

Corn Tortillas

2 Dozen tortillas

2½ cups dent corn

Rinse corn. Put in a large saucepan and cover with cold water to about 1½ inches above corn. Heat slowly to simmer. Do not boil.

2½ teaspoons cal (see sidebar)
1 cup water

Mix water with cal. Pour through a cloth or strainer into the heating corn in the saucepan. Stir well.

Simmer 20 minutes until the kernels turn bright yellow-orange. The outer covering "skin" of the kernel should loosen (check by pulling a kernel out and cooling it). Wrap the saucepan in a towel and let it sit overnight.

The following day, rinse the kernels, rubbing them between your hands to loosen the skins. Drain well and grind in a Corona flour mill or equivalent. The ground substance, called *nixtamal*, is rolled into golfball-sized portions, pressed in a tortilla press, and immediately grilled on a flat griddle or a comal. The *nixtamal* can also be used for tamales.

Carol Moné

Note: cal is available at Mexican groceries

Dent corn, also called "field corn," is higher in starch and lower in sugar than table corn. The stalks of dent corn are larger than those of table corn, and can reach to 15 feet in height. The individual kernels have distinctive dents along their sides, which led to the common name. Dent corn grows best with long, warm summers, which allow the ears of corn to fully mature. When dried properly it keeps for up to two years. In order to be edible, dent corn must be processed to soften the outer shell of the corn.

Soaking the corn in cal (calcium hydroxide) also frees the niacin bound up in the kernels, making it more nutritious.

Food-grade calcium hydroxide (hydrated lime) is used in Native American and Latin American cooking. Corn cooked with cal becomes "nixtamal," which has a significant increase in its nutritional value and is considered tastier and easier to digest. It's also used for pickling cucumbers the old-fashioned way, for that extra crispness.

Crêpes

About 12

Crêpes can be filled with seafood, meat, vegetables, cheese or fruit. (See recipes for fillings on pages 140 and 222)

1 cup flour
1 teaspoon baking powder
Sift dry ingredients into large mixing bowl.

2 eggs, beaten
½ cup milk
½ cup water
Note: You can change the proportions of milk to water, but not the one-cup total amount.
Mix wet ingredients together. Make a well in the dry ingredients. Gradually add the wet ingredients and stir until smooth.

¼ teaspoon salt
Optional: 2 tablespoons butter, melted
Add the salt and optional butter. Beat until smooth.

Lightly oil a crêpe cooker, griddle or skillet. Cast iron is good, for a consistent heat. Heat until pan it is about medium-hot. Pour about ¼ cup batter onto pan and tilt the pan until you have a thin layer of batter about 5 inches round.

Cook the crêpe until the bottom is light brown (about 2 minutes.) Loosen the crêpe and turn it over to cook the other side. Fill with dessert or main dish filling. Use cooked crêpes to make blintzes. Crêpes can be frozen or refrigerated for later use.

Ann Anderson

Plums,
Lauren Cohn-Sarabia, Photographer

Desserts

Grilled Summer Fruit

6 Servings

This is so good you'll be grilling dessert every night during the months of July and August. I especially love to grill peaches, but you can experiment with nectarines, apricots and apples.

6 tablespoons butter or margarine
¼ cup honey

In a 9- to 10-inch frying pan over medium-high heat, melt butter; add honey and stir until well blended. Remove pan from heat.

6 firm-ripe peaches or apples (6 ounces each), cut in half and pitted

Lay fruit, cut side down, on a barbecue grill over a solid bed of medium coals or medium heat on a gas grill (you can hold your hand at grill level only 4 to 5 seconds); close lid on gas grill. Cook until fruit is hot and lightly browned on the bottom. Brush tops with butter mixture, then turn fruit over and brush cooked sides with mixture. Cook until fruits are warm but still hold their shape, 6 to 10 minutes total.

Can be served with vanilla ice cream on top.

Lauren Sarabia
Comfort of Home Catering

Peaches, Neukom Family Farm
Chris Wisner, Photographer

Huckleberry and Hazelnut Squash Pudding

10 Servings

Just our luck! Both the huckleberries and squash are readily available in time to create this delicious marriage of fruit and vegetable.

Heat oven to 375°

5 cups Hubbard squash or other winter squash (about a 5-pound squash)

Cut squash in half and place flesh side down in baking dish with ½ to 1 inch of water. Bake 40-90 minutes, depending on type of winter squash used. Squash is done when fork can be easily inserted through the entire thickness of the thickest flesh of the squash. When done, remove from oven and cool and remove squash pulp from skin.

2 cups huckleberries
1 cup plus 2 tablespoons honey

Slather huckleberries with 2 tablespoons honey and bake in dish at 375° for about 20 minutes.

¾ cup hazelnuts
Up to 3 cups water or milk
7 medium eggs

In a blender, process hazelnuts with a little water. Mix together the blended hazelnuts, water or milk (start with about 1 cup of water or milk), honey and eggs. Pour into a separate bowl and set aside. In the blender, mix about ⅓ of the hazelnut/egg/honey mixture with ⅓ of the squash. Pour into separate mixing bowl. Repeat two more times. Mix the three batches together with a spoon. Consistency should be like cake batter. If not, add water or milk. Pour into 9 x 13-inch baking pan.

Sprinkle huckleberries evenly across the dish. Bake at 375° for 40 to 70 minutes, or until a knife inserted near the center comes out clean.

Optional: whipped cream for topping.

Nathan Helm-Burger

Snow on Mount Olympus
(Iced Goat-Milk with Figs and Honey)
6 Half-cup servings

For those warm days of summer, this is especially good when milk is sweet and figs are fresh. It's no wonder the mythological Greek gods savored these delectable flavors—together, they are divine!

¾ cup honey
2 cups fresh whole goat milk (use whole, non-homogenized cow milk if you don't have access to fresh goat milk)
½ cup chopped fresh or dried figs

Add honey to milk and stir until honey is thoroughly dissolved—this may take several minutes. Add chopped figs. Pour into an ice cream maker to freeze into a mythical delight.

If you don't have an ice cream maker, chill the milk-honey-fig mixture in the refrigerator at least an hour. Chill a sturdy metal bowl (large enough to hold mixture) in the freezer for 15 minutes. Pour the mixture into the metal bowl—be careful not to touch bare hands to frozen metal objects. Use a pot holder or kitchen towel to hold the bowl. With a wire whisk, fork, spoon or other mixing implement, mix well, scraping the frozen sides and stirring back into the mix. Place bowl (but not your mixing implement) back into the freezer, and every 15 minutes or so, remove, stir well (scraping the sides), and return to freezer. The mixture may take an hour or more to freeze until it holds its shape.

This ambrosia is best enjoyed immediately, but if you plan to consume it at a later time, transfer the iced milk to a freezer-appropriate container (not the metal bowl). Be prepared to find a relatively solid mass in your freezer when you return to it (the more honey you use, the softer it will store). Let it thaw at room temperature slightly, and do your best to mix it to the consistency you desire.

Erin Derden-Little

Poached Pears in White Wine

6 Servings

1 bottle (or 4 cups) of dry white wine such as Sauvignon Blanc or Chardonnay
1 cup sugar or ¾ cup of honey
Peel and juice from one Meyer lemon
1-inch piece of fresh ginger, cut into coins

In a large sauce pot, put in everything except the pears. Bring the whole mixture to a boil over a high heat, stirring to incorporate the sugar.

6 firm, ripe pears, peeled and left whole

When the wine mixture comes to a boil, turn down the heat to a simmer and add the pears. Simmer about 10 minutes, until pears are just tender when poked with a knife. Serve the pears in a bowl at room temperature with some of their syrup.

Variation: this recipe works well with peaches and cherries.

If using peaches, first remove their skins by blanching them in boiling water for about 30 seconds then dropping them immediately into cold water. Their skins will slip off easily. Then add them to the syrup as you would the pears. They will take less time to cook, maybe only 4 minutes.

If using cherries, drop them into the syrup as you would the pears, except keep the syrup on a medium heat. The cherries will cook in just a minute or two. Wait for one or two to split their skins, then remove them from the heat.

Patricia Cambianica
LaTrattoria

Chris Wisner, Photographer

Poached Pears in Red Wine

6 Servings

6 firm ripe pears

Boil the pears in water for a few minutes. Remove and immediately put under cold water. Peel as soon as they are cold, leaving the stems.

½ bottle of red wine

Choose either sugar or honey for sweetener. If using sugar, use about a cup and add water until total volume is about 1 cup. If using honey, use about 1 cup. If you want more sweetener, you can add more.

Cinnamon stick, if desired

Make a syrup of the wine and sugar (cinnamon optional) and bring it to a simmer.

Place the pears upright, with enough water to cover them, and simmer until they are tender. Time will depend upon the size of the pears.

Remove pears and reduce the syrup. Serve the syrup over the pears. Chill if desired, or serve warm.

Carol Moné

Goose-Egg Custard

This sweet and creamy custard is similar to a Crème Brulé without the hard sugar brulé on top.

4 Servings

Preheat oven to 275°

1 pint Strauss cream

½ cup sugar

Mix cream and sugar.

2 goose egg yolks (or yolks from 5 eggs from pasture-raised chickens)

1 tablespoon vanilla

Whisk in egg yolks and vanilla.

Pour mixture into a 9-inch pie pan. Bake 1 hour. It's done when you can jiggle it and it all moves as one—there should not be a puddle in the center. Chill and serve.

Shail Pec-Crouse
Tule Fog Farm

Fruit and Honey Sorbets

1 Quart

This recipe can be adapted for use with other summer fruits including peaches, blackberries, blueberries, melons, raspberries, etc., by simply replacing the strawberries in equal amounts. Mint may be replaced, again in equal quantities, by other fresh herbs including rosemary, tarragon and basil.

2 cups fresh strawberries, chopped

2 cups local red wine*, unfiltered apple juice, or a combination of the two (white wine can be substituted for a lighter taste and appearance)

¼ cup fresh mint leaves, chopped

3 tablespoons honey

Heat fruit, wine, mint leaves and honey in a saucepan over medium heat for 5 minutes, stirring occasionally. Remove from heat and refrigerate at least 4 hours but no more than 24 hours. Place mixture in a blender and blend until smooth. Strain if you prefer a sorbet with no seeds.

1 teaspoon grated lemon zest

Stir in lemon zest and process in an ice cream freezer according to manufacturer's directions, or place in a shallow pan in the freezer and stir about once an hour until frozen. Remove sorbet from freezer to soften it before serving.

*Because alcohol has a lower freezing temperature than fruit and water, using wine will make a softer-textured sorbet.

Kathy Marshall

Patrick Sarabia Tending Bees
Lauren Sarabia, Photographer

Lemon-Herb Sorbet

1½ Pints

1½ cups of water, white wine* or mead
½ cup honey
½ cup lemon juice
3 tablespoons chopped fresh herbs (laven-
der, rosemary, mint, tarragon or
basil)

Heat water, honey, lemon juice and herbs in a saucepan over medium heat for 5 minutes, stirring occasionally. Remove from heat and refrigerate at least 4 hours but no more than 24 hours. Place mixture in a blender and process until smooth.

Zest of 1 lemon, finely grated

Stir lemon zest into the first mixture and process in an ice cream freezer according to manufacturer's directions, or place in a shallow pan in the freezer and stir about once an hour until frozen. Remove sorbet from freezer for softening before serving.

*Because alcohol has a lower freezing temperature than fruit and water, using wine will make a softer-textured sorbet.

Optional: fresh or frozen fruit (whole blue-
berries, grapes, raspberries or chopped
strawberries, melon, peaches) may be
added just before freezing

Kathy Marshall

A Meyer lemon tree can be grown in a pot or in the ground in most of our region .

Pumpkin Pie

One 9-inch Pie

Preheat oven to 425°

- **2 cups cooked pumpkin or winter squash**
- **1½ cups heavy cream**
- **¾ cup sugar or ½ cup honey**
- **½ teaspoon salt**
- **½ teaspoon ground ginger**
- **¼ teaspoon allspice**
- **1 teaspoon cinnamon**
- **¼ teaspoon cloves**
- **2 eggs, well beaten**

In a large bowl, mix all ingredients together. Pour into uncooked pie crust. Bake 15 minutes at 425°. Reduce oven heat to 350° and bake an additional 45 minutes, until set. Pie is done when a knife inserted comes out clean.

Ann Anderson

Carrot Cake/Zucchini Cake

6-8 Servings

Preheat oven to 350°

- **3 eggs**
- **⅓ cup oil**
- **1½ cups sugar, or slightly less than this quantity of honey**
- **2 cups shredded carrot or zucchini, or combination of the two**

In large bowl stir together and set aside.

- **2 cups flour**
- **¼ teaspoon baking powder**
- **1½ teaspoons baking soda**
- **1 teaspoon salt**
- **2 teaspoons cinnamon**
- **1 teaspoon vanilla**

Combine dry ingredients and add to the egg mixture. Mix just until all the dry ingredients are moistened. Pour mixture into greased bread pan, cake pan (8- x 8-inches) or muffin tins.

Bake 1 hour for cake; 20 minutes for muffins

Lia Webb

Tip:

Cooking Pumpkin or Winter Squash for Pie

Wash pumpkin or squash and cut in half. Remove seeds. Place in a baking dish, cut side down. Add about ½ inch of water to dish. Bake at 325° for about 1 hour. Pumpkin or squash is done when it can be easily pierced with a fork.

Summary Cobbler

6 Servings

This delicious crustless cobbler couldn't be easier, with all the wonderful fruit we have available here. Apples and pears tend to lend themselves to the fall and winter months, while the softer stone-fruit and berries can be used during summer months or frozen and used later in the year.

Preheat oven to 375°

For Filling:

> **Butter, enough to coat the dish**
> **4 cups peeled, pitted and sliced stone-fruit (peaches, plums, nectarines) or apples, pears or berries**
> **3 tablespoons flour**
> **Juice of one lemon**

Mix fruit, flour and lemon juice in large bowl and pour into prepared 8-inch square glass or metal baking pan.

For topping:

> **⅔ to ¾ cup brown sugar**
> **½ cup flour**
> **½ cup oats**
> **¾ teaspoon cinnamon**
> **¾ teaspoon nutmeg**
> **⅓ cup butter, softened**

Mix topping ingredients together and spread over the fruit mixture.

Bake 30 minutes, or until topping is golden brown.

Debbie Davis

Huckleberry Tart

6 Servings

Preheat oven to 350°

For crust:
Make the crust, using the Los Bagels tart crust recipe. (See page 221)

Roll out the dough into a rectangle large enough to overlap a cookie sheet by about 1 inch.

Place dough on the cookie sheet and pinch the overlapping dough up along the sides of the pan to contain the fruit. Bake for only 10 minutes, but not until it is completely done. Remove from oven.

For fruit filling:
4 cups wild huckleberries, washed and de-stemmed (that's the hard part)*
2-3 tablespoons of sugar or honey

Spread raw huckleberries across the surface of the partially baked crust. Sprinkle with sugar or drizzle with honey. Warm the honey so it will be easier to drizzle. Return the filled tart to the oven; bake until huckleberries are cooked. They will burst open a bit and become more liquid.

Cut into bars about 2 x 3 inches. Eat either hot or cooled. Top with whipped cream if desired.

Ann Anderson

* You can substitute different berries or stone-fruit such as peaches or plums, but huckleberries have a strong flavor and are my favorite.

My granddaughters and I make this every year in the late summer or fall when the huckleberries are ripe in the forest. We go huckleberry picking, come home, make the tart and eat it before they go back home. Sometimes they bring friends—it's a great way to spend an afternoon with children.

HUCKLEBERRY CAKE.

One qt. flour, piece of butter size of an egg, 1 cup sugar, 2 cups milk, 3 tea poons baking powder, 2 cups of huckleberries. Bake in shallow pans and eat hot with butter.

Mrs. E. D. Keck.

Recipe from:
Eureka Cook Book, 1907
The Ladies League of the First Congregational Church

Pear-Plum Applesauce

This recipe is fun to make with fruit that has been frozen, then pulled from the depths of your freezer in the middle of winter. You can freeze the plums whole and use them with the fresh apples and pears later. The amount of each type of fruit is determined by how much sauce you want to make. A good start would be 4-6 pieces of each type of fruit.

Fuji and Gala apples
Asian pears
Plums, very ripe
¼ cup unfiltered water
Optional: honey

Wash, peel and core or pit all fruit. Chop into bite-size pieces. Put into saucepan with water and simmer, covered, over very low heat about 1 hour. Stir occasionally to keep fruit from scorching. Remove fruit from heat. Use a potato masher or a ricer to smooth out the consistency. Sweeten with honey if you want a sweeter sauce. Cool in refrigerator in appropriate containers.

Cyndi Freitas

Apple Pie Filling

One 9-inch Pie

Variations for Pie:

Instead of apples, use fresh peaches or blackberries

Preheat oven to 350°

6 cups of peeled, cored and sliced apples
½ cup sugar
⅛ teaspoon salt
1½ teaspoons cornstarch
1 teaspoon cinnamon

If apples are bland, add 1 tablespoon lemon juice. Mix all ingredients together and spoon into unbaked pie crust (See page 201).

2 teaspoons butter

Dot with butter. Cover with second pie crust and pinch edges together. Perforate crust to allow steam to escape. Bake 45 to 55 minutes, until crust is golden.

Ann Anderson

Apple-Quince Compote

8 Servings

This compote is cooked down to a thick sauce that can be used as apple butter. Cook less for an applesauce

4 cups apples, cored and diced into large pieces

2 cups ripe quince, cored and cut into large pieces (If you wish to make a different taste mixture, use 6 cups apples and 2 cups quince.)

Place apples and quince in a heavy pot. Cover fruit with about 1 inch of water. Cook, stirring occasionally, over low heat until fruit is soft. Run cooked fruit through a food mill or ricer to separate out skins, or cool fruit and remove skins by hand.

4 tablespoons butter (½ cube)
½ stick cinnamon
½ teaspoon ground allspice
½ teaspoon grated nutmeg
Honey to taste

In a heavy pan on a heat-spreader over low heat, melt butter. Add fruit and spices and cook, stirring frequently. Check for taste. Add honey to sweeten if desired. Then cook slowly for several hours, stirring occasionally, until mixture reaches desired thickness. This compote can be canned, using the same canning technique as for jam.

Gail Coonen

Cooked Plums and Yogurt Cheese
6 Servings

2 cups fresh yogurt
Zest of 3 Meyer lemons
Honey to taste

In a bowl, mix together yogurt, lemon zest, and honey. In another medium bowl, spread a linen tea towel. Pour the yogurt mixture into the tea towel. Secure the top and place the towel in a strainer or colander in the sink or over a bowl. Let all the liquid drip out. This generally takes 12 or so hours.

When the mixture is semi-solid, form the yogurt into a ball. Refrigerate if not using immediately.

24 ripe, dark-colored plums, any size or type
1½ cups water
1½ cups port or red wine
½ cup sugar or honey
1 4-inch cinnamon stick
10 whole cardamom seeds, crushed

Cut the plums in half and discard pits. Place in a medium saucepan and add wine and water to cover the plums. Add the sugar, cinnamon and cardamom seeds.

Bring ingredients to boil, then lower heat and simmer until plums are softened, about 10 minutes. Drain and cool.

To serve, put plums on a small dessert plate and add a generous dollop of yogurt cheese to the top.

Both the plums and the yogurt can be made in advance and stored 4-5 days in the refrigerator.

Note: Canned plums work just as well as fresh plums—no need to cook them.

Suzanne Simpson

Los Bagels Peach Tarts

About 12 Tarts

Preheat oven to 350°

1½ cups flour
1½ cups butter
⅓ cup sugar
Pinch salt

Pour flour, sugar and salt into food processor. Cut cold butter into small cubes and scatter across flour mixture. Pulse flour, sugar, salt and butter mixture until butter is about the size of peas.

3 tablespoons iced water

Add and pulse until mixture holds together when pressed between your fingers. Mixture should still be dry and crumbly.

Toss dough onto a well-floured table and work with hands just until dough comes together. You may need to add a touch more iced water and flour during this process. Chill finished dough, (wrapped in plastic wrap) at least an hour before rolling it out.

1 pound fresh peaches, sliced
1 tablespoon lemon juice
¼ cup flour
⅛ cup sugar

While dough is chilling, combine filling ingredients in large bowl and mix by hand. Mix well, but stop before peaches break down. Grease a baking sheet.

On a well-floured surface, roll out dough ⅛- to ¼-inch thick. Cut dough into circles about 5 inches in diameter.

Put filling in the center of circles and fold sides up around the filling. The filling should still be visible—about a silver dollar–size opening.

1 teaspoon cinnamon
Sugar, to taste

Sprinkle each tart with cinnamon-sugar mixture. Arrange on greased baking sheet. Bake 20-30 minutes or until tarts turn golden brown.

Los Bagels

Variations for Peach Tarts:
Use sliced plums, sliced apples or blackberries, blueberries, raspberries, huckleberries or strawberries.

Fruit-filled Crêpes

4 Servings

4 crêpes (See page 204)
1 cup fruit
  Choices: thinly sliced apples, pears,
    peaches, sliced strawberries, or coarsely
    cut raspberries, blackberries or blueber-
    ries
Optional: honey to taste

To cook apples, pears or peaches, heat a tablespoon of butter in a skillet. Add the fruit and
sauté gently. Add honey to taste if you like. Do
not overcook.

For other fruit, heat very slowly in sauce pan so
that the fruit provides its own juice. Do not overcook. Add honey to taste.

Optional: ¼ teaspoon cinnamon mixed
  with sugar

Make crêpes or heat previously made crêpes. Fill
each crêpe with about ¼ cup of fruit. Fold end
up and sides over.

For apples, pears and peaches, sprinkle with the
cinnamon/sugar mixture. Powdered sugar works
best on the other fruits.

Ann Anderson

Lauren Cohn-Sarabia, Photographer

Basics

Vegetable Stock

As you are peeling or processing vegetables throughout the week, keep the tidbits to use for making the broth. Make sure the ingredients are well cleaned. Use peels from carrots, onion skins and ends, tops from celery, beets or other greens, basil and other fresh herbs, potato skins, squash ends and skins. Let your imagination be your guide. Refrigerate or freeze everything until you are ready to make the broth.

Put the ingredients into a big pot with water to cover plus about 2 inches. Bring to boil. Reduce heat and simmer for 3 hours. Cool; then strain, reserving the broth.

Store broth in one- or two-cup containers, or in ice-cube trays. Use at once, or freeze in appropriate containers until ready to use.

Suzanne Simpson

Vegetable broth lends itself easily to the creative cook in each of us. Since vegetable skins hold the highest concentration of nutrients, this broth is a vitamin-rich resource. The yield depends on the amount of ingredients you use. The broth can be made with many kinds of vegetables; use what is easily available to you.

Chicken Stock

About 2 Gallons

5 pounds chicken parts, including feet, necks, backs
4-5 large carrots, trimmed but unpeeled
2 large whole onions, unpeeled
2 heads garlic, unpeeled
4-6 stalks celery, tops on
Handful of parsley or other herbs to taste
3-4 knobs of whole, fresh ginger
Water to cover
Salt and pepper to taste
Optional: 6-7 kaffir lime leaves for an Asian flavored stock

In large stockpot, place all the ingredients. Add enough water to cover 4 inches above the ingredients. Bring to boil, reduce heat, and simmer, covered, 9-12 hours.

When done, let cool, then strain stock into a large bowl. Transfer stock to clean canning jars, filling only to about 3 inches from the top of the jar. Freeze for future use.

Suzanne Simpson

This recipe was given to me by a friend, who got it from a famous Chinese chef in San Francisco. In his recipe, only chicken feet were used. They yield less fat and have more flavor than other parts. Organic chicken feet can be ordered through the North Coast Co-op.

Ginger is the only non-local ingredient.

Many people grow kaffir lime trees here in Humboldt County. The leaves are a mainstay of many types of Asian cooking.

Beef Stock

About 2 Gallons

5 pounds beef bones

Place bones in roasting pan and roast at 500° for 20 minutes.

4-5 large carrots, trimmed but unpeeled
2 large whole onions, unpeeled
2 heads garlic, unpeeled
4-6 stalks celery, tops on
Handful of parsley or other herbs to taste
3-4 knobs of whole fresh ginger
Water to cover
Salt and pepper to taste

In large stockpot, place all the ingredients. Add enough water to cover 4 inches above the ingredients. Bring to boil, reduce heat, and simmer, covered, 9-12 hours.

When done, let cool. Strain stock into a large bowl. Transfer stock to clean canning jars, leaving about 3 inches of head room at the top of the jar. Freeze for future use.

Suzanne Simpson

Sea Salt

About 4 Cups

5 gallons ocean water

Collect 5 gallons of the cleanest ocean water you can find. Pour the water through a coffee filter into a large pot. Boil for 20 minutes to kill bacteria. Filter again.

Pour water into baking trays with rims. Dry by placing trays in oven for about 2 hours at 350°, on top of wood-burning stove, or outside in sun. If you dry it outside, cover with cheesecloth to keep out the local flora and fauna.

Scrape the dried salt from tray and store. Adding a few grains of raw rice to the stored salt helps to keep it dry.

Salt is what makes things taste bad when it isn't in them.
~Anonymous

German Gravy with Mushrooms
1-2 Cups

This is a multipurpose gravy. It's delicious with your Thanksgiving bird, or served over pastas or grains. Try it on a simple dinner of steamed vegetables.

¼ cup whole wheat flour

Toast and stir the flour in a dry pan until quite brown; remove from pan and set aside.

¼ to 1 cup chopped wild mushrooms

Lightly fry mushrooms in dry pan. Remove and set aside.

1 small onion, chopped
1-2 tablespoons oil or local butter
1 whole clove garlic, or more

Sauté onion in oil. Add garlic, stir about 2 minutes. Mash the softened garlic with a fork. Add the mushrooms.

Stir toasted flour into this mixture.

1 cup milk or stock (vegetable, chicken or beef)
½ teaspoon salt
½ teaspoon marjoram
Black pepper to taste

Slowly add milk or stock, stirring, and bring to a boil. Simmer a few minutes, adding salt, pepper and herbs. Correct seasonings.

Thin with water if necessary, or with more stock or milk.

Lia Webb

Authentic Enchilada Sauce
1 Quart

20 dried chili peppers (about 6-inches long) Try ancho or guajillo chili peppers
1½ quarts water

Put in pot and simmer until volume is reduced by about a third to about 1 quart. Cool and put in blender until smooth.

Carol Moné

Grammy Wentz's Chili Sauce

3 to 4 Quarts*

An old family recipe for a delicious chunky ketchup from my mother, grandmother and aunt.

4 quarts tomatoes (16 cups), quartered
2 red sweet peppers, quartered, seeded, pith removed
2 to 2½ onions, half-inch dice
1 cup vinegar
2 teaspoons salt
2 tablespoons sugar or 4 teaspoons honey*

Place in large pot. Bring to a boil; reduce heat and simmer.

1½ teaspoons whole allspice
1½ teaspoons whole cloves

Put allspice and cloves in a cheesecloth bag. Add to tomato mixture, removing when mixture is spicy enough for your taste.

Cook all ingredients until they do not separate, about 1 to 1½ hours.

Ladle hot sauce into warm, sterilized canning jars, leaving a ½-inch headspace. Remove air bubbles. Wipe rim. Add lids and screw on to finger tightness. Immerse jars in water in a canner; cover the canner. Bring water to a boil and process for 15 minutes. Remove lid; wait 5 minutes, then remove jars; cool and store.

Nancy Sheen
Sheen Farms

*Note: Quantity reduced from 8 quarts to 4 by editor. Option for honey added by editor.

Enchilada Sauce

4 Servings

This delicious sauce can be made spicier by adding more hot peppers or by including the seeds from the peppers listed below. The recipe for the sauce does not involve cooking, as you will add the sauce to your enchilada recipe and cook, once the enchiladas have been assembled.

1 pound fresh Roma tomatoes or similarly suitable tomato, seeds removed
2 sweet red bell peppers, quartered, seeds removed
1 hot pepper (more, if you like it spicier), seeds removed
2 medium red onions, coarsely diced
4 large garlic cloves, peeled
½ teaspoon salt
½ teaspoon black pepper
½ teaspoon ground cumin

Purée all ingredients in a blender or food processor. Adjust for spiciness to your taste. The sauce can be refrigerated for up to 2 days, but it's best if used the same day.

Lauren Cohn-Sarabia
Comfort of Home Catering

Tomato Sauce

About 2 cups

4 large tomatoes, skins and seeds removed
Salt and pepper to taste

Mash tomatoes and simmer in a pot until soft. Process tomatoes in a food mill or blender. Use immediately or store in refrigerator for a few days.

As an option, vary the flavor by adding some of the following when cooking:

1 large onion, chopped
1 sweet pepper, seed and membranes removed
4 tablespoons parsley

The Cookbook Team

Italian-Style Tomato Paste

About 1½ to 2 Cups

12 large tomatoes, skinned, seeded and
    chopped. You need 6-8 quarts.
½ medium fennel bulb, chopped
2 small celery ribs, chopped
1 small onion, chopped
Fresh herbs to taste: basil, marjoram, oregano
24 peppercorns

Put all ingredients into a large heavy pot. Simmer,
stirring often until cooked. Sieve or put through
a ricer and return the pulp to a double boiler to
reduce. Stir frequently to avoid scorching. *Not
scorching is important.*

Cook until the mixture is a paste. This will take a
long time.

Carol Moné

White Sauce

1 Cup

*This sauce can be taken in many directions, from savory
to sweet. It begins with a one-to-one relationship between
butter and flour. The more butter and flour, the thicker
the sauce.*

1 tablespoon butter
Melt in a small saucepan.

1 tablespoon flour
Slowly whisk flour into melted butter. Allow the
butter and flour mixture to bubble around together, stirring, for a minute or two before adding
the next ingredients.

1 cup milk, warmed
Slowly whisk milk into the butter and flour mixture.

When the sauce is smooth, add whatever you like:
spices, sautéed onions, garlic or shallots, salt, pepper, or cheese. For a thicker sauce, use 2 tablespoons of butter to 2 tablespoons of flour. For a
really thick sauce, increase these to 3 tablespoons
of each.

Instead of milk, try adding stock or water in
which vegetables have been cooked. Wine can
also be used.

Martha Haynes

Blueberry Ketchup

2 Pints

2 tablespoons vegetable oil
1 large garlic clove, crushed
1 tablespoon fresh ginger, minced

Heat oil in heavy-bottomed 2-quart or larger saucepan. Add the garlic and ginger and cook over low heat 2 minutes

1 medium onion, finely chopped

Add the onion and cook until soft and transparent, stirring often.

2 pints blueberries
1 cup fresh tomatoes, peeled, seeded, and
chopped
2 large purple plums, pitted and chopped
¼ cup dark brown sugar, firmly packed
1 tablespoon blueberry or raspberry vin-
egar
Zest of 1 lemon, cut into julienne strips
1 tablespoon fresh lemon juice
1 medium dried chili pepper, crumbled
1 teaspoon ground cinnamon
1 teaspoon ground cardamom
1 teaspoon ground coriander
1 teaspoon salt
1 teaspoon freshly ground mixed pepper-
corns

Add the rest of the ingredients to the onion mixture, stirring well. Cook over medium heat until the mixture begins to simmer. Reduce the heat and simmer gently 30 minutes, stirring occasionally. Remove from heat. Let the mixture cool slightly, then purée in small batches. Return the purée to the pan. Cook at a simmer until thick, about one hour. Pour into two sterile pint-size containers. Cover and let cool. Store in the refrigerator up to four weeks, or freeze.

Martha Haynes

Homemade Sour Cream

1 Pint

1 pint heavy cream
**2 tablespoons "starter" sour cream (any
   brand that includes live cultures)**

Pour the heavy cream into a pot and heat until almost boiling. Heat slowly and stir often. Monitor the temperature—it should reach 150-160° on a candy thermometer, but not above.

Allow the cream to cool at room temperature or in the refrigerator. Stir; check the temperature frequently. The cream must cool to below 100°, but above 60°; 80-90 ° is optimal.

Warm the starter to room temperature and mix into the warm cream.

Pour cream into a pint-size glass jar and cover with a lid. Incubate 16-24 hours. During incubation, keep cream warm, to encourage bacterial growth; 70-80° is ideal. Keeping the incubating cream in an oven with a pilot light is one option, or wrap the glass jar in a dish towel and keep warm in a small insulated cooler chest that's been warmed. If the cream gets too hot, the bacteria will be killed and the sour cream will not thicken. Start tasting the cream after 15 hours. When it is acid enough, chill in the refrigerator 24 hours before serving.

Sour cream will keep for 1-2 weeks in the refrigerator. You can use your homemade sour cream as a starter for your next batch, but use it within 5-7 days, to ensure that the bacteria still have growing power.

Megan Blodgett
North Coast Co-op's original Locavore Challenger

Butter and Buttermilk

1 Quart cream makes about ¼ pound butter

Heavy cream

Let cream warm to room temperature.

Beat with an electric whisk or food processor as if you were making whipped cream. An option is to pour the cream into a jar and shake it for 20 minutes to a half hour. The cream will begin to form stiff peaks. Keep beating the cream, but reduce the processor speed. The cream will turn a bit yellow in color, then bits of butter will appear, along with a thin liquid (buttermilk). Seconds later, the butter will clump and separate from the buttermilk.

Drain off the buttermilk. It can be used for baking, cooking, or for buttermilk salad dressing (See page 112).

Wash the butter to clean off all the buttermilk. To do this, add clean cold water to the butter in a blender and blend on low speed for 1 minute. Don't use warm water; the butter will melt and run off with the buttermilk.

Drain off the water. Repeat up to seven times, until the drained water runs clean.

Use your hands and the back of a spoon to press remaining water out of the butter.

Shape and wrap the butter however you like and store it in the refrigerator.

Megan Blodgett
North Coast Co-op's Original Locavore Challenger

Suzanne Simpson, Food Stylist
Ann Anderson, Photographer

Food Storage and Preservation

Dilly Beans

Plan to grow a few extra bush bean plants just so you can make this wonderful recipe of pickled beans.

Two recipes follow for your use, depending on how many jars of beans you wish to make.

After the first time, you will surely want to make more!

Prepare canning jars by either boiling or sterilizing in the dishwasher.

The number of green beans depend on the type of bean and the size beans you plan to use.

For each jar of beans, use the following:

1 small garlic clove
1 head of dill
¼ teaspoon red pepper flakes

Put one of each of the above ingredients into each jar.

For Small Batch	For Large Batch
6 eight-ounce jars	18-20 eight-ounce jars
2 cups water	8 cups water
¼ cup salt	1 cup salt
2 cups white vinegar	8 cups white vinegar

Mix together the water, salt and vinegar. Stir to dissolve the salt completely.

Cut off stem end of beans, leaving on the other end, and pack the beans vertically into each jar with the stem-ends down.

Pour vinegar-salt solution around the beans to fill jars to about ½-inch from the top.

Cap the jars and process in a water bath for 10 minutes. Let sit for a couple of weeks before opening.

Best if chilled before serving.

Giovanna DeJohn and Annie DeKruse

Suzanne Simpson
Sharon Letts, Photographer

Sweet Red Pepper Jam

Six 8-ounce jars

12 large red peppers

Remove the stems, seeds and white pith. Dice peppers.

1 tablespoon salt

Place in a bowl, sprinkle with salt and allow to stand 3 to 4 hours. Rinse off salt and pat dry with a cloth towel.

3 cups sugar
1 pint vinegar

In a large saucepan, mix the peppers, sugar and vinegar. Boil until the mixture forms a jam.

Use standard preserving process for jams and jellies.

Jams, Jellies and Marmalades

Specific instructions for making fruit-based preserves can be found in the instructions that come with pectin. It is important to follow the instructions specific to the pectin. Some pectins are made to be used with reduced sugar or with honey. Good local choices for fruit are any of our berries, peaches, plums, figs or Meyer lemons.

Apple Butter

About 8 pint-size jars

6-7 pounds apples, washed, cored and quartered
3 cups water

Simmer apples in water until they soften. Cool and put through fine strainer or ricer to remove skins.

½ cup sugar or ⅓ cup honey for each cup of pulp
1½ teaspoons cinnamon
¾ teaspoon cloves
½ teaspoon allspice
Juice and grated rind of 2 lemons

Cook over low heat, stirring constantly, until sugar dissolves. Continue cooking until thick. Pour into hot, sterilized canning jars.

Ann Anderson

Kim Chee

About 8 Servings

1 large head Chinese cabbage, sliced
Set in large bowl and sprinkle with 1 handful of coarse sea salt. Toss every 15 minutes for a couple of hours until the cabbage is quite wilted. Don't drain off liquid.

3-4 (or more) cloves garlic, crushed
3-4 quarter-size fresh ginger slices
Add to cabbage at the first tossing.

Sprinkling of chili pepper flakes
Add to cabbage. Adjust to your taste and tolerance for hot food. You can taste the liquid at the bottom to get an idea of how things are mixing.

⅓ to ½ cup sesame or sunflower seeds,
alone or mixed
Roast sesame seeds in oven or dry iron skillet with a lid. Stir frequently and mash gently with the back of a wooden spoon or mallet.

Add the seeds to the cabbage.

¾ cup sliced cucumber
¼ cup daikon radish
¼ cup coarsely chopped onion
Press mixture into jars and pour liquid equally in each jar to ½-inch from top.

Cover top of jar with wax paper, then put on the top. Refrigerate a couple of days before eating.

Serving suggestion: eat Kim Chee alone or place on crackers with some peanut butter—sounds strange but give it a try.

Lia Webb

Grandpa Lew's Kosher Dill Pickles

Three 1-quart jars

3 quarts water
6 tablespoons coarse kosher salt

Heat the water in a saucepan. Add the salt and mix until it is dissolved. Remove from heat.

Enough cucumbers, sliced lengthwise into quarters, to tightly fill three 1-quart canning jars

Wash the jars, then heat in an oven for five minutes at 250° to sterilize.

Place the sliced cucumbers vertically into the hot jars, packing them full.

9 cloves garlic, peeled an crushed
1 tablespoon pickling spice
3 bay leaves
¼ cup fresh dill weed

Distribute the ingredients evenly to all of the jars. Pour the salted water into each of the jars, over the cucumbers and the spices. Leave room at the top for brine to form.

Close up the jars and allow the pickles to ferment three days or longer at room temperature. When they taste just the way you like, refrigerate.

Lewis Litzky

Steve Gregory's Sauerkraut

8-10 Servings

Steve lives in Manila, near Eureka, and makes sauerkraut crock pots, among other talents.

2 pounds cabbage, finely sliced
4 teaspoons salt

Mix well and pack tightly into clean, sterile crock. You may need to pound the mixture down with your fist. Cover with clean cloth (cotton works best) large enough to support weight holding it down. Keep kraut covered with liquid, adding salted water as needed.

Secure the cloth cover with a weight. such as a big jar of water or anything to hold the crock top down. Allow kraut to ferment 2 to 6 weeks.

Clean the cloth and the weight daily. This is important.

Rita Carlson

Pickle Party

*Cookbook Team, Food Stylists
Ann Anderson, Photographer*

Food Preservation

As we move toward eating more regionally, we soon realize that our favorite foods are not available all year. While awareness of seasonality was common knowledge to our ancestors, our children, who see everything in the fresh fruit and vegetable section of the grocery all year long, might not consider foods as seasonal.

In order to have our favorite flavors year-round, as well as to conserve the bounty of the harvest, we need to learn how to preserve food. In the future, we may have a local cannery, but for now we are on our own.

This chapter provides an introduction to the subject of food preservation. It is by no means complete. If you want more details, we suggest seeking out the books referenced or downloading information from the web sites listed at the end of this chapter. There are also food preservation classes offered locally.

Food can be kept for extended periods in several ways: cold storage (root cellars or colder rooms), refrigerated, frozen, dried, pickled or canned. Various foods do better than others with differing techniques and the period of time a food can be stored varies by food and technique.

Take note of when each food is at the height of its season—the price will be lower and the quality higher. Appendix A has a chart showing which foods are in season, by month.

Cold Storage - Root Cellar and Refrigerator

People have had "root cellars" for centuries, and we can do the same. See the web site at the end of this chapter for information on how to build one. A cellar, basement or even a cool room—ideally on the north side of the house—will work for storage. Some foods need to be stored below 40° and these are best kept in a refrigerator unless you have a true root cellar. They include beets, broccoli, Brussels sprouts, cabbage, carrots, cauliflower, celery, Chinese cabbage, collards, eggplant, horseradish, kohlrabi, parsnips, potatoes and turnips. Note for potatoes: Cure by storing in warm, dark environment for 7-10 days to allow the potato to dry and develop a thick skin.

Fruits and vegetables that can be stored at temperatures between 40° and 50° include cucumbers, cantaloupe, watermelon and eggplant. Foods that can be stored at above 50° include dry hot peppers, onions, pumpkins and winter squash.

Freezing Vegetables and Fruit

Freezing is one of the quickest and easiest ways to preserve food. Even a freezer in your refrigerator can be organized to accommodate a lot of food. Use only fresh, ripe, unblemished fruits and vegetables.

Freezing Vegetables

Good candidates for freezing are asparagus, green beans, broccoli, Brussels sprouts, cauliflower, corn, peas, hot peppers, sweet peppers, summer squash. Onions, pumpkins and other winter squash may also be considered.

Some vegetables, such as onions and peppers, can be frozen raw, but most need to be blanched and a few need to be fully cooked.

Onions: Wash, peel and chop into about ½-inch pieces. Put the onions into freezer bags in a single flat layer. Freeze the bags on a cookie sheet to keep the bags flat until frozen, then you can stack them directly in the freezer. You can add the frozen onions directly into your cooking pot or pan without thawing them first. Onions will keep from 3-6 months.

Bell Peppers (sweet peppers): Use crisp, fresh peppers. Wash peppers and remove stems, seeds and membrane. Dice peppers or cut them into strips. Place the cut peppers onto a cookie sheet and freeze for an hour or longer. Freezing before placing peppers in the bag will help them not stick together. Then transfer the frozen peppers into a freezer bag and seal, removing as much air as possible. Frozen peppers can be kept for up to 8 months and can be added to your cooking pot or pan while still frozen.

Hot Peppers: Freeze raw, as for bell peppers, or roasted first.

Most vegetables need to be blanched. Trim off the ends and any bad spots and cut to the desired size before blanching. The table below shows blanching times for some common vegetables. Remove the blanched vegetables and immediately put them in a big container of ice water to stop the cooking. Drain and then store in freezer bags or jars.

Blanching can be accomplished by putting the vegetables into boiling water or by steaming. If steaming, make sure the water is boiling before you put the vegetables into the steamer. Blanching for the recommended amount of time is important.

Vegetable	Boiling Time to Blanch (Minutes)	Steaming Time to Blanch (Minutes)
Asparagus	3	4
Green Beans	2½	3
Broccoli, split	3 to 4½	3 to 5
Brussels sprouts	3 to 4½	3 to 5
Cauliflower, florets	2½	3
Corn, kernels	3 to 7	4 to 8
Peas	1½ to 2½	2 to 3
Summer Squash	3	4

Zucchini is superabundant in late summer and makes wonderful breads. Wash and grate the zucchini. Steam-blanch in small quantities 1-2 minutes until translucent. Measure the quantity required for specific recipes in the future. Pack portions into freezer containers. If using jars, leave about ½ inch between the top of the zucchini and the lid of the jar. Place the filled jars in cold water to chill before freezing. When ready to make bread, thaw and use.

Vegetables that require complete cooking before freezing include pumpkin and winter squash. Wash, peel and cut into cubes. Blanch until tender, cool and pack into freezer containers. Cooked squash purée can also be frozen.

Freezing Fruit

Many fruits can be frozen raw. Pit fruits such as peaches, plums or apricots, and peel if necessary. Halve or slice fruit and spread it on a large tray. Do not let the pieces touch. Put the tray in the freezer overnight. After the fruit is frozen, place it in freezer bags or jars and store in the freezer. Small fruits such as berries can be frozen with the same technique. This method eliminates clumping and makes it easier to remove only what is needed from the container. Do not allow fruit to thaw until just before use, and do not refreeze thawed fruit.

If you have an abundance of tomatoes, and no time to can or dehydrate them, put them on a tray so they are not touching and freeze them whole until they are ready to use. Using this method, you can run hot water over the tomatoes and the skins will slide right off, which saves peeling when you are ready to be use them for canning or cooking.

Method to Dry Fruit and Vegetables
By Susan Ornelas, edited by Suzanne Simpson

Why Dry Fruit and Vegetables?

Drying fruit and vegetables is one of the easiest ways to put up food for winter. Dried foods don't take any energy to store. They're easy to process, and they add color and important nutrients to a winter diet. The drying process was discovered thousands of years ago and is still in use today.

Uses for Dried Fruit and Vegetables

Dried fruit has many healthy and tasty uses. It makes great snacks for after-dinner munching, kids' lunches, and for a snack after exercising. Soaked overnight and added to hot cereal or yogurt, the fruit makes for a sweet and delicious breakfast. Dried figs and apricots are a tasty addition to green salads and Middle-Eastern meat stews. Sun-dried tomatoes are incredibly useful and economical for adding to winter stews, soups and frittatas. Their sweet intensity brings back memories of warm summers.

How to Dry Fruit and Vegetables

Use only ripe, not over-ripe, fruit and vegetables. Wash and dry them and cut out all dark spots and bruises.

You will need the following to start: a bucket or sink containing clean, cold water; a knife and chopping block; a large bowl of cool water mixed with 1-2 tablespoons of citric acid or powdered vitamin C (for fruit only); an electric dehydrator with drying racks; or if using the sun, drying trays; muslin to cover and protect the produce from pests; and a compost bucket.

To dry large fruit, such as apples, pears, melons or peaches, cut the fruit into thin slices. To dry small fruit, such as figs and apricots, cut them in half.

Drop the fruit into a bowl of citric acid water for a few seconds, then lay them out in a single layer on the drying trays, skin-side down. Pack them in tightly—they will shrink.

Small canning tomatoes, such as the Romas, are the easiest tomatoes to dry. Cut tomatoes in half and scoop out the seeds. Place on a tray, skin-side down. With larger tomatoes, cut them into ¼-inch slices.

If using an electric dehydrator, follow the manufacturer's directions. Most fruit and vegetables will require 6-24 hours at 135-140° F. It is best to use a dehydrator that has a fan in order to evenly dry the produce.

In inland Humboldt, Del Norte Counties and in Trinity County, it is possible to dehydrate food in the sun. It is a lengthy process, and can take from 2-5 days depending on the temperature, humidity and thickness of the fruit and vegetables. Place produce on screens and cover with cheese-cloth to keep the bugs off. If possible, move the trays around, following the sun. In the evening, move them to a safe, warm place away from moisture and animals. If using the sun-drying method, it is important to put your dehydrated food in a freezer for 2-3 days to kill any insect eggs that may be on the food. Store in sealed jars or plastic bags.

Another way to dehydrate food is to buy or make a solar dehydrator. Instructions for building several versions can be found on the Mother Earth News web site.

Most solar dryers are closed, which prevents bugs or dirt from getting onto the food. Temperatures generated in a solar dryer are higher than those generated by the sun alone, and food will dry faster.

When drying vegetables, blanch them first in boiling water for 1-2 minutes. Remove them from the hot water and immediately put them in cold water. Pat dry and proceed with the dehydrating process.

The dried produce should be supple, but have no moisture. Err on the side of the fruit being a bit too dry, but don't let it get brittle. Let dried food cool to room temperature before packing it in the glass jars or plastic bags.

Pickling

Pickled food comes in many varieties such as pickles, relishes, chutneys or sauces. Cucumber, watermelon rind, peaches, pears, hot pepper, cabbage (sauerkraut or kim chee) and corn are just a few of the vegetables and fruits that are commonly pickled. The first part of this chapter provides a few recipes.

Canning

Many fruits, vegetables and fish are suitable for canning. Instructions for canning need to be followed precisely and references for canning are at the end of this chapter. Much of the information is free from the web.

Fruit made into jams, jellies and marmalades is the easiest of the canning items. Sugar is a natural preservative. To be strictly locavore, you can also make these items with honey. Read the label on the pectin packages and choose one made to be used with honey. Jams and jellies made with honey cannot be kept as long as those made with sugar, especially after the jar is opened, but the flavor is wonderful. Use the honey-based jams and jellies quickly.

In order to be safe, fruits and vegetables, especially those with a low acid content, need to be canned with great care. That being said, canning is a joyful process as noted by one of our editors.

Joys of Canning
by Suzanne Simpson

One of the fondest memories I have of my mother is when we canned peaches together when I was a young girl.

We lived in the Central Valley of California, where summer canning was a hot and sweaty experience. Although I was not always a willing student, as many pre-teens are prone to being, I now look back on those days fondly, and realize that the domestic skills my mother taught me—cooking from scratch, canning, freezing, growing food, and even plucking and cleaning chickens and wild fowl—have brought me much pleasure over the years.

On "peach day" Mom awakened me at the first bird chirps. It was the coolest part of the day, when the dew was still on the fields. The flowers and plants around our house pulsed with cool, delicious aromas before the heat of the day settled in.

With our old black-and-white dog, Lucky, loping along beside us, we headed out to the peach trees with our lug boxes and a ladder. Slipping up the ladder through the cool, green dappled leaves, it was my job to pick the beautiful, aromatic pink- and orange-skinned peaches. Mom was below to take them from me and carefully place them in the wooden boxes, so they wouldn't bruise.

After the picking was done, we washed and peeled the peaches, halved them, and sprinkled a little lemon juice over them to keep the fruit from turning brown.

Next, we made a simple syrup with water and sugar, and kept it simmering. The peach halves were placed flat side down in the jars. It made a lovely design. To finish, I put a cinnamon stick in each jar. Mom poured the hot syrup over the peaches, sealed the jars and put them in the boiling water of the 33-quart Granite Canner.

On canning days, Mom always had the radio on some classical music station. She'd sing along with the Metropolitan Opera or the Mormon Tabernacle Choir, depending of the day of the week.

When the canning was finished, we put the jars on the kitchen table to cool; jars and jars of peaches, glowing like orange jewels, bathed in the afternoon sun that poured through the window. It had been a good canning day.

Canning was only part of the process, for in those days the county fair was an important part of the community. It had not only the animal barns, but a special building where women would bring their canned fruits, vegetables, and baked goods to be judged. Mom always hoped for the first place blue ribbon, and many times she got it. On the other hand, I thought it would be more fun to be a judge and get to sample everything.

After the judging, we would walk through the building to look at all the inviting jars of food. There they sat, tables of dilled pickles, bread-and-butter pickles, sauerkraut, pickled beets and figs, rows and rows of every imaginable variety of canned fruits, vegetables, and jams and jellies.

My mother has been gone many years now, but those wonderful memories live on in me, and now I am teaching canning to my family as well as to our community.

Being a dyed-in-the-wool experimentalist, I expanded my canning repertoire to include pasta sauces made with Trinity wild mushrooms; Italian caponata with eggplant and pine nuts; figs canned with Meyer lemon zest; plums in port; pears with cinnamon; an assortment of chutneys that go so well with Indian food; and local albacore (my favorite), purchased from the local fishing boats at the Woodley Island docks.

It wasn't until recently that I knew why my mother sang along with the radio while she was canning. It is such a basic human need, one so satisfying, to take food and preserve it, to know that in the deepest part of winter when it's cold and dreary and we long for spring, we can take a jar of cinnamon peaches off the shelf and enjoy not only their delicious flavor but memories of summer's past.

Note: With any kind of food processing, it is necessary to follow the strict guidelines. Because of the controversy over using certain plastics that may have toxins in them, I personally do not store any acidic food in plastic.

Information Resources for Food Storage and Preservation

Books

Bubel, Mike and Nancy, *Root Cellaring: Natural Cold Storage of Fruits & Vegetables*, Storey Publishing, North Adams, MA, 1991

University of Georgia Cooperative Extension and the United States Department of Agriculture, *Complete Guide to Home Canning; So Easy To Preserve*, 5th Edition.

Kingry, Judi and Devine, Lauren, Editors, *Ball Complete Book of Home Preserving*, Publisher, Robert Rose, 2006

Madison, Deborah and Coleman, Eliot. *Keeping Food Fresh, Old World Techniques and Recipes*, The Gardeners and Farmers of Terre Vivante, Chelsea Green Publishing Company, White River Junction, VT, 2007

See also, Rombauer, Joy of Cooking in main reference, page 302

Web Based Resources
Food Preservation
National Center for Home Food Preservation, University of Georgia
www.uga.edu/nchfp
California Extension Service
cesacramento.ucdavis.edu/Master_Food_preservers
The University of Georgia Cooperative Extension Program has an excellent series of articles on various types of food preservation techniques. They can be downloaded and printed.
Freezing Fruit
www.pubs.caes.uga.edu/caespubs/pubs/PDF/FDNS-E43-4.pdf
Canning Fruit
www.pubs.caes.uga.edu/caespubs/pubs/PDF/FDNS-E43-1.pdf
Canning Vegetables
www.pubs.caes.uga.edu/caespubs/pubs/PDF/FDNS-E43-3.pdf
Drying fruits and vegetables
www.pubs.caes.uga.edu/caespubs/pubs/pdf/FDNS-E43-10.pdf
Jams and Jellies
www.pubs.caes.uga.edu/caespubs/pubs/PDF/FDNS-E43-8.pdf
Uncooked Jams and Jellies
www.pubs.caes.uga.edu/caespubs/pubs/PDF/FDNS-E43-9%20.pdf
University of Nebraska-Lincoln Extension in Lancaster County
www.lancaster.unl.edu/food/foodpres.shtml
Recommended Food Storage Times Cold and Dry Refrigerated and Frozen Foods from University of Kentucky Cooperative Extension
www.ca.uky.edu/hes/fcs/factshts/FN-SSB.085.PDF
Search "How to Build a Root Cellar" or "How to Build a Solar Food Dryer" on Mother Jones News. There are several options for each.
www.motherearthnews.com

Classes on Canning

Check with the following organizations:

UC Cooperative Extension
5630 S. Broadway
Eureka CA 95503
707-445-7351
www.cehumboldt.ucdavis.edu

Campus Center for Appropriate Technology
1 Harpst St.
Arcata CA 95521
707-826-3551
www.humboldt.edu/~ccat

Community Kitchen
North Coast Co-op (Eureka store)
25 4th St.
Eureka CA 95501
707-443-6027
co-opeka@northcoastco-op.com

Potawat Health Village
United Indian Health Services
1600 Weeot Way
Arcata CA 95521
707-825-5030 (Nutrition office)
www.uihs.org

Part III Appendices and References

The information in the appendices will help you find sources for local food as well as provide a starting point for those who want to read more about food systems, cooking, gardening or who wish to become involved with one of the organizations supporting local agriculture.

The information in the appendices is believed to be correct as of the date of publication. We have attempted to contact the farmers, restaurants, groceries and other organizations to verify the information. If we did not get a response from an organization, we used the latest information publicly available. We may have omitted some organizations even after our best attempts to find them all. If we have, we apologize.

Appendix A: Seasonality of Produce

The seasonality charts can help you in your meal planning. As you plan your meals, consider what is in season first and then choose your recipes, instead of choosing what to cook and then looking for the ingredients.

Information for the seasonality charts is from three sources that are shown on the charts themselves. These are:

1. Humboldt Community Alliance with Family Farmers
2. Anderson Valley Foodshed Group
3. Suzanne Simpson

For a beautiful Humboldt Seasonality Chart, go to www.caff.org/regions/Produce_Availability.pdf and print it on a color printer.

Six Rivers Region Produce Availability Chart for Fruit

	Jan	Feb	Mar	Apr	May	June	July	Aug	Sept	Oct	Nov	Dec
Apples[1]									X	X	X	
Asian Pears[3]								X	X			
Bartlett Pears[1]							X	X	X			
Blackberries[1,3]							X	X	X	X		
Blueberries[1]							X	X	X	X	X	
Cherries						X						
Figs[1]								X	X	X		
Grapes[1,3]								X	X	X	X	
Huckleberries[3]								X	X	X		
Melons							X	X	X			
Peaches[1]							X	X	X			
Pears[2]								X	X	X		
Persimmons[2]											X	X
Plums[1]							X	X	X			
Pluots[1]							X	X	X			
Raspberries[1]						X	X	X	X	X		
Strawberries[1]						X	X	X	X	X		

Six Rivers Region Produce Availability Chart for Vegetables

	Jan	Feb	Mar	Apr	May	June	July	Aug	Sept	Oct	Nov	Dec
Artichokes[1]					X	X	X	X	X	X		
Arugula[1]				X	X	X	X	X	X	X	X	
Asian Greens[3]	X	X	X	X	X	X	X	X	X	X	X	X
Asparagus[1,3]				X	X	X	X	X				
Basil[1]						X	X	X	X	X	X	
Beans (Dry)[3]								X	X	X	X	
Beets-red and gold[1]						X	X	X	X	X	X	
Black-eyed peas[3]								X	X	X		
Bok Choy	X	X	X	X	X	X	X	X	X	X	X	X
Broccoli[1,3]				X	X	X	X	X	X	X	X	X
Broccoli Rabe[3]				X	X	X	X	X	X	X	X	X
Brussels Sprouts	X											X
Cabbage[1]				X	X	X	X	X	X	X	X	X
Carrots[1]					X	X	X	X	X	X	X	X
Cauliflower[1,3]				X	X	X	X	X	X	X		
Celeriac, Rutabaga, Parsnips[1]										X	X	
Celery[3]						X	X	X	X	X		

Six Rivers Produce Availability Chart for Vegetables

	Jan	Feb	Mar	Apr	May	June	July	Aug	Sept	Oct	Nov	Dec
Chards[1]	X	X	X	X	X	X	X	X	X	X	X	X
Chick Peas (Garbanzo Beans)[3]							X	X				
Chives[1]						X	X	X	X	X	X	
Cilantro[1]				X	X	X	X	X	X			
Collard greens[1]						X	X	X	X	X	X	
Corn, yellow and white[1]							X	X	X	X		
Corn (Dent)								X	X	X		
Cucumbers[1]						X	X	X	X	X		
Daikon Radish[3]					X	X	X	X	X	X		
Eggplant[1,3]							X	X	X	X		
Fava Beans[2]				X	X	X	X					
Fennel						X	X	X	X			
Garlic[1,3]					X	X	X	X	X	X	X	X
Green Beans							X	X	X	X		
Jerusalem Artichoke[2]								X	X	X	X	
Kale Varieties[1]	X	X	X	X	X	X	X	X	X	X	X	X
Leeks[1]	X	X	X	X	X	X	X	X	X	X	X	X

Six Rivers Produce Availability Chart for Vegetables

	Jan	Feb	Mar	Apr	May	June	July	Aug	Sept	Oct	Nov	Dec
Lentils[3]							X	X	X			
Lettuce varieties[1]				X	X	X	X	X	X	X		
Mustard Greens[1]					X	X	X	X	X	X		
Napa Cabbage[1]	X	X	X	X	X	X	X	X	X	X	X	X
Onions-yellow and red[1]						X	X	X	X	X	X	
Parsley[1]					X	X	X	X	X	X	X	X
Peas, sugar snap[1]					X	X	X	X	X	X	X	
Peppers-green, red, yellow[1]							X	X	X	X		
Potatoes-red, Yukon, russet[1]							X	X	X	X	X	X
Pumpkins[1]									X	X	X	
Radishes[1]				X	X	X	X	X	X	X	X	
Spinach[1,3]				X	X	X	X	X	X	X	X	X
Squash-zucchini, crookneck[1]						X	X	X	X	X		
Squash- winter varieties[1]								X	X	X		
Tomatoes[1]							X	X	X	X		
Turnips, Rutabagas[1]					X	X	X	X	X	X	X	

Appendix B: Farmers' Markets

The U.S. Department of Agriculture (USDA) estimates more than a million people visit a Farmers' Market each week they are open. More than 20,000 farmers use Farmers' Markets to sell to consumers. On average, the produce you find in your local supermarket has been transported about 1,500 miles to its destination. Compare this distance to the average of 50 miles of travel for produce appearing at a Farmers' Market. Starting in 1979 with a few farmers selling off the backs of their trucks in an empty lot in Arcata, our region now boasts Farmers' Markets from Garberville northward as far as Crescent City, and from Shelter Cove eastward to include Weaverville.

The largest and oldest Farmers' Markets organization in our region is the North Coast Growers' Association, managing five markets in Northern Humboldt County. The Southern Humboldt Farmers' Markets manages four markets. Dates, locations and times of markets may change from year to year. Contacts are provided if you wish to check for changes.

North Coast Growers Association (NCGA)
www.humfarm.org

Humboldt Community Alliance with Family Farmers (Humboldt-CAFF)
www.caff.org/regions/humboldt.html

Local Harvest
www.localharvest.org

North Coast Growers Association (NCGA)

P.O. Box 4232
Arcata CA 95518
707-441-9999

www.humfarm.org

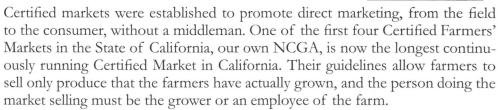

Certified markets were established to promote direct marketing, from the field to the consumer, without a middleman. One of the first four Certified Farmers' Markets in the State of California, our own NCGA, is now the longest continuously running Certified Market in California. Their guidelines allow farmers to sell only produce that the farmers have actually grown, and the person doing the market selling must be the grower or an employee of the farm.

Certified Markets are helping to bring back the small family farm by giving local farmers an opportunity to sell directly to the consumer at fair market value. They also ensure that the consumer buys a genuinely local product, not something picked underripe and shipped thousands of miles. The consumer gets the freshest, naturally ripened fruit and vegetables, in addition to local honey, oysters, beef, mushrooms, cheese, flowers, herbs, trees, and bedding plants, directly from the producer. Regional wine that's been certified organic is now also available at some of the North Coast farmers' markets.

April through November

Arcata
Saturdays, on the Arcata Plaza
9 a.m. to 2 p.m.
Live music starts at 10 a.m.

Tuesdays, across from
the Co-op at the parking lot
on 8th and I
3:30 to 6:30 p.m.

Eureka
Tuesdays, in Old Town
10 a.m. to 1 p.m.

Thursdays,
Henderson Center
10 a.m. to 1 p.m.

McKinleyville
Thursdays, McKinleyville
Shopping Center
3 to 6:30 p.m.

Southern Humboldt Farmers' Markets (SHFM)
Everett King
P.O. Box 218
Redway CA 95560
707-986-7230
stamps@whitethorne

May though October

Garberville
Fridays, Garberville Town
Square
11 a.m. to 3 p.m.

Shelter Cove
Next to the marina
Tuesdays, 11 a.m. to 3 p.m.

Miranda (Avenue of the Giants)
Tuesdays, near the Miranda
Post Office
1 to 5 p.m.

Ferndale
Saturdays, next to the Victorian Village Inn, end of
Main St.
10 a.m. to 1 p.m.

Fortuna
Holly Kreb
707-722-4330
May 25 through late October
Tuesdays, 10th and Main Sts.
3 to 6 p.m.

Del Norte County
Linda LaMarr
www.northerncalifornia.net
Crescent City CA 95531
707-464-3174
June to October
Saturdays, Del Norte Fairgrounds parking lot
9 a.m. to 12 noon

Trinity County
May to November
Hayfork
530-623-5947
Fridays, on Main Street
4 to 7 p.m.

May to October
Weaverville
Sue Corrigan, Market Mgr.
530-623-6821
Call 9 a.m. to 5 p.m.

Wednesdays, Highland Art
Center Meadow
4 to 7 p.m.

Appendix C:
Farms, Dairies, Ranches and Fishers

Our appendices have been checked and we believe they are correct as of the date of publication. We attempted to contact each of the farms listed but not all replied. If we did not receive a reply, we used the most recent public information we could find and talked with some of the Farmers' Market managers. However, specifics for farmers may have changed, new farms may exist and some may have stopped farming. If we missed finding someone or made an error, we apologize. The following web sites can help you find more information or changes.

NCGA www.humfarm.org

Humboldt Community Alliance with Family Farmers (H-CAFF)
www.caff.org/regions/humboldt.html

Local Harvest
www.localharvest.org

Web Direct Agricultural Sales
This web site is a tool for sellers and buyers in Humboldt, Del Norte and Trinity Counties. Buyers can search for products by type or grower. Sellers can list products that are ready for distribution. The goal is to enhance communication and ease of connection within our local food system. Encouraging local production and purchasing will be a win-win situation for all consumers and producers.

The web site is sponsored by the University of California Cooperative Extension Office in Eureka with collaboration from Humboldt-CAFF, and the Humboldt County Farm Bureau. www.redwoodag.com

U-Picks

Lost Coast Blueberry Farm
Rio Mattole
P.O. Box 137
Honeydew CA 95545
707-629-3528 or 497-4602
riomattole@gmail.com
Products: Organic blueberries
Markets: U-Pick on Saturdays. Farmers Markets: Arcata Plaza; Eureka Old Town and Henderson Center; Fortuna; Ferndale; and Garberville

Wolfsen Farms
Herb and Elaine Wolfsen
2103 Baird Rd.
McKinleyville CA 95519
707-839-2017
ewwolfsen@suddenlink.net
Products: Organic blueberries
Markets: Arcata Plaza
On-site sales: Seven days a week, 10 a.m. to 5 p.m.

StarBrite Farm
Dezh Pagen
3003 Highway 96
Willow Creek CA 95573
530-629-3516
Products: Organically-grown produce. Farm tours.

Farm Stands

Alexandre EcoDairy Family Farms
Blake and Stephanie Alexandre
8371 Lower Lake Rd.
Crescent City CA 95531
www.ecodairyfarms.com
707-487-1000
Products: Certified organic milk, eggs, grass-fed pork
Markets: Farm Stand Monday-Friday 8 a.m.to 5 p.m. or by appointment

Chan Saechao Strawberries
Eel River Drive (Kenmar Exit)
Fortuna CA 95540
707-845-3930
Products: Strawberries
Markets: NCGA markets, and Ferndale
On-site sales: Farm Stand

Clendenen's Cider Works
96 - 12th St.
Fortuna CA 95540
707-725-2123
clif@clendenensciderworks.com
Products: Apples, fresh apple cider, produce
On-site sales: Open daily, August-February

Flood Plain Produce
Holly Kreb
31117 Avenue of the Giants
Pepperwood CA 95565
707-732-4330
hollisruth@asis.com
Products: Fruit, vegetables, cut flowers
Markets: Fortuna
On-site sales: Farm Stand July-August. Farm stays available.

High Oak Farm
Larry Ogden
Shelter Cove Rd.
P.O. Box 309
Whitethorn CA 95589
707-986-7481
hioak@asis.com
Products: Strawberries, raspberries
On-site sales: Farm stand

McIntosh Farm Country Store
Loren McIntosh
1264 Giuntoli Ln.
Arcata CA 95589
707-822-0487
Products: Produce from McIntosh Farms, jams and jellies from Vista Rose
Markets: Store and Restaurant year round

StarBrite Farm
See listing under U-Picks

Trinity River Farm
Tom, Kay, Molly and Susan
O'Gorman
2443 Highway 96
Willow Creek CA 95573
530-629-3200
tom@trinityriverfarm.com
Products: Fruits and vegetables, bedding plants, local jams, jellies, sauces.
On-site sales: Farm Stand April-October and also tent in Willow Creek.

Farms

The following farms may be available by appointment for direct sales. Check each listing for details. You may find their products at Farmers' Markets and/or local grocery stores or restaurants. You can check directly with the farmer for changes.

Abbreviations: CSA, Community Supported Agriculture (See Appendix G for list of CSA Farms).
Markets are Farmers' Markets unless otherwise indicated.

Amity Heritage Roses and Garden Nursery
Tracy and Janet Sclar
P.O. Box 357
Hydesville CA 95547
707-768-2040
tanj@amityheritageroses.com
www.amityheritageroses.com
Products: Rose plants, perennials, herbs, lilacs, summer produce, apples
Markets: Arcata Plaza
On-site sales: By appointment only

Bayside Family Farm
Susan Ornelas & Ashley Wellington
2182 Old Arcata Rd.
Kokte Ranch & Nature Preserve
Jacoby Creek Land Trust
Bayside CA 95524
707-826-2722
jclandtrust@yahoo.com
www.jclandtrust.org
Products: Pasture-raised poultry, raspberries, garlic, winter squash, greens and flowers
On-site sales: Yes

Bayside Farms
Products: Artichokes, mixed produce
Markets: Garberville

Betty's Country Shop
Betty Teasley
P.O. Box 250
Weott CA 95571
707-946-2465
Products: Produce, cut flowers, plants, wreaths
Markets: Arcata Plaza

Blake Richard Farm
Blake Richard, Wild Rose Farm
P.O. Box 1233
Blue Lake CA 95525
707-834-4115
Products: Mixed vegetables, including spinach, cilantro, cooking greens
Markets: Arcata Plaza

Blue Jay Nursery
Eric and Christine Justesen
P.O. Box 208
Carlotta CA 95528
707-768-9201
bluejaynursery@suddenlink.net
Products: Bedding plants, annuals, perennials, certified organic vegetable and herb starts
Markets: Arcata Plaza
On-site sales: By appointment

Briceland Family Farms
Products: Mixed produce
Markets: Ferndale

Chan Saechao Strawberries
See listing under Farm Stands

Charlotte's Perennial Garden
Charlotte Grigsmiller
P.O. Box 485
Whitethorn CA 95589
707-986-7229
Products: Salad mixes, cucumbers,
squash, onions, garlic, herbs
Markets: Shelter Cove; Garberville

Claudia's Organic Herbs
Claudia Holzinger and Von Tunstall
P.O. Box 233
Orleans CA 95556
530-627-3712
claudiaholzinger@yahoo.com
Products: 20 varieties fresh and dried
herbs, sweet and specialty basil, garlic,
onions, tomatoes, garlic braids
Markets: Arcata Plaza; Eureka Old
Town
On-site sales: Call for appointment

Deep Seeded Community Farm
P.O. Box 4380
Arcata CA 95518
707-825-8033
deepseeded@gmail.com
www.ArcataCSA.com
Products: Assorted vegetables, strawberries
Markets: Arcata Plaza; McKinleyville; CSA membership

Double J & J Produce
John and Jacqueline Sherman
P.O. Box 4687
Arcata CA 95518
707-822-2629
jsherman1@humboldt1.com
Products: Mixed produce
Markets: Arcata Plaza and 8th and
I; Eureka Old Town and Henderson
Center; McKinleyville

Earth N Hands Farm
Dean Gilkerson and Missy Gruen
P.O. Box 119
Kneeland CA 95549
707-599-7570
strawberryfields@gotsky.com
Products: Organic strawberries, rasp-
berries, peppers, onions, lettuce, basil,
cucumbers and more
Markets: Arcata Plaza, 8th and I;
Eureka Old Town and Henderson
Center

Earthly Edibles Family Farms
Ed Cohen
P.O. Box 5184
Arcata CA 95518
707-822-8841
ravensluch@hotmail.com
Products: Mixed produce
Markets: Arcata Plaza

ECO Gardening Farm

Boyd Smith
P.O. Box 5169
Arcata CA 95518
707-834-2239
eocgardening@hotmail.com
www.ecogardening.com and
www.econeem.com
Products: Seeds, plant starts, artichokes, potatoes, radishes, tomatoes, bok choy, chard, cherries, peaches, pears, apples, hops and Econeem products
Markets: Arcata Plaza
On-site sales: yes

Camp Grant Ranch
aka Eel River Farms at Camp Grant Ranch

John LaBoyteaux
P.O. Box 2163
Redway CA 95566
707-923-2670
helenthemelon@earthlink.net
Products: Beets, carrots, chard, peaches, apples, apple cider, squash, cucumbers, corn, melons
Markets: Gaberville; Ferndale; Miranda

Eel River Produce

William Reynolds
56 Shively Flat Rd.
Scotia CA 95565
707-722-4309
eelriverproduce@earthlink.net
Products: Fresh beans, melons, seed crops, summer and winter squash, tomatoes
Markets: Southern Humboldt

Feral Family Farm

Autumn, Dave, Misha and Ray
134 Esther Ln.
Arcata CA 95521
707-822-2514
theferals@asis.com
Products: Apples, pears, berries, tomatoes, wheatgrass, fresh apple juice, berry juice, mixed vegetable juice.
Markets: Arcata Plaza and 8th and I

Fieldbrook Nursery

Jim Polly
155 Cidermill Rd.
McKinleyville CA 95519
707-839-0524
Products: Apples, plums, nursery trees, artichoke plants, garlic, onions and other fruits and vegetables
Markets: Arcata Plaza; Eureka Henderson Center; McKinleyville

Fieldbrook Valley Apple Farm
Richard and Bettie Lovie
336 Rock Pit Rd.
Fieldbrook CA 95519
707-839-4289
loviesgotapples@suddenlink.net
www.fieldbrookfarms.tripod.com
Products: 50 varieties of apples
Markets: Arcata Plaza; Eureka Henderson Center
On-site sales: Every day, August-October, 9 a.m. to 5 p.m.

Fishman Farm
Robert Fishman
4721 Sprowel Creek Rd.
Garberville CA 95542
Products: Tomatoes, peppers, grapes, squash, plums, pears, apples
Markets: Southern Humboldt

Flood Plain Produce
See listing under Farm Stands

Flora Organica
Andreas, Lisa and Faye Zierer
P.O. Box 206
Arcata CA 95518
707-839-3405
Zierer@suddenlink.net
Products: Cut flowers, lavender, landscape plants, herbs, succulents
Markets: Arcata Plaza; Eureka Old Town and Henderson Center
On-site sales: By appointment

Flying Blue Dog Farm and Nursery
Rita Jacinto and Laurie Levey
P.O. Box 1486
101 Christian School Rd.
Willow Creek CA 95573
530-629-1177
flyingbluedog@gotsky.com
www.flyingbluedogfarm.com
Products: Culinary and medicinal herbs, heirloom veggie starts, jams and jellies, native plants, over 20 varieties of garlic, specialty chili peppers, heirloom tomatoes
Markets: Arcata Plaza
On-site sales: Wednesday-Sunday, 9 a.m. to 6 p.m., Tuesday-Sunday in July. After July, by appointment only

Freya's Garden
Lisa Bianchi
3748 Old Railroad Grade Rd.
Fieldbrook CA 95519
707-840-9164
freya@humboldt1.com
Products: Organic plants including starts especially for Humboldt coast; flower and perennial starts
Markets: Arcata Plaza

G Farm

John Gary
P.O. Box 4597
Blue Lake CA 95525
707-498-2319
Products: Lettuce, broccoli, cabbage, cauliflower, spinach, peas, artichokes, chard, green beans, garlic
Markets: Arcata Plaza and 8th and I; Eureka Old Town and Henderson Center

Garberville Community Farm

John Finley
P.O. Box 994
934 Sprowel Creek Rd.
Garberville CA 95542
707-223-4996
garbervillefarm@gmail.com
Products: Artichokes, beans, brassicas, chard, corn, cucumbers, eggplant, flowers, fruits, nuts, garlic, herbs, leeks, melons, onions, peas, peppers, potatoes, pumpkins, root crops, salad mix, soybeans, winter squash, tomatoes
Markets: Garberville and CSA membership

Gopher Gardens

Robert Ducate
1469 Walker Point Rd.
Bayside CA 95524
707-441-1663
Products: Flowers, fruit, plants
Markets: Arcata Plaza and 8th and I; Eureka Old Town

Gratefully Grown Gardens

Deena Fabbri and Aaron Colvin
1582 Freshwater Rd.
Eureka CA 95503
707-442-7105
colvinfabb@aol.com
Products: Green beans, summer squash, cucumbers, artichokes, raspberries, potatoes, wide variety of potted dahlias
Markets: Arcata Plaza and 8th and I; Eureka Old Town and Henderson Center
On-site sales: By appointment

Green Fire Farm

Grady Walker and Linda Hildebrand
P.O. Box 608
Hoopa CA 95546
530-625-1667
greenfirefarm@gotsky.com
Products: Tomatoes, peppers, greens, squash, root crops, orchard fruit, wine grapes

Markets: Arcata Plaza and 8th and I; Eureka Old Town and Henderson Center

Green Gold Nursery
Products: Tomatoes, lettuce, herbs
Markets: Ferndale

Greenmantle Nursery
Ram and Marissa Fishman
3010 Ettersburg Rd.
Garberville CA 95542
707-986-7504
www.greenmantle.com
Products: Nursery-grown trees, apples, figs
Markets: Garberville

High Oak Farm
See listing under farm stands

Hillbelly Farm
Ty Johnson and Hilary Schwartz
337 2nd Ave.
Rio Dell CA 95562
707-764-3670
Products: Apples, artichokes, asparagus, basil, beans, beets, blackberries, Brussels sprouts, cabbage, carrots, celery, cherries, chives, cilantro, corn, cucumbers, dill, eggplant, fennel, figs, garlic, horseradish, kale, kiwifruit, lemons, marjoram, melons, okra, onions, oregano, parsley, pears, fresh peas, peppers, potatoes, radishes, raspberries, rhubarb, sage, salad mix, spinach, summer squash, winter squash, strawberries, sunflowers, thyme, tomatoes, turnips
Markets: Arcata Plaza

Hilltop Farm
Julie Steiner
3472 Mitchell Heights Dr.
Eureka CA 95503
707-445-0744
jerjukama@yahoo.com
Products: Organic greens, including lettuce, arugula, mizuna, kale, mustard, cress, herbs, cut flowers. Bags are biodegradable.
Markets: Arcata Plaza

Honey Apple Farms
Ron and Shelly Honig
11251 West End Rd.
Arcata CA 95521
707-822-6186
shellyhonig@gmail.com
Products: Apples, plums, Asian pears, summer and winter squash, pumpkins, organic greens, blueberries, farm fresh eggs
Markets: Arcata Plaza and 8th and I; Eureka Old Town and Henderson Center; McKinleyville

Huckleberry Farm and Nursery

Kathy McDonald
77 Fieldbrook Heights
Fieldbrook CA 95519
707-839-3684
hucklebrry3684@aol.com
Products: Perennial and deer-resistant plants, produce, eggs, fruit trees
Markets: Arcata Plaza and 8th and I; Eureka Old Town and Henderson Center; McKinleyville

Humboldt Honey/Ace in the Hole

Products: Honey, other bee products
Markets: Southern Humboldt

I and I Farm

Ino Riley
P.O. Box 1584
Willow Creek CA 95573
707-845-9504
Products: Strawberries, carrots, salad mix, onions, artichokes, tomatoes, squash, cucumbers
Markets: All

Jacobs Greens

Karina Gilkerson
P.O. Box 1272
Blue Lake CA 95525
707-668-1684
arugula14@yahoo.com
Products: Kitchen garden starts, salad greens, herb starts
Markets: Arcata Plaza

Jacquie's Garden

Products: Mixed produce, fruit preserves
Markets: Ferndale

Little River Farm

John Severn
140 Ole Hanson Rd.
Eureka CA 95503
707-441-9286
littleriverfarm@sbcglobal.net
Products: Spring salad, mesclun mix, spinach, arugula, braising mix and many specialty greens, carrots, herbs, endive, escarole, radicchio, strawberries, blueberries, raspberries, broccoli, broccoli rabe, broccolini
Markets: Arcata Plaza and 8th and I; Eureka Old Town and Henderson Center
On-site sales: By appointment

Lost Coast Blueberry Farm

See listing under U-Picks

Loving Earth Gardens

2950 Janes Rd.
Arcata CA 95521
707-825-9298
Products: Mixed produce, fruit, cut flowers
Markets: Arcata Plaza and 8th and I; Eureka Old Town and Henderson Center; McKinleyville

Luna Farms

Alissa Pattison and
Frederic Dietmeyer
95 Neighbor Ln.
P.O. Box 184
Willow Creek CA 95573
530-355-4191
farmfred@gmail.com
Products: Vegetables, strawberries, melons, flowers, herbs, tomatoes, eggplant, peppers, tomatilloes, summer and winter squash
Markets: Arcata Plaza and 8th and I; Eureka Old Town and Henderson Center; McKinleyville; Weaverville and CSA membership

Luscious Gardens

Kashi Albertson and Naomi Withers
707-834-2698
lusciousgardens@gmail.com
Products: Perennial food plants, wide range of berries and fruit trees
Markets: Arcata Plaza; also landscaping with edible plants

Maggie May Farms

Abram Stark
3719 Sunny Side Ave.
Eureka CA 95503
707-442-7435
Products: Apples, carrots, beets, greens, radishes, turnips, kohlrabi, rabbit, eggs
Markets: Arcata Plaza and 8th and I; Eureka Old Town and Henderson Center
On-site sales: yes

Magic Finger Organic Garden

Clifford Kitts
P.O. Box 104
Miranda CA 95553
707-943-3347
Products: Tomatoes, squash
Markets: Southern Humboldt

Maple Creek Farm

Merit Cape and Wilathi Weaver
P.O. Box 5103
Arcata CA 95518
707-839-9135
Products: Medicinal and culinary herbs, gardening plants, dried herbs and teas, dried wreaths, bottled herb syrups, willow trellises, vines
Markets: Arcata Plaza
On-site sales: Please call for an appointment (any day, any time)

Mattole River Organic Farms

Products: Peppers, melons, tree fruits, berries
Markets: Ferndale

McIntosh Farms

Clayton McIntosh and Family
P.O. Box 924
Willow Creek CA 95573
530-629-4145
Products: Tomatoes, peaches, peppers, figs, cherries, plums, Asian pears, chestnuts
Markets: Arcata Plaza; Eureka Old Town and Henderson Center; McKinleyville; Fortuna
On-site sales: Any day, any time

Moonshadow Farms

Toni Stoffel
P.O. Box 488
Miranda CA 95553
707-943-3025
Products: Mixed produce, cherries, plums, apples, figs, chestnuts
Markets: Miranda

Morning Glory
Matthew Brockmeyer
P.O. Box 175
Garberville CA 95542
570-301-7338
Products: Garlic, kale, onions, tomatoes, squash
Markets: Southern Humboldt

Mountain Home Farm
Sarah Post
P.O. Box 99
Orleans CA 95556
530-627-3423
Products: Tomatoes, peppers, carrots, onions, potatoes, other assorted vegetables
Markets: Arcata Plaza
On-site sales: Please call first

Mycality Mushrooms
Michael Egan
2577 Fickle Hill Rd.
Arcata CA 95521
707-834-6396
Products: Mushrooms
Markets: Arcata Plaza and 8th and I; Eureka Old Town and Henderson Center

Nai's Strawberries
Nai Saechao
371 9th St.
Fortuna CA 95540
707-498-0736
Products: Strawberries
Markets: Arcata Plaza and 8th and I; Eureka Old Town and Henderson Center; McKinleyville

Neukom Family Farm
Jacques and Amy Neukom
P.O. Box 312
Willow Creek CA 95573
530-629-1909
spinningweb@hotmail.com
Products: Peaches, strawberries, melons, tomatoes, peppers, peas
Markets: Arcata Plaza; Eureka Old Town and Henderson Center; Fortuna

Norton Creek Farm
Roger L. Smith
3040 Central Ave.
McKinleyville CA 95519
707-839-0786
rlsmith3040@sbcglobal.net
Products: Dahlias, vegetables, raspberries
Markets: Arcata Plaza; McKinleyville
On-site sales: By appointment

Ocean Air Farm
Paul Madeira and
Julie Jo Ayer Williams
Crescent City CA 95531
707-616-1632
oceanairfarms@gmail.com
Products: 40 vegetables, lettuce, salad greens, summer squash, onions, potatoes, pasture-raised chickens
Markets: Crescent City and CSA membership
On-site sales: Once or twice a year for chicken

Paul Lohse
P.O. Box 429
Arcata CA 95521
707-668-5432
auroracaldris@hotmail.com
Products: Basil, carrots, heirloom tomatoes, specialty crops, sunflowers
Markets: Arcata Plaza; Eureka Old Town and Henderson Center; Fortuna

Pierce Family Farm
Marguerite Pierce
P.O. Box 93
Orleans CA 95556
530-627-3320
Products: Tomatoes, peppers, carrots, basil, cucumbers, squash, assorted seasonal greens, melons
Markets: Arcata Plaza and 8th and I

Potato Rock Nursery
Dan Southard
P.O. Box 902
Trinidad CA 95570
707-839-9175
potatorocknursery@gmail.com
www.potato-rock.com
Products: Choice herbs and native ornamentals from around the world
Markets: Arcata Plaza and online

Potter's Produce
Denis Potter
P.O. Box 1011
Blue Lake CA 95525
707-668-5387
dap3@suddenlink.net
Products: Lettuce, summer and winter squash, chard, kale, kohlrabi, spinach, cherry tomatoes, peas, green beans, snap peas, beets, basil, mint, blueberries, pumpkins, corn, corn maze
Markets: Arcata Plaza and week-day markets when figs and apples are ripe

Dan Primerano
P.O. Box 982
Redway CA 95560
dprimerano@asis.com
Products: Wheat flour, wheat berries
Market: CSA

Rain Frog Farm
1697 Henry Ln.
McKinleyville CA 95519
707-498-9837
kmmorris1@yahoo.com
Products: Summer and winter squash, celery, radish, corn, mixed vegetables, tomatillos, shelling peas, tomatoes, broccoli, eggplant

Markets: Arcata Plaza and 8th and I; Eureka Old Town and Henderson Center

Redwood Roots Farm
Janet Czarnecki
P.O. Box 793
Arcata CA 95518
707-826-0261
janetcz@humboldt1.com
www.redwoodrootsfarm.com
Products: Lettuce heads, herbs, broccoli, cauliflower, lettuce mix, braising mix, root crops
Markets: Arcata Plaza
On-site sales: CSA

Reed's Bees
David Reed
911 Bayview St.
Arcata CA 95521
707-826-1744
Products: Honey, beeswax, beeswax candles, propolis
Markets: Arcata Plaza

River Bees
Seth Rick
156 Ewan Ave.
Shively CA 95565
707-722-4669
onemorebee@yahoo.com
Products: Honey, bee pollen, beeswax, lavender honey, Humboldt Gold Honey brand
Markets: Arcata Plaza
On-site sales: Please call first

Rock n' Rose
Cindy Annotto-Pemberton
1785 Mygina Ave.
McKinleyville CA 95519
707-839-3761
Products: Starts, plants, trees, fresh and dried flower bouquets, leis
Markets: Arcata Plaza and 8th and I; Eureka Old Town and Henderson Center; McKinleyville

Rolling Dunes Farm
Jessica Phillips
950 Kellogg Rd.
Crescent City CA 95531
707-954-1269
Products: Jams, jellies, goats-milk soap, home-grown produce
Markets: Brookings OR

Rolling River Farm and Nursery
Marc Robbi and Corrina Cohen
P.O. Box 332
Orleans CA 95556
530-627-0012
corrinaandmarc@rollingrivernursery.com
www.rollingrivernursery.com
Products: Fresh fruit, flowers, and fruit trees, shrubs, vines for the edible landscape
Markets: Arcata Plaza
On-site sales: By appointment

Saechao Strawberries
Chan Yan Saechao
1665 Thelma St.
Fortuna CA 95540
707-745-3930
Products: Strawberries
Markets: Arcata Plaza; Eureka Old Town and Henderson Center

Salmon House Farm
Matt Myers and Erin Hamann
2950 Janes Rd.
Arcata CA 95521
605-254-8568
eleigh@wapda.
com
salmonhouse-
farm@riseup.net
Products:
Strawberries,
root vegetables,
legumes, cucum-
bers, pumpkins,
flowers, herbs (edible and medicinal),
salad greens
Markets: Arcata Plaza and 8th and I
On-site sales: Yes

Shakefork Community Farm
Kevin Cunningham and Melanie
Olstad.
7914 Highway 36
P.O. Box 4846
Carlotta CA 95528
shakeforkcommunityfarm@gmail.com
Products: Wheat, rye, oats, barley,
buckwheat, corn, edible seeds, dried
flowers
Markets: Arcata Plaza and CSA
membership

Small Fruits
Spencer Hill
P.O. Box 526
Hoopa CA 95546
530-625-4042
Products: 100% organic tayber-
ries, Loch Ness blackberries, golden
raspberries, red raspberries, charentais
melons, white nectarines, miniature
vegetables
Markets: Arcata Plaza and 8th and I;
Eureka Henderson Center

Sun Green Farms
Linda and Jeffrey Vandyke
P.O. Box 304
Miranda CA 95553
707-943-1780
vandyke@asis.com
Products: Tomatoes, squash
Markets: Southern Humboldt

Sunny Slope Farms
Harry and Jan Vaughn
P.O. Box 589
Miranda CA 95553
jdvaughn@northcoast.com
Products: French prunes, apples
plums, berries, mushrooms, assorted
vegetables, chestnuts, walnuts.
Markets: Miranda; Garberville

Sweet Pea Gardens
Shelley Ruhlen
1205 Lincoln Ave.
Arcata CA 95521
707-499-3363
Products: Flowers, herbs, herbal teas,
shiso, shiso sprinkle
Markets: Arcata Plaza

Tanoak Hill Farm
Patty Clary and Bill Verick
P.O. Box 1447
Hoopa CA 95546
530-625-5153
patty@tanoakhill.com
Products: White peaches, kiwi, plums, cherries, apples
Markets: Arcata Plaza

Trident Lightning Farm and Orchard
Will Randall and Danielle Newman
P.O. Box 202
Phillipsville CA 95559
707-943-1713
druidozone@yahoo.com
Products: Apples, Asian pears, cucumbers, corn, flowers, garlic, melons, peaches, pears, plums, potatoes, pumpkins, walnuts, winter squash
Markets: Arcata Plaza and 8th and I; Eureka Old Town

Trinity River Farm
See listing under Farm Stands

Two-Mule Farm
Products: Plant starts, strawberries, tomatoes, squash
Markets: Garberville and Miranda

Valley Flower
William L. Fales
665 Centerville Rd.
Ferndale CA 95536
707-786-7827
Products: Melons, mixed vegetables, peppers, potatoes, summer and winter squash, tomatoes
Markets: Ferndale

Vista's Roses
Vista McIntosh
P.O. Box 296
Willow Creek CA 95573
530-629-4145
vistarose2@aol.com
Products: Flowers, berries, corn, cucumbers, beans, bitter melons, Chinese okra, rhubarb
Markets: Arcata Plaza

Warren Creek Farms
Paul Giuntoli
1264 Warren Creek Rd.
Arcata CA 95521
707-822-6017
Products: Potatoes, winter squash, pumpkins, dry beans, sweet corn, green beans, peas, broccoli, cauliflower, pickling cucumbers, onions
Markets: Arcata Plaza; Ferndale
On-site sales: October weekends, 9 a.m. to dark. Corn Maze, pumpkin patch and produce stand at 1171 Mad River Rd.

Willow Creek Farms
Michael and Jennifer Peterson
P.O. Box 1392
1000 Country Club Dr.
Willow Creek CA 95573
530-629-4950
www.willowcreekorganicfarms.com
Products: Sweet corn, beans, tomatoes, peppers, melons, onions, Brussels sprouts, broccoli
Markets: Arcata Plaza and 8th and I; Eureka Old Town and Henderson Center; McKinleyville

Windborne Farm
Jennifer Greene
530-468-4340
windborne3csa@yahoo.com
Products: Grain CSA

Winsmuir Farm
David and Mary Margaret Smith
92611 Airport Rd.
The Sixes OR 97476
541-348-2832
Products: Organic cranberries
Markets: Arcata Plaza

Wolfsen Farms
See listing under U-Picks

Yew Bear Ranch
Products: Mixed produce, garlic and blueberries
Markets: Garberville

Ziganti's Orchards
Lisa Ziganti
Products: Cherries, herbs, eggs
Markets: Garberville

Seafood

The following fishers raise or catch and sell their products. Markets that sell local fish and seafood are listed under Retail Stores, Appendix D.

Aqua Rodeo Farms
Sebastion Elrite
P.O. Box 371
Eureka CA 95502
707-444-3854
sebastian@aqua-rodeofarms.com
www.aqua-rodeofarms.com
Products: Oysters, seaweed
Markets: Arcata 8th and I; Eureka Henderson Center; Mckinleyville
On-site sales: April through October on Saturdays, off the boat at the Woodley Island Marina, Dock B-00

North Bay Shellfish and Succulents
Catherine Peterson and Scott Sterner
1167 Driver Rd.
Trinidad, CA 95570
707-677-3509 or 839-4723
micatjoy@aol.com
Products: Kumamoto oysters, Japanese pacific oysters, mussels and large assortment of succulent plants
Markets: Arcata Plaza
On-site sales: Call to order

Cap'n Zach's Crab House Inc.
1594 Reasor Rd.
McKinleyville CA 95519
707-839-9059
Products: Crab in season
Markets: Store in McKinleyville

Hoopa Processing Corporation
Carmeli Begay
P.O. Box 8
Hoopa CA 95546
hpchoopa@yahoo.com
530-625-4389
Products: Canned smoked wild salmon
Markets: Arcata Plaza or call

Jenna Lee's Seafood
Woodley Island B Dock
Eureka CA
707-498-8552
Products: Crab
Markets: At Dock

Beef

Bear River Valley Beef
Hugo and Elizabeth Klopper
P.O. Box 342
4415 Upper Bear River Rd.
Ferndale CA 95536
707-786-9460
info@bestgrassfedbeef.com
www.bestgrassfedbeef.com
Product: 100% grass-fed beef
Markets: Eureka Henderson Center;
McKinleyville; Garberville
On-site sales: Online sales

Chapman Ranch
Mark and Tammie Chapman
P.O. 368
Miranda CA 95553
707-599-0516 or 707-599-0518
mtchapman@starband.net
www.theranchonasalmoncreek.blog-
spot.com
Products: Beef
On-site sales: July to fall

Ferndale Farms
Jill Hackett
1787 Howe Creek Rd.
Ferndale CA 95536
707-845-0752 hackett.jill@gmail.com
or jill@ferndale-farms.com or
Products: Beef, lamb, goat meat
Markets: Arcata Plaza

Gold'n Bare Ranch
Mario de Solenni
3275 Railroad Ave.
Crescent City CA 95531
707-464-6181
Products: Beef
On-site sales: Pick up at ranch or in
Crescent City

J. Russ Ranch
Jack "Jay" Russ
P.O. Box 391
Ferndale CA 95536
707-786-4407
jruss@jrusscompany.com
www.JRussRanch.com
Products: Beef
Market: Arcata Plaza
On-site sales: By phone or e-mail

Goat

Kneeland Glen
Kathy Muller
707-443-1424
kneelandglengoats@msn.com
Check at Farmer's Market on Arcata
Plaza

Ferndale Farms
See listing under Beef

Wild Iris Farm
Joan Crandell
Fieldbrook CA 95519
crandellj@gmail.com
Products: Rabbits, goats
On-site sales: Contact regarding
processed rabbit. Goats sold live.

Lamb

Ferndale Farms
See listing under Beef

Pork

Alexandre EcoFarm Family Dairy
See listing under Dairy

Poultry

Tule Fog Farm
Shail Pec-Crouse
1887 Q St.
Arcata CA 95521
707-826-1450
tulefogfarm@gmail.com
Products: Chicken eggs, goose eggs, geese, pork in future
Markets: Arcata Plaza
Goose and Goose eggs, CSA, Goat Milk CSA (milk share in 2010)
On-site sales: Call or e-mail

Wild Chick Farm
Sarah Brunner
2911 Stover Rd.
Blue Lake CA 95525
707-845-4718
wildchickfarm@gmail.com
www.wildchickfarm.com
Products: Free-range chicken eggs, poultry products, chicken meat
Markets: Arcata Plaza
On-site sales: Please e-mail first

Ocean Air Farm
See listing under Farms
Free-range chickens. Chickens once or twice a year on-site.

Bayside Family Farm
See listing under Farms

Rabbits

Buck and Daisy's Rabbit Tree
David and Ash MacCuish
Eureka CA
707-496-8324
david@orchidcomputers.com
www.buckanddaisy.com
Products: Rabbit
On-site sales: By appointment

Maggie May Farms
See listing under Farms

Wild Iris Farm
See listing under Goat

Dairy

Alexandre EcoDairy Family Farms
Blake and Stephanie Alexandre
8371 Lower Lake Rd.
Crescent City CA 95531
www.ecodairyfarms.com
707-487-1000
Products: Eggs, grass-fed pork, beef, milk. Some products wholesale
Markets: Farm Stand
Monday-Friday 8 a.m.-5 p.m. or by appointment

Eggs

See Farmers at Farmers' Market and

Alexandre EcoDairy Family Farms
See listing under Dairy

Huckleberry Farm and Nursery
See listing under Farms

Tule Fog Farm
See listing under Poultry

Appendix D:
Retail Markets that Sell Local Foods

Unlike predominantly urban areas, we on the North Coast have the enormous good fortune of still having small neighborhood groceries. Eureka alone has more than a dozen of these corner stores. In interviewing the store owners and managers, it quickly became evident that we could not list all the local products each store offered because most of them carried an impressive array of local packaged products, dairy, and frequently even local produce, eggs, meats and fish. Some rural stores buy produce informally from their customers on an irregular or seasonal basis.

Overwhelmingly, we heard store managers and owners say that they listen to their customers, which of course they must do to stay in business. Their willingness to provide what their customers want is only limited by their ability to find suppliers. Every grocer, even in the big-box chains, realizes that customer satisfaction keeps the doors open, so our advice is to talk to the owner or manager of your neighborhood store and request regional products. Keep at it until the shelves are overflowing with fresh local produce, eggs, dairy, meat and fish.

General Grocery Stores

Chautauqua Natural Foods
436 Church St.
Garberville CA 95542
707-923-2452
www.chautauquanaturalfoods.com
Sources fruits and vegetables from local farmers and local farmers market. Also local honey, bee pollen, eggs.

Eureka Natural Foods
1450 Broadway
Eureka CA 95501
707-442-6325
www.eurekanaturalfoods.com
800-603-8364
orders@eurekanaturalfoods.com
Web site has an excellent reference section. Meats, fruits and vegetables, dairy and cheese, and locally-produced grocery items.

Murphy's Markets
Murphy's has family-owned groceries in Sunny Brae, Cutten, Blue Lake, and Trinidad. Each store is responsive to the needs and requests of shoppers.

All stores supply various local seasonal fruits and vegetables, local honey, grass-fed beef, crab (in season) and oysters, fresh fish (as available), smoked fish, and local dairy and cheese. Additionally, numerous locally-produced grocery items line the shelves.

Murphy's Sunny Brae
785 Bayside Rd.
Arcata CA 95521
707-822-7665

Murphy's Cutten
4020 Walnut Dr.
Eureka CA 95503
707-443-7388

Murphy's Glendale
1451 Glendale Dr.
Blue Lake CA 95525
707-822-1157

Murphy's Trinidad
Saunder's Shopping Center
Trinidad CA 95570
707-677-3643

North Coast Cooperative (Co-op)

The Co-op has two cooperatively-owned organically-certified grocery stores. Both stock numerous local products: meats, dairy, produce and packaged items. Produce is labeled with its place of origin, and if within our immediate region, by the farm that grew it. The Co-op researches the practices of its suppliers and makes the information available to customers. Education regarding local and organic food is another part of their mission

North Coast Cooperative, Arcata
811 I St.
Arcata CA 95521
707-822-5947

North Coast Cooperative, Eureka
25 4th St.
Eureka CA 95501
707-443-6027
www.northcoastco-op.com

Ray's Food Place
Nine Stores in region
Ray's has started to sell more local produce and packaged products. Be sure to encourage you local store to increase the number of locally produced items.

Wildberries Marketplace
747 Thirteenth St.
Arcata CA 95521
707-822-0095
www.wildberries.com
Wildberries is a locally-owned, full-line retail grocery store offering many local products.

Meat Markets
Loleta Meat Market
350 Main St.
Loleta CA 95551
707-733-5319
Products: Meat; sausage made at market

Fish Markets

Botchie's Crab Stand
6670 Fields Landing Dr.
Fields Landing CA 95537
707-442-4134
Products: Crab

Capt'n Zach's Crab House, Inc.
1594 Reasor Rd.
McKinleyville CA 95519
707- 845-4100
Seasonal. Closed until December 1
Products: Crab

Crab-E-Tom's
1815 Main St.
Fortuna CA 95540
707-725-6558
Products: Crab

Jenna Lee's Seafood
Woodley Island B Dock
Eureka
707-498-8552
Products: Crab

Mr. Fish Seafood
2740 Broadway
Eureka CA 95501
707-443-2661
Products: Fresh crab and salmon in season; complete line of fresh seafood

Katy's Smokehouse
740 Edwards St.
Trinidad CA 95570
707-677-0151
www.katyssmokehouse.com
Products: Fresh, canned, smoked fish

Appendix E:
Restaurants Featuring Local Food

Restaurants in this list use some local food. When you visit them, please let them know that you appreciate this effort and ask if they can do more.

Humboldt Community Alliance with Family Farmers has launched innovative partnerships with local restaurants to promote their use of products from local farms.

Look for participating restaurants displaying the "Buy Fresh Buy Local" decal in their windows. This CAFF identification shows that they are buying from local farmers and have special menu items using foods from our regional farmers. Restaurants with a * next to their name are participants in the CAFF program.

3 Foods Café
835 J St.
Arcata CA 95521
707-822-9474
Grass-fed beef, produce; they grow their own greens and garnishes

Abruzzi
780 7th St.
Arcata CA 95521
707-826-2345
Produce, fruit, dairy

The Alibi
744 9th St.
Arcata CA 95521
707-822-3731
Tofu, produce

Amillia's Gourmet to Go
443 Melville Rd.
Garberville CA 95542
707-923-4340
Lettuce, basil, bok choy, tomatoes, watermelon, goat cheese, rabbit

Arcata Pizza and Deli
1057 H St.
Arcata CA 95521
707-822-4650
Grass-fed beef

Arcata Scoop
1068 I St.
Arcata CA 95521
707-825-7266
Fruits, lavender, herbs, honey

Avalon*
3rd and G Sts.
Eureka CA 95501
707-445-0500
www.avaloneureka.com
Oysters, cheese, meat, herbs, mushrooms, produce, honey, potatoes, beans, squash, huckleberries, blackberries

Baked in Humboldt
Goods available at the Fernbridge Market
Fernbridge CA
707-725-3701
Fruits and vegetables, dairy, cheese

Beachcomber Café
363 Trinity St.
Trinidad CA 95570
707-677-0106
Eggs, chicken, duck, smoked fish, produce, grass-fed beef, all greens, potatoes

Benbow Inn
445 Lake Benbow Dr.
Garberville CA 95542
707-923-2124
www.benbowinn.com
Herbs and vegetables from their own gardens; dairy, cheese, fish, mushrooms, beef, oysters, berries, stone fruit, honey

The Big Blue Café
846 G St.
Arcata CA 95521
707-826-7578
Grass-fed beef, produce

Big Pete's Pizzeria
1504 G St.
Arcata CA 95521
707-826-1890 and

1709 5th St.
Eureka CA 95501
707-441-1151
Grass-fed beef, produce, smoked salmon

Bon Boniere
Jacoby Storehouse
791 8th St.
Arcata CA 95521
707-822-6388 and

215 F St. at Opera Alley
Eureka CA 95501
707-268-0122
Cheese, dairy, tofu, produce

Café Brio
791 G St.
Arcata CA 95521
707-822-5922
www.briobaking.com
Grass-fed beef and lamb, produce, goat cheese, dairy

Café Minou, Chautauqua Natural Foods
436 Church St.
Garberville CA 95542
707-923-2452
Produce, eggs, cheese

Café Nooner
Opera Alley (E St. between 2nd and 3rd)
Eureka CA 95501
707-443-4663
www.cafenooner.com
Grass-fed beef, goat cheese, lamb, cheese, produce

The Cantina
At Fernbridge Market
Fernbridge CA 95540
707-725-3701
Beef, produce

Calico's Café
808 Redwood Dr.
Garberville CA 95542
707-923-2253
Produce, goat cheese, grass-fed beef, tofu

Catch Café
355 Main St.
Trinidad CA 95570
707-677-0390
Grass-fed beef, goat cheese, tofu, produce

Cecil's New Orleans Bistro
773 Redwood Dr.
Upstairs at Jacob Garber Square
Garberville CA 95542
707-923-7007
Produce, goat cheese, seafood, mushrooms

The Cove Restaurant
10 Seal Ct.
Shelter Cove CA 95589
707-986-1197
Seafood, vegetables, blueberries

Crosswinds
860 10th St.
Arcata CA 95521
707-826-2133
www.arcatacrosswinds.net
Tofu, cheese

Cutten Inn
3980 Walnut Dr.
Eureka CA 95503
707-445-9217
Grass-fed beef, produce, goat cheese,
ice cream, chicken, oysters, fish

**Eel River Brewing Company's
Taproom and Grill**
1777 Alamar Way
Fortuna CA 95540
707-725-2739
Smoked albacore, sausage, cheese,
grass-fed meat, tofu

Eureka Natural Foods
1450 Broadway
Eureka CA 95501
707-442-6325
Grass-fed beef, produce, cheese, dairy

F Street Café*
1630 F St.
Eureka CA 95501
707-268-8959
www.fstreetcafe.com
Greens, corn, tomatoes, squash, onions,
mushrooms, spinach, goat cheese,
olives, herbs, fruit, strawberries, beans,
grass-fed beef, lamb, fish

Folie Douce
1551 G St.
Arcata CA 95521
707-822-1042
www.holyfolie.com
Produce, herbs, goat cheese, potatoes,
lamb, oysters, olives, mushrooms,
grass-fed beef occasionally

Gallagher's
139 2nd St.
Eureka CA 95501
707-442-1177
Grass-fed beef

Golden Harvest Café
1062 G St.
Arcata CA 95521
707-822-8962 and

1707 W. Allard at Broadway
Eureka CA 95501
707-442-1610
Grass-fed beef

The Groves Restaurant
12990 Avenue of the Giants
Myers Flat CA 95554
707-943-9907
www.riverbendcellars.com
Grass-fed beef, produce, goat cheese,
cheese, dairy, oysters, crab, seafood
when available

**Hank's Coffeehouse & General
Store**
1602 Old Arcatra Rd.
Bayside, CA 95524
707-822-4423
Local food items whenever possible

Hansen's Truck Stop and Coffee Shop
Hwy. 101, 3 miles south of Fortuna
Fortuna CA 95540
707-725-2206
Grass-fed beef

Humbrews
856 10th St.
Arcata CA 95521
707-826-2739
Grass-fed beef, tofu, goat cheese

Hurricane Kate's
511 2nd St.
Eureka CA 95501
707-444-1405
Produce, goat cheese, oysters, seafood, dairy

Jambalaya
915 H St.
Arcata CA 95521
707-822-4766
Grass-fed beef, tofu, oysters, produce, goat cheese

Japhy's Soup and Noodles*
1563 G St.
Arcata CA 95521
707-826-2594
www.japhys.com
Grass-fed beef, produce, tofu

Kyoto
320 F St.
Eureka CA 95501
707-443-7777
Seafood, wild salmon

Larrupin Café
1658 Patricks Point Dr.
Trinidad CA 95570
707-677-0230
Greens, fish, grass-fed beef, goat cheese

La Trattoria
30 Sunny Brae Center
Arcata CA 95521
707-822-6101
Grass-fed beef, produce, potatoes, beans, dairy, cheese, wines, olives

Paul's Live From New York
670 9th St.
Arcata CA 95521
707-822-6199
Grass-fed beef

Loleta Bakery
348 Main St.
Loleta CA 95551
707-733-1789
www.loletabakery.com
Produce, dairy, honey, cheese, meat, beans, apples, local grain (coming soon)

Los Bagels
1085 I St.
Arcata CA 95521
707-822-3150 and

2nd and E Sts.
Eureka CA 95501
707-442-8325
Berries, basil, peaches

Lost Coast Brewery
617 4th St.
Eureka CA 95501
707-445-4480
Produce, grass-fed beef

Mateel Café
3342 Redwood Dr.
Redway CA 95560
707-923-2030
www.mateelcafe.com
Vegetables, fruit

Mazzotti's
773 8th St.
Arcata CA 95521
707-822-1900 and

305 F St.
Eureka CA 95501
707-445-1912
Produce, including basil, tomatoes,
zucchini, cucumbers, lettuce

Moonstone Grill
100 Moonstone Beach Rd.
Trinidad, CA 95570
707-677-1616
Produce, fruit, dairy

Pacific Rim Noodle House
1021 I St.
Arcata CA 95521
707-826-7604
Produce

Plaza Grill
780 7th St.
Arcata, CA 95521-6319
707-826-0860
Produce, fruit, dairy

Restaurant 301 (at the Carter House Inns)
301 L St.
Eureka CA 95501
707-444-8062
800-404-1390
www.carterhouse.com
Produce (some from their own garden), cheese, meats, seafood

The Sea Grill
316 E St.
Eureka CA 95501
707-443-7187
Produce

Six Rivers Brewery
1300 Central Ave.
McKinleyville CA 95519
707-839-7580
www.sixriversbrewery.com
Grass-fed beef, cheese, fish, produce

Smug's Pizza
1034 G St.
Arcata CA 95521
707-822-1927 and

626 2nd St.
Eureka CA 95501
707-268-8082 and

2720 Central Ave.
McKinleyville CA 95519
707-839-7684
Vegetables, basil

Stars
1535 G St.
Arcata CA 95521
707-826-1379 and

2009 Harrison St.
Eureka CA 95501
707-445-2061
Grass-fed beef

Tomo
708 9th St.
Arcata CA 95521
707-822-1414
Produce, albacore, ling cod, other local seafood

Wildflower Café Vegetarian Restaurant*
1064 G St.
Arcata CA 95521
707-822-0360
Lettuce, kale, chard, beans, beets, cheese, squash

Woodrose Café
911 Redwood Ave.
Garberville CA 95542
707-923-3191
Produce

Caterers

Most caterers will try to accommodate the wishes of their clients. When you work with a caterer, let them know that you want them to use local foods.

Abbruzi Catering
Arcata
707-826-2377
lauren@abruzzicatering.com

A Taste of Class
Eureka
707-496-6133
www.tasteofclasscatering.com

Blackberry Bramble BBQ and Catering
Blue Lake
707-668-1616
bbq@gmail.com

Brett Shuler Fine Catering
707-822-4221
shunada@sbcglobal.net

Cassaro's Catering
Arcata
707-822-8009

Catch Café
Trinidad
707-677-0390

Catering by Aimee
Trinidad
707-677-3224

Celebrations
Arcata
707-826-1224
celebrate@arcatanet.com

Classic Catering
McKinleyville
707-839-1730

Comfort of Home Catering
707-822-1781 or
707-496-6720
www.comfortofhomecatering.com

Michelle Miller Fine Catering
Ferndale
707-786-4636
www.michellemillerfinecatering.com

Savory Thyme
Eureka
707-4444-2266
www.savorythymecatering.com

Moonlight Catering
Fortuna
707-725-3524

Ms. M's Fine Event Catering
McKinleyville
707-845-3225
www.msmcatering.com

Sweet Basil Catering
Loleta
707-733-8003
www.sweetbasilcatering.net

Teri's Custom Catering and Cakes
Eureka
707-444-8791

Appendix F: Local Package-Product Producers

Information in this list is from many sources, including the North Coast Co-operative, Humboldt Local, Humboldt-CAFF, various web sites and personal contacts. Where we have the information as to whether products are certified organic, we have added it. However, if the organic designation is not shown, it does not mean that the products are necessarily not organic.

We have added the Trust Your Source (TYS) designation for the sources from the North Coast Cooperative:

> Trust Your Source is the Co-op's new project to promote awareness of food grown or produced within the Klamath/North Coast Bio-region of California and whose producers use sustainable production methods.
>
> *North Coast Co-operative*

The Co-op lists suppliers on their web site and in many cases the supplier has included the source of their ingredients. You can read the full definition of TYS as well as details on many of the TYS suppliers on the Co-op's web page at: www.northcoastco-op.com/healthy.htm#recipes. Scroll down to the "Trust Your Source" description and click on the name of the supplier of interest to read more about them.

We realize not all of these packaged products use local ingredients exclusively. But we hope, over time, the local content will increase. We also believe the transportation costs for these products are probably less than equivalent product made outside our region.

Some listings show **TYS** (Trust Your Source) and/or **O** (Certified Organic).

Baked Goods, Candies and Desserts

Auntie's Candies
Egret Bites

Bien Padre Foods
1459 Railroad St.
Eureka CA 95503
707-442-4585
Tortilla chips, tortillas

Barry's Theatre Cookies
yummers@barrytheatrecookies.com
Cookies

Bon Boniere
100 Ericson Ct.
Arcata CA 95521
707-822-1612
Fudge sauce

Brio Bread
1309 11th St.
Arcata CA 95521
707-822-0791
brio@humboldt.com
Artisan French breads, pastry

Desserts on Us
57 Belle Falor Ct.
Arcata CA 95521
707-822-0160
www.dessertsonus.com
Cookies

Drakes Glen Creations
100 Ericson Ct. #115
Arcata CA 95521
www.chocolatedragon.com
707-825-7788
Chocolate bars, candy

Comfort of Home Catering
Old World Cookies
Fieldbrook CA 95519
707-822-1781
www.comfortofhomecatering.com
Cookies, catering services

Hearts Content Baked Goods
100 Ericson Ct.
Arcata CA 95521
707-826-9352
Cookies, Delcos Cookies

Los Bagels (TYS)
1061 I St.
Arcata CA 95521
707-822-3150
Bagels, cream cheese spreads

North Coast Bakery
North Coast Co-operative
Arcata and Eureka locations
707-826-2706
Breads, pastry

Royal Cookie Capers
100 Ericson Court #145
Arcata CA 95521
707-822-0492
Sweet breads, cakes, cookie dough, vegan

Sjaak's Fine Chocolates O
Eureka CA 95501
800-869-6506
www.sjaaks.com
Chocolate candy

Beverages (non-alcoholic)

Bayside Roasters (TYS)
Eureka CA
www.baysideroasters.com
Coffee

Humboldt Bay Coffee Company
535 3rd St.
Eureka CA 95501
707-444-3969
roaster@humboldtcoffee.com
Coffee

Clendenen's Cider Works
96 12th St.
Fortuna CA 95540
707-725-2123
Apples, cider

Kinetic Koffee
550 South G St.
Arcata CA 95521
707-825-9417
www.kinetickoffee.com
Coffee

Muddy Waters Coffee (TYS)
330 Commercial
Eureka CA 95501
707-268-1133
chris@ilovemud.com
Coffee

Planet Chai (TYS)
P.O. Box 5178
Arcata CA 95521
707-832-9717
www.planetchai.com
Chai tea

Sweet Pea Garden Teas
1205 Lincoln Ave.
Arcata CA 95521
707-499-3363
Organic teas

Sacred Grounds Coffee
65 Ericson Ct. #3
Arcata CA 95521
707-822-3711
info@sacredgroundsorganics.com
Organic coffee

Cheese and Dairy

Alexandre Dairy (TYS) O
8371 Lower Lake Rd.
Crescent City CA 95531
707-487-1001
www.ecodairyfarms.com
Cheese, milk, eggs

Butterchef Organic Flavored Gourmet Butter
888-435-5156
www.butterchef.com
Infused gourmet butters

Cheese Queseria Michoacan
9701 West Rd.
Redwood Valley CA 95470
707-485-0579
Mexican cheeses

Cypress Grove Cheese
1330 Q St.
Arcata CA 95521
707-825-1100
info@cypressgrovechevre.com
Award-winning artisanal chevre

Humboldt Creamery
572 Highway 1
Fortuna, CA 95540
707-725-6182
info@humboldtcreamery.com
Butter, milk, cream, ice cream

Loleta Cheese Factory (TYS) O
252 Loleta Dr.
Loleta CA 95551
707-733-5470
www.loletacheese.com
Cheese

Rumiano Cheese Company
Baird Rumiano
511 Ninth St.
Crescent City CA 95531
Jack (including dry), Cheddar, goat

Cheese -Outside Tri-County Area

Rogue Creamery
311 North Front St.
Central Point OR 97502
866-396-4704
www.roguecreamery.com
Blue, Gorgonzola, Cheddar, TouVelle cheese

Straus Family Creamery
P.O. Box 761
Marshall CA 94940
415-663-5465 FAX
family@strausfamilycreamery.com
www.strausfamilycreamery.com
Milk, cream, eggnog, butter

Marin French Cheese Company
7500 Red Hill Rd.
Petaluma CA 94952
800-292-6001
www.marinfrenchcheese.com
Handmade Brie, Camembert

Sierra Nevada Cheese Company
6505 County Rd. 39
Willows CA 95988
530-934-8660
www.sierranevadacheese.com
Gina Marie Cream Cheese

Dressings, Sauces

Olive Oil: We do not have any commercial olive oil producers in Del Norte, Humboldt or Trinity Counties at this time. However, our neighboring counties of Mendocino, Shasta, Lake, Tehema, Sonoma and Napa have more than we can list here. Read the labels where you shop, or order directly from the source.

Abruzzi
Jacoby Storehouse
791 8th St.
Arcata CA 95521
707-826-2345
chris@abruzzicatering.com
House salad dressing

Boehm's Cafe Specialty Foods
P.O. Box 561
Fortuna CA 95540
707-725-7830
kjkeljoy@suddenlink.net
www.boehmscafe.com
Sauces, jelly, pickled food

Calhoun Barbeque Sauce
100 Ericson Ct.
Arcata CA 95521
calhounsbbq@live.com
Barbeque sauce

Casa Lindra Salsa/
Trinidad Bay Company
5425 Ericson Way
Arcata CA 95521
707-822-7933
Burritos, salsa

Larrupin Goods
1658 Patricks Point Dr.
Trinidad CA 95570
707-677-0230
www.larrupin.com/sauces
Barbeque, dill mustard sauces

Mas Salsa Por Favor
P.O. Box 908
Blue Lake CA 95525
Salsa

Mazzotti's Italian Food
12 West 4th St.
Eureka CA 95501
707-445-1987
www.mazzottis.com/arcata.html
House Italian dressing

Nonna Lena's (TYS)
P.O. Box 357
Arcata CA 95518
707-822-1517
www.nonnalena.com
Pesto, hummus, spreads

Pacific Rim Noodle House
1021 I St.
Arcata CA 95521
707-826-0240
www.pacificrimnoodle.com
Southeast Asian and Asian sauces

Rita's Café
427 West Harris
Eureka CA 95503
707-476-8565
www.Ritascafe.com
Burritos, salsa, frozen meals

Roy's Club Italian Restaurant
218 D St.
Eureka CA 95501
707-442-4574
www.Roys_Club_Italian_Restaurant.
com
Marinara sauce, basil vinaigrette,
pasta, polenta mix, orzetto

Shamus T Bones
5437 Hwy. 36
Carlotta CA 95528
707-768-3316
www.shamustbones.com
Barbeque Sauce

Smokey Jim's BBQ Sauce
Bigfoot Gourmet Baskets
888-560-0941
Barbeque sauce

Smokin' Moses Bar-B-Que Sauce
395 Sequoia Rd.
Miranda CA 95553
707-677-0506
Barbeque Sauce

Sweet Mama Janise's
P.O. Box 5667
Eureka CA 95502
support@sweetmamajanisse.com
Caribbean sauces

Weitchpec Chile Company (TYS)
Weitchpec CA 95546
Humboldt Green, Habañero,
Klamath Red chili sauces

Wildflower Specialty Foods (TYS)
853 Spring St.
Arcata CA 95521
707-825-1004
Tofu tahini salad dressing, herbal
vinaigrette salad dressings

Fish, Shellfish and Meat

Carvalho Fisheries Inc.
Eureka CA 95501
800-301-3270
Canned albacore

Fish Brothers (TYS)
203 Taylor Way
Blue Lake CA 95525
707-668-9700
www.fishbrothers.com
Smoked fish

Humboldt Grass-fed Beef (TYS)
P.O. Box 313
Fortuna CA 95540
707-845-7188 or 707-845-7878
grassfed@northcoast.com
www.humboldtgrassfedbeef.com
Grass-fed beef

Katy's Smokehouse (TYS)
740 Edwards
Trinidad CA 95570
707-677-0151
Smoked albacore, canned fish

Lazio Gourmet Albacore Tuna
P.O. Box 6146
Eureka CA 95502
800-737-6688
onfo@laziotuna.com
Canned tuna

North Bay Shellfish and Succulents
1167 Driver Rd.
Trinidad CA 95570
707-677-3509
Shellfish

Honey

Barbata Honey Farms (TYS)
1773 Ambosini Lane
Ferndale CA 95536
707-786-4382
Honey

Big D Ranch Honey (TYS)
7680 Myrtle Ave.
Eureka CA 95503
707-442-1914
Honey

Humboldt Honey (TYS)
2125 Whitlow Rd.
Meyers Flat CA 95554
Honey

Loleta Farms Honey
M. P. Muessig
P.O. Box 141
Loleta CA 95551
Honey

Monastery Honey
18104 Briceland-Thorn Rd.
Whitethorn CA 95589
707-986-7419
www.redwoodsabbey.org
Flavored and creamed honey

Reed's Bees
www.reedsbees.com
Honey, bees wax candles, propolis

River Bees
156 Ewan Ave.
Shively CA 95565
707-722-4669
onemorebee@yahoo.com
Honey, bee pollen, beeswax, lavender
honey, Humboldt Gold Honey brand

Jams and Jellies

Centerville Farms
P.O. Box 906
Ferndale CA 95536
877-780-4666
info@centervillefarms.com
Spreadable fruit, agave nectar honey blend

Diane's
707-839-2919
www.dianessweetheat.com
Spicy jams

Hunter Orchards (TYS) O
14431 Old Westside
Grenada CA 96038
530-436-2532
hunterorchards@jeffnet.org
Jams

Mad River Farm Food
100 Ericson Ct. #104
Arcata CA 95521
707-822-0248
info@mad-river-farm.com
Jam, jelly, preserves, barbeque sauce

Zimmerman's Country Kitchen
Distributed by Tomaso's Specialty Foods
P.O. Box 141
Blue Lake CA 95525
707-668-1868
Jam

Other Foods and Products

Beautiful Earth
707-839-7269
www.beautifulearthbags.com
Veggie bags, flour sacks, bath bags

Curley's Grill
P.O. Box 247
Ferndale CA 95536
707-786-9696
Tomato-basil soup

Hasta Be Pasta
5425 Ericson Ct.
Arcata CA 95521
707-825-0178
Antipasto spreads, ready-to-eat meals

Henry's Olives (TYS)
4177 Excelsior Rd.
Eureka, CA
707-445-9527
henrysolives@reninet.com
Olives

The Healthy Alternative Soy Strips
P.O. Box 221
Blocksburg CA 95514
707-383-2903
Soy products

Sergios
707-444-8870
Ravioli, pasta

Tofu Shop Specialty Foods, Inc. (TYS) O
65 Frank Martin Ct.
Arcata CA 95521
707-822-7401
www.tofushop.com
Nigari bulk, grilled and baked tofu, burgers, spreads, soy milk

Tomaso's Specialty Foods O
201 Taylor Way
Blue Lake CA
707-668-1868
Frozen meals, pasta sauce, pesto, alfredo sauce, salad dressing

Vegan Dream
100 Ericson Ct. Suite 125
Arcata CA 95521
707-826-1101
www.vegandream.com
Vegan jerky

Breweries

Eel River Brewing Company O
1777 Alamar Way
Fortuna CA 95540
Brewery in Scotia
707-725-2739
www.eelriverbrewing.com

Mad River Brewing Company
195 Taylor Way
Blue Lake CA 95525
707-668-4151
www.madriverbrewing.com

Lost Coast Brewery
(Café and brewhouse)
617 4th St.
Eureka CA 95501
707-445-4480

Six Rivers Brewery
1300 Central Ave.
McKinleyville CA 95519
707-839-7580
friends@sasquatchllc.com
www.sixriversbrewery.com

Wineries

Briceland Vineyards (TYS)
5959 Briceland Rd.
Redway CA 95560
707-923-2429

Butter Creek Ranch Winery
Hyampom
530-628-4890
marnie@buttercreekranch.com
www.buttercreekranch.com

Cabot Vineyards
209 Ferris Ranch Rd.
Orleans CA 95556
530-469-3397
cabotvin@sisqtel.net
www.cabotvineyards.com

Coates Vineyards (TYS) O
3255 Red Cap Rd.
Orleans CA 95556
530-627-3369
norman@coatesvineyards.com
www.coatesvineyards.com

Curtis and David Winery
1800 Q St.
Arcata CA 95521
707-822-5633
info@curtisanddavid.com
www.curtisanddavid.com

Dogwood Estate Winery
3995 Campbell Ridge Rd.
Salyer CA 95563
530-629-3750
dogwoodestates@snowcrest.net
www.dogwoodestatewinery.com

Ed Oliveira Winery
156 Center St.
Arcata CA 95521
707-822-3023
edoliveirawinery@aol.com

Elk Prairie Vineyard (TYS)
11544 Dyerville Loop Rd.
Myers Flat CA 95554
707-943-3498
alan@elkprairievineyard.com
www.elkprairievineyard.com

Fieldbrook Valley Winery
4241 Fieldbrook Rd.
Arcata CA 95521
707-839-4140
bob@fieldbrookwinery.com
www.fieldbrookwinery.com

Heidrun Meadery
55 Ericson Ct., Suite 4
Arcata CA 95521
707-825-8748
info@heidrunmeadery.com
www.heidrunmeadery.com
Naturally sparkling dry meads made
from honey

Lost Coast Vineyards (TYS)
795 Conklin Creek Rd.
Petrolia CA 95558
707-629-3671

Old Growth Cellars (TYS)
500 Quail Valley Rd.
Eureka CA 95503
707-444-2333
wine@oldgrowthcellars.com
www.oldgrowthcellars.com

Moonstone Crossing
1000 Moonstone Cross Rd.
Trinidad CA 95570
707-677-3832
donbremm@yahoo.com
www.moonstonecrossing.com

Riverbend Cellars (TYS)
12990 Avenue of the Giants
Myers Flat CA 95554
707-943-9907
RiverbendCellars@gotsky.com
www.riverbendcellars.com

Robert Goodman Wines
937 10th St.
Arcata CA 95521
707-826-WINE (9463)
www.robertgoodmanvines.com

Rosina Vineyard
751 Sorenson Rd.
Redcrest CA 95569
707-722-4331

Sentinel Winery
2263 Patterson Ln.
Willow Creek CA 95573
530-629-2338
sentinel@onemain.com

Violet-Green Winery (TYS)
P.O. Box 165
Bayside CA 95524
707-445-8679
wine@violetgreenwinery.com
www.violetgreenwinery.com

Whitethorn Winery
545 Shelter Cove Rd.
Whitethorn CA 95589
707-986-1642

Winnett Vineyards (TYS)
655 Peach Tree Ln.
Willow Creek CA 95573
530-629-3478
www.winnettvineyards.com

Wittwer Winery
2121 Table Bluff Rd.
Loleta CA 95551
707-733-5292

Appendix G:
Community Supported Agriculture (CSA) Farms

CSA farmers enjoy the security of knowing that their crops are sold right from the start of the season. Community members purchase shares in the output of a particular CSA farm and in return receive a box or bag of fresh food each week during the season. Buying a share in a CSA is a way to lower the overall cost of the food for the consumer, and at the same time get the freshest produce available. This subscription method of food shopping also helps support and extend local food production. You can even go see your food growing—what a treat.

Democracy Unlimited Humboldt County

Arcata Educational Farm
930 Old Arcata Rd.
Arcata CA 95521
707-825-1777
The Arcata Educational Farm is a student-run CSA farm. Educational opportunities are available including work-trades and farm tours and the farms always welcome volunteers.
Products: More than 60 kinds of seasonal organic vegetables, herbs, and flowers

College of the Redwoods Sustainable Agricultural Farm
409 Shively Flat Rd.
Shively CA 95565
707-845-6977
franz-rulofson@redwoods.edu
This is another student-run CSA farm.
Products: Wide variety of vegetables and orchard fruit

Don Primerano
P.O. Box 982
Redway CA 95560
707-923-4660
dprimerano@asis.com
Products: Wheat flour, wheat berries

Community Farm in Garberville
John Finley, Manager
934 Sprowel Creek Rd.
Garberville CA 95542
707-223-4996
garbervillefarm@gmail.com
The Community Farm is located in the 431-acre Southern Humboldt Community Park. The park hosts other farms, as well as trails and other recreational opportunities.
Products: Arugula, onions, beets, potatoes, lettuce, peppers, carrots, melons, bunch onions, squash, kale, sweet corn, chard, beans, garlic, herbs, broccoli, radishes, cabbage, tomatoes, flowers, cucumbers

Deep Seeded Community Farm
Eddie Tanner, Farmer
P.O. Box 4380
Arcata CA 95518
707-825-8033
deepseeded@gmail.com
www.ArcataCSA.com
Products: Beets, chard, fava beans, snap peas, broccoli, onions, spinach, potatoes, cucumbers, cherry tomatoes, bell peppers, zucchini, garlic, carrots, Brussels sprouts, kale, cauliflower, leeks, winter squash, strawberries

Green Fire Farm

Linda Hildebrand and Grady Walker, Farmers

Contact through Democracy Unlimited

707-269-0984

info@duhc.org

greenfirefarm@asis.com

Green Fire Farm is a certified organic farm located along the Trinity River in the Hoopa Valley of northeastern Humboldt County.

Products: Tomatoes, peppers, greens, squash, root crops, orchard fruit, wine grapes

Luna Farms

Alissa Pattison and Frederic Dietmeyer, Farmers

95 Neighbor Lane

P.O. Box 184

Willow Creek CA 95573

530-355-4191

farmfred@gmail.com

Products: Tomatoes, eggplant, peppers, tomatillos, summer and winter squash, strawberries, melons, flowers, herbs

Ocean Air Farm

Paul Madeira and Julie Jo Ayer Williams, Farmers

190 Bolen Ln.

Fort Dick, CA 95531

707-616-1632

oceanairfarms@gmail.com

Products: 40 kinds of vegetables, lettuce, salad greens, summer squash, onions, potatoes, pasture-raised chickens

Pierce Family Farm

Margarite Pierce, Farmer

P.O. Box 93

Orleans CA 95556

530-627-3320

piercefarm@toast.net

Pick-ups in Orleans and Arcata

Products: Seasonal vegetables from arugula to zucchini

Redwood Roots Farm

Janet Czarnecki, Farmer

P.O. Box 793

Arcata CA 95518

707-826-0261

janetcz@humboldt1.com

www.redwoodrootsfarm.com

Products: Vegetables, flowers, herbs, berries

*Redwood Roots Farm
CSA Pick-up Day*

Shakefork Community Farm and Grain Share Program

Kevin Cunningham and
Melanie Olstad, Farmers
7914 Highway 36
Carlotta CA 95528
shakeforkcommunityfarm@gmail.com
Products: Wheat, rye, oats, barley, buckwheat, corn, edible seeds, dried flowers

Tule Fog Farm

Shail Pec-Crouse and
Sean Armstrong, Farmers
1887 Q St.
Arcata CA 95521
707-826-1450
tulefogfarm@gmail.com
Products: Goose eggs, geese, pork in future, chicken eggs, chicken

Humboldt Times, August 20, 1864

For the Harvest
We now have on hand CRADLES, SNATHS, RAKES, FORKS, etc.
Also CULTIVATORS, horse hoes, plows of different descriptions and other implements of the use of Farmers.

L. C. Schmidt & Co.
Eureka Hardware Store

The United Indian Health Services (UIHS)
Potawot Community Food Garden

Ed Mata, Food and Garden Resource Specialist
T Griffin, Garden Food Specialist
1600 Weott Way
Arcata CA 95521
707-826-8476

Incorporated in 1970, UIHS is a non-profit tribal health consortium serving American Indians and their families in Humboldt and Del Norte Counties. The UIHS Potawot Community Food Garden has more than two acres of organic gardens producing fruit, produce and herbs. Members buy shares and shop at the weekly market. Each week, an item in season is made into a dish to be sampled. Recipes are available for the all the products of the garden. The garden is part of the "Food Is Good Medicine Project" based on a nutritional model that honors traditional native foods and recognizes the spiritual connection existing between gathering, preparing and sharing food. The emphasis is on the health of the people in "body, mind and spirit."

In addition to the garden, UIHS offers classes that are open to the public. Contact Ed Mata for upcoming classes and space availability. An outreach component provides services and workshops at Weitchpec, Smith River Clinic and the Margaret Keating School. The garden project encourages home gardens and can supply starts. The garden does not have a formal intern program, but opportunities for interning on an informal basis are available.

Appendix H: Growing Your Own Food

Several options are available for growing your own food. You can grow in your own garden, share a friend's garden, or participate in a community garden. If you have land but can't do the gardening yourself, you might find someone to grow the food on your land and both of you can share in the bounty. You can also hire a foodscaper.

What to Grow

Every garden has room for some edibles. A useful herb garden can pass for landscaping. A small vegetable garden can fit next to a sunny fence. A single fruit tree can grace a small front lawn. Larger yards, of course, offer greater opportunities, but remember that an entire movable garden can be planted in three-pound coffee tins!

A Suggested Herb Garden

Buying fresh herbs each time you need them can be expensive, but we are lucky in that they are so easy to grow. Many are even perennial. Karina Green, of Jacob's Greens, suggests some all-around useful perennial culinary herbs that will do well in coastal cool and inland heat: thyme, oregano, sage, marjoram, chives, rosemary, and tarragon. Annual herbs include basil, cilantro, dill and parsley.

Basil prefers heat, but planted in the greenhouse along with tomatoes, it does well on the coast. There are far too many herbs to mention here, but these are Karina's favorites. Even within this short list there are many varieties, for example: lemon thyme, or Thai basil. Karina gets most of her seeds from Johnny's Selected Seeds. Seeds of Change also has a wide selection of old-world varieties.

Fruit Trees

Fruit trees best suited to our region are apples, Asian pears, pears, peaches and plums. Fruit bushes includes blueberries, raspberries and blackberries. Strawberries are also a favorite.

Vegetables

The list of vegetables that grow well in this region is long. Look at the seasonality chart in Appendix A for some of the most popular. See also the growing charts in Eddie Tanner's book *The Humboldt Kitchen Gardener*. The charts list plants best suited to coastal and inland areas.

Humboldt Times, December 10, 1864,
GARDEN SEEDS
A large quantity of Garden Seeds, fresh and of the best quality, just arrived, for sale low by

A. L. WALLER

Where to find plants to grow

Plants can be started from seeds, from starts or established plants, from bare-root or established trees.

Seeds

Synergy Seed Exchange
George Stevens
www.synergyseeds.com
Willow Creek CA 95573
synergy67@hotmail.com
Hundreds of varieties of seeds for produce, grains, oils, fruit and flowers including many heirloom varieties.

Most of the following list is courtesy of Eddie Tanner and is from his book, *The Humboldt Kitchen Gardener*. Bountiful Gardens and Kitazawa are seed companies used by one of our editors.

Bountiful Gardens
18001 Shafer Beach Rd.
Willets CA 95490
707-459-0150
www.bountifulgardens.org

Johnny's Selected Seeds
955 Benton Ave.
Winslow ME 04901
www.Johnnyseeds.com
User-friendly catalog, best selection of F1 (hybrid) seeds, some certified organic.

Kitazawa Seed Company
P.O. Box 12220
Oakland CA 94661
610-5951188
www.kitazawaseed.com
Wide selection of Asian greens

Native Seeds/SEARCH
526 N. 4th Ave.
Tucson AZ 85705
www.nativeseeds.org
Source for indigenous varieties from the Americas; all open pollinated.

Peaceful Valley Farm Supply
P.O. Box 2209
Grass Valley CA 95945
888-784-1722
www.groworganic.com
Good prices on bulk certified-organic, open-pollinated seed, various suppliers.

Seeds of Change
P.O. Box 15700
Santa Fe NM 97592
999-762-7333
Great selection of heirloom and traditional seeds. All certified organic and open pollinated.

Seed Saver's Exchange
3094 North Winn Rd.
Decorah IA 52101
www.seedsavers.org
Source for rare and heirloom seeds

Territorial Seed Company
P.O. Box 158
Cottage Grove OR 97424
www.territorialseeds.com
Open-pollinated and F1 (Hybrid) varieties selected for the Pacific Northwest, some certified organic.

Plant Starts

Shop the farmers' markets for plant starts, especially in the spring and early summer months. Many of the local grocery stores sell starts. Local nurseries also have them available.

Trees

Trees can be purchased bare-root in the early spring or potted all through the year. Bare-root trees are generally less expensive but may take longer to become established than potted trees. Look for trees at your local nursery or at farmers' markets.

Where to grow a garden if you don't have land

Community Gardens

We have identified a few community gardens and hope more will become established in the future.

Arcata Educational Farm
930 Old Arcata Rd.
Arcata, CA 95521-67766
Contact: Karen Diemer
707-825-1777

Trinidad
Carol Moné 707-677-0862
or cemone@humboldt1.com

Eureka
Deborah Giraud
debra-giraud@redwood.edu

What to do if you can't or don't want to do your own gardening, but have some land.

Find someone without land, maybe a student or someone who lives in an apartment. You provide the land and they supply the labor and you share in the products of the garden. We do not yet have a "match-making" service like the one available in Seattle, Washington (www.urbangardenshare.org), but maybe some enterprising person will start one. For now, check with neighbors, friends, put a note on bulletin boards at the local colleges, or try craigslist.

You can hire someone to foodscape your garden. Local landscapers may be able to do the work but there are at least two companies that have made this their business focus. You can also check with a local farmer who may be interested in creating your foodscaped garden.

Luscious Gardens
Kashi Anderson and Naomi Withers
P.O. Box 976
Arcata CA 95518
707-834-2698
lusciousgardens@gmail.com

Neighborhood Farms and Victory Gardens
3441 K St.
Eureka CA 95503
707-498-1659
info@humboldtexchange.org

How to grow your own food

We have neither the space nor the expertise to tell you everything you need to know about growing your own food. But the good news is that we have many resources in our community that can help.

Books

Tanner, Eddie. *The Humboldt Gardener: A Concise Guide to Raising Organic Vegetables and Fruits in the Greater Humboldt County Region.* Published by Eddie Tanner, Arcata, CA, 2008. Available at local bookstores.

——*Food is Good Medicine: A Practical Guide to Growing Food in Northwestern California.* Published by United Indian Health Services, Inc. Arcata, CA, 2008. Available at Potawot Health Village, 1600 Weeot Way, Arcata, CA

Olkowski, Helga, et al. *The Integral Urban House: Self-Reliant Living in the City*, New Catalyst Books, Gabriola Island,. BC, Canada, 2008

Stewart, Amy. *The Earth Moved.* Workman Publishing, Chapel Hill, NC, 2004

Government Printing Office, United States Department of Agriculture. *Victory Garden: Leader's Handbook*. Washington , 1943. Available as a free download from digitalcollections.smu.edu/cgi-bin/showfile. exe?CISOROOT=/hgpandCISOPTR=353andfilename=354.pdf

The reference librarian at your public library can also steer you to numerous appropriate books.

Online information

Path to Freedom shows how one group created a micro-farm at a suburban home in Pasadena, CA. www.pathtofreedom.com

Classes

Redwood Roots Farm
Classes are offered on many aspects of farming including soil, compost, propagation and starting seedlings. See specific list and class schedule on the Redwood Roots web page. www.redwoodrootsfarm.com

Flying Blue Dog Nursery
Check their web site for class locations and listings. They may also be willing to answer questions. www.flyingbluedog.com

Humboldt State University Extension
Recent classes have included: Backyard Poultry and Organic Gardening: From the Backyard to the Kitchen Table www.humboldt.edu/~extended.

College of the Redwoods (CR)
7351 Thompkins Hill Rd.
Eureka CA 95501
707-722-4640 (farm)
707-476-4558 (Division office)
www.redwoods.edu

Formal classes coupled with practical experience on the CR Community Supported Agriculture Farm.

Internships

Redwood Roots Farm
P.O. Box 793
Arcata CA 95518
707-826-0261
www.redwoodrootsfarm.com

Deep Seeded Community Farm
P.O. Box 4380
Arcata CA 95518
707-825-8033
www.deepseeded.com

Volunteer Opportunities

The Arcata Educational Farm
Contact arcataedfarm@yahoo.com

Potawot Community Food Garden
needs on-going volunteers to tend garden. Call 707-826-8476 for more information.

Other Resources

Humboldt County Cooperative Extension
The Extension office has many resources available to home gardeners. They also run the 13-week Master Gardener training program, offered every other year.
Agricultural Center
5630 South Broadway
Eureka CA 95503
707-445-7351
www.cehumboldt.ucdavis.edu
Deborah Giraud is the contact for plant science.
ddgiraud@ucdavis.edu

Appendix I: Foraging, Fishing and Hunting

Foraging on the North Coast

Foraged food adds both richness and variety to our diets. Humboldt County is absolutely loaded with free foods from the ocean and the hillsides.

Mushrooms are available from the coast through the inland areas from fall through early summer. The light fall rains bring out chanterelles, boletus and hedgehog mushrooms. After the first frost, tan oak mushrooms can be found at the higher elevations. In the spring, morels thrive in burned-over areas. Our region has a very active mycological society that offers monthly education and field trips. These are free, they're fun, and they teach mushroom identification techniques and the areas where mushrooms can legally be picked.

Clams are available in the bay and during minus tides on the ocean-side beaches. Humboldt Bay has an unlimited supply of large clams that are good for chowders or clam fritters. They can be harvested around Fields Landing and off the mud islands in the middle of the bay. Large clams such as Martha Washingtons can easily fill a gunny-sack. Razor clams can be found at a minus tides on Clam Beach, if the ocean is calm. These are the most delicious of all the local clams. Farther north, on Indian Beach, below the Memorial Lighthouse in Trinidad, cockle-like clams, great for steaming, can be found.

We North Coast residents can fish on almost all our waterways: ocean, lagoons, creeks and rivers. Some creeks and all rivers produce trout, steelhead or salmon. Most of the small creeks have cut-throat trout that are always hungry and are easy to catch. Ruth Lake and Fish Lake are consistent producers of trout, bass and blue-gill. In the fall, the salmon and steelhead come into all our rivers. There is also a steelhead run in the winter. River fishing usually begins in the later part of August on the Klamath and Trinity rivers. Once the rains start, the Eel, Van Duzen and Mad Rivers and Redwood Creek become productive. The Department of Fish and Game has two "free fishing days" each year. On these days, you don't need a license to fish either on the ocean or in the rivers.

The ocean provides a wide variety of bottom fish. It's very easy to catch ling cod and snapper from a boat. Halibut fishing continues to be very productive, with fish in the 40- to 70-pound range being common. California halibut has a short run in Humboldt Bay from June through August, with fish weighing from two to 20 pounds. Fishing boat charters are available in Eureka, Trinidad, Crescent City and Brookings, OR.

Red-tail perch can be caught off the beaches from Mad River Beach to Gold Beach and from all the lagoon spits. Starting in late spring, they can also be taken from the jetties and the rock wall in front of the PG&E plant at King Salmon. For a little more adventure, small sardine-like fish that are present much of the year at Gold Beach, Freshwater and Mad River Beach can be caught, using an A-frame or throw net. If it suits you better, commercial boats sell fresh or fresh-frozen albacore from the docks in Eureka during the summer and early fall. Live Dungeness crabs are generally for sale around Christmas for a few months.

For the hunters, fall is the season for upland birds such as quail, blue grouse and banded pigeons. Deer hunting also starts in the fall, with separate seasons for bow hunters and rifle hunters. Ducks and geese are hunted in the late fall. Goose populations have rebounded so successfully that their numbers have become problematic. Local dairy ranchers now allow hunters to enter their fields to "thin" the bird population. Hunters are allowed two geese per day over a very long season. If you're not a hunter, get to know one. Hunters are a generous lot and may give you one of their extra birds.

Two wonderful programs are available for children to learn how to hunt. On the second and third weekend in October, there is a free junior pheasant hunt at Ocean Ranch. Birds are "planted" on ranches down at the mouth of the Eel River, and the kids are put into a field with an expert hunter and a dog. The dog will point and flush out the birds. The kids are allowed two pheasant apiece. It's a good way for kids to learn how to hunt safely. There is also a junior deer hunt, for kids ages 10 to 16, where they are allowed to hunt in areas that are generally off limits to older, experienced hunters.

And the berries! Salmonberries and native blackberries ripen in June and July. The Himalayan blackberries come a little later, usually late July and August, earlier in the upland region. Almost any country road will provide good berry picking. Try the railroad grade on Samoa Boulevard in Arcata or Murray Road, going toward Fieldbrook from McKinleyville. Snow Camp and Maple Creek Roads out of Blue Lake, and many more, have fruit for berry pies, jams and cobblers awaiting ambitious pickers. The coastal hillsides and forests produce large crops of huckleberries in the fall. Berries are easy to pick and make delicious treats. Stick to the roadside patches if you don't know an area, as you may run into another type of grower who may be grumpy about your intrusion.

Sometimes we gather more than we can eat. Canning, drying and freezing allows you to enjoy our bounty all year long.

The following plants are in such abundance in our area that we want to add a few more words. References on edible plants are listed at the end of this Appendix. **Always make sure you know how to correctly identify any wild plant that you plan to eat. Some wild plants are poisonous.**

Berries

Salmonberries. This orange or red-orange berry is the first to appear in sunny portions of forest edges in early summer. It may be difficult to find enough for a pie, but you can add them to salads as a bright garnish, or eat them just as you find them.

Thimbleberries. This prolific plant can be found in many parts of the county and is plentiful in our coastal forests. Thimbleberries are a relative of the raspberry and are shaped like a shallow thimble. Bright red and intense in flavor, they ripen in late summer. Use in salads, as a garnish or just eat them. If you are persistent, collect enough for a tart.

Native Blackberries. These are smaller and more conical in shape than the non-native Himalayan blackberry. Their flavor is stronger. The berries are ready to eat in June or July—earlier in the year than Himalayans. The native blackberry is not as common or as productive as the Himalayan.

Himalayan Blackberries. This plant is non-native and invasive, but produces an abundance of sweet fruit. The vines seem to be everywhere but the berries are sweeter in the inland areas. It is easy to pick plenty of these berries for pies, cobblers, tarts or to make jam or jelly.

Huckleberries. A relative of the blueberry, the huckleberry is found in abundance in our coastal forests where the sun is able to penetrate the forest canopy. The berries are small, with an intense flavor. It is easy to find plenty of berries but they are time-consuming to pick and to clean. Use them for pies, tarts, jam, to make syrup or to use in other desserts.

Salalberries. We usually see salal foliage used in floral arrangements, but the medium-size dark berries are edible. They, too, are related to blueberries, but are not as sweet and have a slightly "vegetable taste." Eat them raw or use them in cooking. The skins are a bit tough, which makes for an interesting jam.

Note: Berries may be picked in California State Parks.

Teas
Herbal teas can be made from many of our native plants, including dandelion greens, Douglas Fir needles, nettle, huckleberry, blackberry, miner's lettuce, purslane, wild rose (hips) and Yerba Buena. (Nettles can also be made into a lovely Cream of Nettle soup or stir-fried with other vegetables. Be very careful harvesting nettles, as the spines can sting before the nettles are cooked.)

Mushrooms
The North Coast region is a perfect climate for mushrooms, and many of the local varieties are edible. Before collecting them, it is important to know how to identify them and know where it is legal to pick. We urge caution and education if you collect on your own, as a wrong choice can cause illness and even death. References on mushrooms are at the end of this chapter including how to contact the local Mycological Society.

Note: Mushrooms may NOT be gathered in California State Parks or National Parks.

Other plants
Lamb's quarters, chickweed, sheep sorrel, miner's lettuce, dandelion, purslane, beach strawberry and wood strawberry, black-cap raspberry, spice bush, red flowering current, manzanita, acorns, Oregon crabapple, Indian potatoes, wild onion, bay nuts, hazelnuts, fennel, acorns, redwood sorrel and brodiaea are all edible.

Seaweed
Seaweed is another native food readily available in our region. Most marine algae are edible. Get a good book at the library to help identify the following locally abundant marine algae and make sure you know which are NOT edible. As an example, avoid *Desmaresria,* which contains dilute sulfuric acid, evident because it bleaches other algae on contact.

When harvesting, cut the algae away from the attachment base. Removal of the attachment destroys the plant, preventing future growth and propagation.

Lamanaria are large brown kelp found in the lowest inter-tidal and sub-tidal zones. These kelp are marketed as kombu.

Alaria is the winged kelp sold as wakame. Alaria grows in the lower inter-tidal zone on exposed rocky shores.

Porphyra, known as laver in Europe, is known here as nori. There are numerous varieties.

Pelvetiopsis, also known as rockweed, is not commercially harvested, but is very easy to access since it grows in the high intertidal zone and is usually exposed. It keeps well when refrigerated, unlike others that must be dried to preserve. *Pelvetiopsis* is good snipped into salads and added to cooked vegetable and meat dishes.

Nereocystis, or bull kelp, can be pickled as you would cucumbers. The bulbs can also be stuffed and served for a main dish. It is generally found offshore, but fresh specimens often drift onto the beach.

Note: Permits are required to gather seaweed.

A note on processing and preserving fish and wild game: Check with a local meat market. Some will butcher deer for you. Fish Brothers in Blue Lake will can your fish, if you don't want to can it yourself.

Information Resources

Native Plants
Pojar, Jim and McKinnon, Andy. *Plants of the Pacific Northwest Coast.* Lone Pine Publishers, Vancouver, BC, Canada, 1994

Tilford, Gregory L. *Edible and Medicinal Plants of the West.* Mountain Press Publishing Company, Missoula, MT, 1997

The United States Department of Agriculture has a useful web site for researching plants: www.plants.usda.gov/java/nameSearch

Mushrooms
Humboldt Bay Mycological Society
P.O. Box 4419
Arcata CA 95521
Coordinator: 707-822-8856
www.groups.yahoo.com/group/H-B-M-S e-mail: h_b_m_s@yahoo.com

Arora, David. *Mushrooms Demystified.* Ten Speed Press, Berkeley, CA, 1986

———*All That the Rain Promises, and More ...: A Hip Pocket Guide to Western Mushrooms.* Ten Speed Press, Berkeley, CA, 1991

Seaweed
Mondragon, Jennifer and Jeff Mondragon. *Seaweeds of the Pacific Coast: Common Marine Algae from Alaska to Baja California,* Sea Challengers, Los Osos, CA, 2003

Druehl, Louis. *Pacific Seaweeds.* Harbour, Madeira Park, BC, Canada, 2003

Appendix J:
Organizations Supporting Local Agriculture

California Farm Bureau Federation
The California Farm Bureau Federation is a non-governmental, non-profit, voluntary-membership California corporation, the purpose of which is to protect and promote agricultural interests throughout the state of California and to find solutions to the problems of the farm, the farm home and the rural community.

Del Norte Farm Bureau
P.O. Box 789
Smith River CA 95567
707-487-0612
www.cfbf.com.delnorte

Humboldt County Farm Bureau
5601 S. Broadway
Eureka CA 95503
707-443-4844
www.humboldtfarmbureau.org

Trinity County Farm Bureau
HC 62
Box 72
Zenia CA 95595
trincofb@gotsky.com

Democracy Unlimited of Humboldt County (DUHC)
P.O. Box 610
Eureka CA 95502
707-269-0984
www.duhc.org
Democracy Unlimited is a community-organizing group dedicated to making the promise of democracy a reality. They help to design and implement grass-roots strategies to exercise democratic control over corporations and governments.

As part of their effort, they operate a "Food and Democracy" Program.

Specifically, they partner with Green Fire Farm to offer Community Supported Agriculture shares for residents of Eureka and Arcata. They also partner with Redwood Roots CSA to offer a workshop, "The Revolution Will Not Be Microwaved." This workshop investigates the rise of industrial agriculture and what folks are doing in response. Through history, economics, and ecology, participants explore the potential for community food that benefits people, not corporations.

Humboldt-Community Alliance with Family Farmers (H-CAFF)
922 E St., Suite 202
Eureka CA 95501
707-444-3255
www.caff.org
Humboldt-CAFF is the North Coast Regional CAFF organization. The Community Alliance with Family Farmers is building a movement of rural and urban people to foster family-scale agriculture that cares for the land, sustains local economies and promotes social justice.

Humboldt County Agriculture Commissioner
5630 S. Broadway
Eureka, CA 95503
707-441-5273
www.co.humboldt.ca.us/ag
Provides environmental protection through agricultural pest exclusion, detection, pesticide use enforcement, and support of the USDA animal damage control program; protects consumers by inspecting/testing all commercial weighing devices and enforcing package label laws.

National Future Farmers of America Organization (FFA)

FFA agricultural education prepares students for successful careers and a lifetime of informed choices in the global agriculture, food, fiber and natural resources systems. Chapters are at high schools in Arcata, Eureka, Ferndale, Fortuna, Hayfork and Del Norte.

North Coast Cooperative (Co-op)

811 I St.
Arcata CA 95521
707-822-5947
www.northcoastco-op.com
The Co-op is a member-owned community market guided by cooperative principles emphasizing a diverse selection of organic, bulk, and local food products. The Co-op provides consumer education so that shoppers can make informed choices, and promotes community building and environmental sustainability while maintaining financial stability. The foundation of their work is meeting member needs.

North Coast Growers Association (NCGA)

P.O. Box 4232
Arcata CA 95518
707-441-9999
www.humfarm.org
The NCGA Farmers' Market was established in 1979 by a handful of farmers. They began selling from the backs of their trucks in the vacant lot at the foot of 7th and F Streets in Arcata. This is their 31st season, and they now have more than 100 members. Membership in the NCGA is open to residents of Humboldt County.

Humboldt Bay Center for Sustainable Living (HBCSL)

P.O. Box 309
Eureka CA 95502
707-822-5583
Suzanne.simpson@eco-hostel.org
The Humboldt Bay Center for Sustainable Living is concerned with the search for globally-sustainable, whole and ecologically sound technologies and ways of life. Within this search, their role is to explore and demonstrate through experiential living a wide range of alternatives, communicating to other people the options for achieving positive change in their own lives. This process involves:

Inspiring - Instilling the desire to change by practical example through experiential living

Informing - Feeding the desire to change by providing the most appropriate information

Enabling - Providing effective and continuing support to put the change into practice

UC Cooperative Extension

5630 S. Broadway
Eureka CA 95503
707-445-7351
www.cehumboldt.ucdavis.edu
The Extension's mission is to develop and extend the use of research-based knowledge to improve specific practices and technologies in agriculture, natural resource management, nutrition education and youth development.

Appendix K: Information Sources

Cookbooks

Chesman, Andrea. *Serving Up the Harvest, Celebrating the Goodness of Fresh Vegetables.* North Adams, MA: Story Publishing, 2007

Dubin, Margaret, and Sara-Larus Tolley. *Seaweed, Salmon and Manzanita Cider, A California Indian Feast.* Berkeley, CA: Heydey Books, 2008

Fallon, Sally. *Nourishing Traditions.* Winona Lake, IN: New Trends Publishing, Inc., 2001

Fletcher, Janet. *Fresh From the Farmers' Market*, Chronicle Books LLC, San Francisco, 2008

Haugen, Scott, and Tiffany Haugen. *Cooking Salmon and Steelhead.* Portland, OR: Frank Amato Publications, 2003

Jaffrey, Madhur. *World Vegetarian.* New York: Crown Publishing Group, 1999

Madison, Deborah. *Local Flavors; Cooking and Eating from America's Farmer's Market*, New York: Broadway Books, 2008

Madison, Deborah, with Edward Espe Brown, *The Greens Cookbook, Extraordinary Vegetarian Cuisine From the Celebrated Restaurant.* New York: Bantam Books, 1987

Only, Nancy. *Managing the Munchies, A Celebration of the Phenomenal Fare of Humboldt County, California.* Eureka, CA: Creyr Publishing, Inc., 2005

Rombauer, Irma, A. Becker, Marion Rombauer, et al., *Joy of Cooking.* New York: Simon and Schuster, Inc., 2006

Traunfeld, Jerry. *Herb Farm Cookbook.* New York: Scribners, 2000

Waters, Alice. *Chez Panisse Vegetables.* New York: Harper Collins, 1996

Woods, Rebecca. *The New Whole Foods Encyclopedia, A comprehensive Resource for Healthy Eating. New York:* Penguin Group, 1999

Fishing, Foraging and Hunting

See resources at end of Appendix I Fishing, Foraging and Hunting on page 309.

Food Preservation

See resources at end of recipe chapter on food preservation on page 245.

Growing Your Own Food

See resources at end of Appendix H Growing Your Own Food on page 304.

General Background

Bendrick, Lou. *Eat Where You Live*. Seattle, WA: Skipstone Press, 2008

Lappé, Frances Moore. *Diet for a Small Planet*. New York: Ballantine Books, The Random House Publishing Group, 1991

McNamee, Thomas. *Alice Waters and Chez Panisse*. New York: Penguin Books, 2007

Pollan, Michael, *The Omnivore's Dilemma: A Natural History of Four Meals* New York: Penguin Group, 2006

————*In Defense of Food: An Eater's Manifesto*. New York: The Penguin Press, 2008

Kingsolver, Barbara, et al. *Animal, Vegetable, Miracle: A Year of Food Life*. New York: Harper Collins, 2007

Roberts, Paul. *The End of Food: How the Food Industry is Destroying Our Food Supply--And What We Can Do About It*. Boston: Mariner Books, Houghton Mifflin Harcourt, 2009

Waters, Alice. *The Art of Simple Food: Notes, Lessons, and Recipes from a Delicious Revolution. New York:* Clarkson Potter, 2007

On-line

Know Your Farmer - Know Your Food
United State Department of Agriculture website
http://riley.nal.usda.gov/nal_display/index.php?info_center=8&tax_level=1&tax_subject=619

Works Cited:

Chapter One

1. National Institute of Health.
   http://www.nieehs,nih.gov/news/media/questions/sya-bp.cfm
2. Nochi, Kim, Stern, Anna, Piebel, Doug, "Just the Facts, When Corporations Rule Our Food", *YES Magazine*, Spring, 2009; p. 24
3. Community Alliance with Family Farmers, www.caff.org
4. Roberts, Paul, *The End of Food*. New York; Houghton Mifflin Harcourt; 2008. p. 154
5. Everybody Eats, *YES Magazine*, Spring 2009; p. 32.
6. Institute for Local Self-Reliance. *"The Economic Impact of Locally Owned Businesses vs. Chains, A Case Study in Midcoast Maine"*, http://www.livingeconomies.org/sites/default/files/file/midcoaststudy.pdf, September 2003
7. http://www.dickinson.edu/storg/sisa/The Dirt08/100milediet.html
8. Roberts, *End of Food*; p. 217
9. YES Magazine Spring 2009; p. 24
10. Roberts, *End of Food*, p. 217
11. Roberts, *End of Food*, p. 221
12. Roberts, *End of Food*, p. 217
13. Ibid
14. US Environmental Protection Agency, Consumer Fact sheet on Atrazine, Mar. 21, 2007, http://www.epa.gov/safewater/contaminants/dw_contamfs/atrazine.html
15. Roberts, *End of Food*, p. 218
16. Ibid
17. Roberts, *End of Food*, p. 77
18 Roberts, *End of Food*, p. 185
19. Ibid
20. Roberts, *End of Food*, p. 180
21. Roberts, *End of Food*, p. 186
22. Roberts, *End of Food*, p. 187
23. Roberts, *End of Food*, p. 29
24. Roberts, *End of Food*, p. 186
25. YES Magazine, Spring, 2009, p. 19
26. YES Magazine, Spring, 2009, p. 24
27. Ibid
28. Kahn, Laura, et al, Recommendations and Reports, Volume 58; No. RR – 7, Center for Disease Control, July 24, 2009

Chapter Two

1. Wilkinson, Renee, American Victory Gardens in World War II, January 2009; http://www.hipchickdigs.com/wordpress/we-content/uploads/2009/01/american-victory-gradens-in-wwii.pdf

Chapter Three

1. Roberts; *End of Food*, p. 221
2. Finkelstein, Eric A., et al, *Annual Medical Spending Attributable To Obesity: Payer-And Service-Specific Estimates*, Health Affairs 28, no. 5 (2009): w822-w831 (published online 27 July 2009; 10.1377/hlthaff.28.5.w822)
3. Jones, Timothy, "Half of US Food Goes to Waste", www.foodproduction-daily.com/Supply-Chain/Half-of-US-food-goes-to-waste
4. National Chicken Council, "Per Capita Consumption of poultry and Live-stock" (current as of October 15, 2008), www.nationalchickencouncil.com/statistics/stat_detail.cfm?id=8
5. United State Department of Agriculture, Vegetarian Diets Tips and Re-sources, www.mypyramid.gov/tips_resources/vegetarian_diets.html
6. Organics Consumers Association, www.organicconsumers.org
7. The Cornucopia Institute, http://www.cornucopia.org

Chapter Four

1. *History of Humboldt County*, *California*. Wallace W. Elliott and Co., San Francisco CA, 1881.
2. *History and Business Directory of Humboldt County*; http://bood.google.com
3. Eddy, J. M. *In the Redwood's Realm; By-ways of Wild Nature and Highways of Industry as Found Under Forest Shades and Amidst Clover Blossoms in Humboldt County, California*. Humboldt Chamber of Commerce, 1893. Available in the Humboldt State University library
4. California Genealogy and History Archives, http://www.calarchives4u.com
5. *The Times*, "Humboldt County Captures Many Awards at State Fair," 1927
6. *The Times*, "Agriculture Returns to This County High," March 10, 1941
7. *The Times*. "Humboldt Turkey Trot...March on Thanksgiving," November 12, 1941
8. Department of Agriculture, Humboldt County, Annual Crop Reports to the County Board of Supervisors, 1951-2008.
9. *The Times Standard*, "Humboldt Potato Farming Booms After Bad Weather," May 9, 1971
10. Annual Crop Reports
11. National Agricultural Statistics Service. USDA, Quick Stats. www.nass.usda.gov/QuickStats/PullData_US_CNTY.jsp
12. United States Department of Agriculture, 2007, Census of Agriculture. www.agcensus.usda.gov/Publications/207/indes.asp
13. University of California, Agricultural Issues Center, Organic Agriculture. Detail report for Humboldt County supplied by Humboldt County Agriculture Commission, Bruce Bryan

14. Farm Bureau of Humboldt County and Humboldt State University, Humboldt County Agriculture Survey, Summary Report, September 2003.
15. The state of California web site provides a description of the Williamson Act:

   The California Land Conservation Act of 1965—commonly referred to as the Williamson Act—enables local governments to enter into contracts with private landowners for the purpose of restricting specific parcels of land to agricultural or related openspace use. In return, landowners receive property tax assessments which are much lower than normal because they are based upon farming and open space uses as opposed to full market value. Local governments receive an annual subvention of forgone property tax revenues from the state via the Open Space Subvention Act of 1971. Williamson Act.

Recipe Chapter for Vegetable-Based Entrées
References

1. Lappé, Frances Moore. *Diet for a Small Planet*. New York: Ballantine Books, 1991, pp. 76, 129
2. National Chicken Council, "Per Capita Consumption of Poultry and Livestock" (Current as of October, 15, 2008) http://www.nationalchicken-council.com/statistics/stat_detail.cfm?id=8
3. USDA http://www.mypyramid.gov/tips_resources/vegetarian_diets.html
4. Roberts, *End of Food*, p. 210
5. Lappé, *supra*, pp. 10, 74
6. *YES* magazine, Spring 2009, p. 24
7. Lappé, *supra*, p. 75
8. Lappé, *supra*, p. 224

Photo Credits
©2009 All photographs are copyright by the individual photographers

Ann Anderson: Pages back cover, 22, 24, 26, 41, 42, 47, 52 mushrooms, 64 oregano, 64, 68, 72 oysters, 75, 78, 82, 83, 84 turnips and apples, 85, 86, 90, 91, 92, 93, 99 kale, 100, 101 cabbage and apples, 102, 103, 108, 109 fish, 111 lemon, 113, 114, 124, 125, 128, 129, 131, 133, 136, 139 zucchini, 144, 149, 154 onion, 161, 163, 169, 171, 177, 178, 180, 181, 182, 183, 194, 195, 198, 208 squash, 209 figs, 211, 212, 214, 217, 219, 220, 221, 226, 230, 233, 236, 238, 239, 248 apples, 254, 255, 256 apples, 257, 259 hops and watermelons, 260 apples, 261 G-Farm, 262, 263 mixed vegetables, 267 River Bees, 287, 288, 290

Lauren Cohn-Sarabia: Pages 26, 44, 45, 48, 54, 65, 66, 76, 84 bees, 89, 95, 96, 101 salad, 107, 110, 117, 119, 139 peppers, 148, 151, 152 peppers, 154 pepper, 155, 160 zucchini, 166, 168, 170, 192, 200, 201, 205, 209 beekeeper, 213, 218, 223, 227, 237 cabbage, 256 farm stand, 260 starts and Freya's Garden, 268 plums

Sharon Letts : Page234

Harvey Raider: Pages 51 sunflower, 56, 64 peppers, 69, 73, 94, 118, 145, 146, 152 beans, 158, 208 huckleberry, 231, 272

Chris Wisner: Pages front cover, vi, 9, 11, 21, 28, 39, 43, 46, 50, 51 kale, 52 tomatillo, 53, 55, 57, 59, 62, 71, 72 Scott Sterner, 74, 79, 80, 81, 87, 88, 97, 98, 99 goat, 104, 105, 109 artichoke, 111 chicken, 120, 122, 127, 132, 134, 138, 140, 141, 147, 150, 152 green beans, 156, 157, 159, 160 eggplant, 162, 164, 165, 167, 172, 174, 179, 184, 185,187, 189, 190, 196, 193, 206, 210, 215, 216, 222, 228, 229, 237 daikon, 247, 248 corn, squash and lettuce, 253, 256 strawberries, 258, 259 tomatoes, 261 squash, grapes and Green Fire Farm, 263 eggs and cucumbers, 264, 265, 266, 267 farm, 268 pumpkins and farm, 269, 270, 291

Karen Wehrstein: Page 137

Recipe Index

C

Cabbage
Cole Slaw 101
Kim Chee 237
Nina's Borscht 79
Sweet and Spicy Cabbage with
    Cranberries 178
Cake
Carrot Cake/Zucchini Cake 215
Carrots
Carrot Cake/Zucchini Cake 215
Carrot Casserole 173
Carrot Soufflé 61
Carrot Soup 73
Mustardy Braised Rabbit With Carrots 134
Cauliflower
Cauliflower-Cheese Pie 147
Savory Cauliflower Salad
    with Fresh Herbs 105
Sweet Cauliflower Salad
with Fresh Herbs 106
Cheese
cheese - cow milk
    Au Gratin Potatoes 179
    Butternut Squash and
    Fontina Risotto 144
    Cauliflower-Cheese Pie 147
chevre - goat cheese
    Crunchy Baked Chevre 41, 42
    Cucumber "Crackers" and Cheese 45
    Cypress Grove Chevre Olive Spread 42
    Garlic and Sun-Dried Tomato Spread 44
    Quiche with Kale Crust 69
    Stuffed Cherry Tomatoes 50
    Stuffed Nasturtium Flowers 44
    Truffredo (Truffle Tremor Alfredo) 148
cream cheese
    Los Bagels Pesto Spread 45
    Smoked Fish and Cheese Stuffing 50
    Stuffed Cherry Tomatoes 50
Chestnuts
Glazed Mushrooms and Chestnuts 177
Winter Harvest Soup 89
Chicken
Casa Chicken 124
Chicken Stock 224
Iranian Eggplant Stew 120
Moroccan Chicken with Green Olives 128
Mu Shu Chicken 126
Roasted Chicken Salad 111
Roasted Lemon Chicken with
    Green Beans and Potatoes 125
Rx: Chicken Soup 77

Stir-Fry 129
Tacos (Meat- or vegetable-based) 118
Chili 117
Chili sauce
Grammy Wentz's Chili Sauce 227
Clams
Clam Chowder 83
Cobbler
Summer Cobbler 216
Corn
Cheddar Corn Chowder 94
Clark Family Corn Pudding 70
Colache (Aztec Stir-Fry) 150
Corn and Black Bean Salad 100
Corn Tortillas 203
Easy Corn Chowder 82
Roasted Red Pepper Corn Tart 146
Crab
Crab Dip 56
Crab Meat Crêpes 140
Deviled Crab 56
Crackers
Basic Crackers 199
Cucumber "Crackers" and Cheese 45
Rye Crackers 198
Cream
Butter and Buttermilk 232
Homemade Sour Cream 231
Cream sauce. *See* White sauce
Crêpes 204
Crab Meat Crêpes 140
Fruit-filled Crêpes 222
Crookneck squash. *See* Summer squash
Croutons
Savory Croutons 89
Crust
Flaky Pie Crust 201
Cucumbers
Cucumber "Crackers" and Cheese 45
Cucumber Sauce 138
Gazpacho 86
Kosher Dill Pickles 238
Custard
Goose-Egg Custard 215

D

Delicata squash. *See* Winter squash
Dill
Dill Sauce 136
Kosher Dill Pickles 238

About the Authors and Editors

The team of authors and editors, aka, The Heirloom Tomatoes, is a group of six woman who live in Humboldt County, California. They come from across the country and from many backgrounds but share a devotion to our community as well as a love of food.

Ann Anderson is a retired publisher of books and patterns on quilting. She spent most of her career in computer sales and marketing after earning a Master's Degree in Cellular and Molecular Biology.

Martha Haynes grew up in the Garden State. After 32 years as a teacher, in retirement, she has finally found the time to go more deeply in to what to cook, why to cook it, and how to cook. Working on this book has changed her in all three categories.

Ann King, Editor, retired and retried. Diverse experiences include joyful times involving theatre, dance, art and music (including singing, learning guitar and playing gut-bucket bass in a jug band). Biggest joys in life: Two sons and a granddaughter. One of the nicest things anyone has said about her: "She understands cooking."

Carol Moné is a school teacher and is a long-term community activist and serious locavore.

Lauren Cohn-Sarabia is a professional caterer in Humboldt County. She enjoys teaching cooking to children and adults, taking photographs and growing vegetables for her family in her home garden.

Suzanne Simpson is a retired public relations professional and is presently a professional artist, ardent home gardener, canner and cook. She is on the board of the Humboldt Bay Center for Sustainable Living (the Eco-Hostel Project).

You can reach the editors at info@locally-delicious.com
Keep track of future projects and ideas on www.locally-delicious.com